The Ottoman Empire, the Great Powers, and the Straits Question 1870-1887

Mehmed Emin Âli Pasha

BARBARA JELAVICH

The Ottoman Empire, the Great Powers, and the Straits Question

1870-1887

INDIANA UNIVERSITY PRESS
Bloomington and London

This book was brought to publication with support from
Ford Foundation funds made available by the
International Publications Advisory Committee through the Office of
Research and Advanced Studies, Indiana University.

Published in Canada by Fitzhenry & Whiteside Limited,
Don Mills, Ontario
Library of Congress catalog card number: 72-88631
ISBN: 0-253-34276-7
Manufactured in the United States of America

CONTENTS

PREFACE

Of the great powers principally engaged in the game of international diplomacy in the nineteenth century, the clear loser in each succeeding contest was undoubtedly the Ottoman Empire. Throughout this period this state had to defend itself against attacks both from within launched by the subject nationalities and from without from the European governments with designs on its territory and independence. The problem of the subject peoples will be dealt with in another book, *Nationalism in the Balkans, 1804-1918.* This narrative will, in contrast, concentrate on the second question, that of the difficult and dangerous relationship of the Ottoman government with the European powers. This issue will be examined in connection with the Black Sea Conference of 1871, which was called to discuss the Russian denunciation of certain clauses of the Treaty of Paris, and the fate of the settlement concerning the Straits which was formulated at this meeting.

The question of the status of the Straits was for the Ottoman Empire perhaps the most important single diplomatic issue which arose in the years before the First World War. At stake was not only the control of a strategic body of water, but also the independence of the Ottoman government. In these years naval or military control of the Straits meant in fact domination over the Ottoman state. As will be shown in the following pages, this danger remained a constant preoccupation of the Ottoman leaders and also the great powers.

The main portion of this narrative is divided into two parts. The first deals in detail with the background of and the discussions in the Black Sea Conference held in London from January 17 to March 14, 1871; the second covers the fate of the settlement and the interpretations given to it in the years before 1887. In the first section the emphasis has been placed on the position of the Ottoman government. At the conference the Ottoman representative was able to play an active, leading role in the discussions. The questions under consideration there concerning the regulation of the Danube and the status of Rumania have been included here, since they relate directly to the Straits. The second half deals primarily with the main episodes in diplomatic history in the following years, when the stipulations of the treaty became a matter of international concern: for instance, the British entrance into the Straits in 1878, the Salisbury declaration at the Congress of Berlin, the Penjdeh incident, and the place of the Straits in the Three Emperors' Alliance of 1881 and the Mediterranean Agreements of 1887. In this section more attention is devoted to the activity of the great powers, particularly Britain, because of the relatively passive and defensive role of the Ottoman Empire in these events. The emphasis here, it will be noted, is placed on the specific incidents involving the application of the Treaty of London; relatively less attention is given to the Straits question in general.

The years from 1870 to 1887 are a well defined period in the diplomatic history of the Eastern Question. During this time the dominant European alliance system was, with the exception of a short period after 1878, the Three Emperors' Alliance of Russia, Germany, and Austria-Hungary. On the world stage the primary rivalries were between the powers with active imperial policies involving Asia and African territories – France, Britain, and Russia. The significance of the Straits in this configuration lay in the fact that it was the entrance to the Black Sea. Without continental allies or an effective land army, Britain's only practical means of countering Russian activity in any part of the world was her ability to use her naval power in the Black Sea. This condition led the British government in the years under discussion to pursue usually a policy of seeking to assure that it could, legally or by force, enter the Black Sea through the Straits at will. With quite opposite interests, backed by a strong alliance and an army in the area, the Russian government feared chiefly a repetition of the events of the Crimean War, when a hostile coalition carried through a successful invasion through the Black Sea. With grossly inadequate naval strength to challenge Britain, Russia, even after 1871, consistently supported the maintenance of the closure of the Straits and the international treaties. After 1887 with the radical shift in the European alliance system, involving the breakup of the Three Emperors' Alliance and the conclusion of the Franco-Russian pact, both Britain and Russia gradually altered their stand on the Straits question. For both the entire issue became of decreasing importance; both found other, more effective ways of dealing with their imperial and national defense problems.

For the Ottoman Empire the fact that the Straits was a major strategic area for these two powers was undoubtedly a disaster. These governments were continually drawn into the internal problems of the empire, particularly in times of national crisis – and certainly for the Ottoman government the 1870s and 1880s marked a clear turn downwards in the fortunes of the empire. Although the Porte[1] had previously been forced to accept the establishment of an independent Greece and autonomous governments in Serbia and Rumania, it was now to suffer even greater losses. At the Congress of Berlin in 1878 the empire was compelled not only to recognize the independence of Serbia, Montenegro, and Rumania and the autonomy of Bulgaria, but also to surrender control of Bosnia-Hercegovina to Austria-Hungary, Cyprus to Britain, and some Asiatic territories to Russia. Egypt and Tunis were soon to fall into other hands. As the empire weakened, the importance of the maintenance of the international treaties concerning the Straits increased. Lacking the military or naval power to defend its position, the Ottoman government had to depend on the operation of the European balance of power system. The enormous difficulties which it faced in this period of continuing crisis are well illustrated in the following narrative.

Throughout this discussion much attention will be given to the question of the formulation, interpretation, and violation of treaties. As a weak state, the Ottoman Empire was usually a strong supporter of legality in international relations and the observance of international law. This attitude was maintained both in relation to the Straits question and toward the subject nationalities. In this regard, and in general, the attempt has been made here to present where possible the Ottoman viewpoint. The attitude of the powers and the Balkan

1. The term *Porte* or *Sublime Porte* was used to refer to the Ottoman government. More specifically it was the designation for the building which contained the principal offices of state at this time. See Roderic H. Davison, *Reform in the Turkish Empire, 1856-1876* (Princeton, 1963), pp. 35-36.

Christians has been well represented in the extensive literature on the Eastern Question. The problem of whether the Ottoman state of the nineteenth century was in fact worth preserving – whether it would have been better had it been either partitioned at once among the great powers or divided into its national units – will not be considered. Instead the empire will be treated as a political unit equal to the other great nations of Europe with similar rights and historical interests to defend.

The spelling of names and geographic points in a study such as this presents certain problems because of the variety of forms used both in the nineteenth century and at present. Complete consistency is not possible, but in general modern spelling has been used unless the person or place is better known in historical literature under another form. It is thus *Giers* and not *Girs* and *Kuchuk Kainardji* not *Küchük Kaynarji*. *Constantinople* has been chosen over *Istanbul* because that is the form used in international diplomacy in the nineteenth century; it also appears in the Ottoman archival material which is the basis of this book. In the citation of documents the spelling, punctuation, capitalization, and abbreviations follow those of the original except where changes have been necessary for consistency and clarity. This material has been translated in the body of the paper, but left in the original in the footnotes and the appendices. The dates are in the western style (the Gregorian calendar) with the exception of those referring to some Russian material, which are double-dated. In the nineteenth century the Russian calendar (the Julian) ran twelve days behind that of western Europe.

The author wishes to thank Professors Vaclav Benes, Robert F. Byrnes, Bradford Martin, and Edward Najam of Indiana University for their assistance with this manuscript and Professor Norman J. G. Pounds who prepared the maps. She is also greatly indebted to Professor Roderic H. Davison of George Washington University and Professor Stanford J. Shaw of the University of California at Los Angeles, who read and commented on the text, and to Mr. Robert Olson of Indiana University who translated the Turkish language materials. Miss Nancy Ann Miller of the Indiana University Press gave excellent editorial advice.

The preparation of this study was made possible by grants from the National Endowment for the Humanities and the American Council of Learned Societies. Support from Ford Foundation funds made available by the International Publications Advisory Committee through the Office of Research and Advanced Studies, as well as research grants from the Office of Research and Advanced Studies, Indiana University, are also most gratefully acknowledged.

This book is based primarily on research done in the *Hariciye Arshivi* in Istanbul, and also in the *Haus-, Hof- und Staatsarchiv* in Vienna and the Public Record Office in London. Without the expert advice and aid given by the staffs, this work could not have been completed. The author wishes to express her thanks to the Ministry of Foreign Affairs of Turkey for permission to use the Ottoman archives and to Mr. Kâmil Ayhan and Mr. Turgut Ishikal for their assistance with this material. Finally, particular gratitude must be expressed for the contributions of Charles, Mark, and Peter Jelavich to all aspects of this publication.

The Ottoman Empire, the Great Powers, and the Straits Question 1870-1887

I

INTRODUCTION

The Great Powers and the Ottoman Empire Throughout the nineteenth century the question of the viablity of the Ottoman Empire was a recurrent issue in international relations. The so-called Eastern Question, which concerned the fate of this state and its widespread territories, was the single major theme in great power diplomacy in this period. The control of the Ottoman possessions and the central government was constantly the object of discussion, negotiation, controversy, and open warfare between the four major powers, Austria, Britain, France, and Russia, who, after 1871, were joined by Italy and Germany. The dangerous international position of the Ottoman state was a reflection of even more unfortunate internal conditions. From the eighteenth century onward the history of the empire was characterized by lost battles, financial disasters, and administrative chaos, a situation which was to give the great powers further opportunities for interference in and domination over the affairs of the state.

Although the great losses to Austria and Russia occurred in the eighteenth century, the process through which the empire steadily lost territory and peoples through the intervention of outside powers and internal disorder continued thereafter. The chief territorial threat remained Russia; in 1812 she took Bessarabia. Through the treaties of Akkerman (1826) and Adrianople (1829) she gained the recognition of her predominant position in the Rumanian principalities of Moldavia and Wallachia and in Serbia. In 1829 she annexed the delta of the Danube River. Previously, in the Treaty of Kuchuk Kainardji (1774), she had laid the basis for a future claim to be the protecting power of the Orthodox Christians.

By the first half of the nineteenth century France joined Austria and Russia as a power with a direct interest in control over Ottoman lands. In 1830 France annexed Algiers and started to influence and control Tunis, another Ottoman possession. Her attempt, however, to build a powerful Egypt around the dynasty of Mehmed Ali failed. Thereafter her chief interest centered in the extension of her influence in North Africa and the maintenance of her predominant position in Egypt.

The process by which European powers gradually detached territories from the empire, whether these actions resulted in direct annexations or in the establishment of autonomous or independent political units, was, as could be expected, accompanied by fierce rivalry and deep suspicion among the participants. In general, the governments agreed here also upon the principle of the balance of power. No one state was to be allowed to gain more lands or influence over more territory than its rivals. In the 1830s Britain, Russia, and Austria joined against French influence in Egypt; in 1854 France, Britain, the Ottoman Empire, and Sardinia went to war with Russia because of their fears of Russian predominance in the Balkans. In 1878 Britain, Austria, and Germany forced Russia to the Congress of Berlin for the same motives. The plans for partition of the empire, devised in various epochs, took care that the powers shared equally in the division of the Ottoman lands.

In the second half of the century as in the first, the Ottoman Empire had to adopt a defensive position and guard against the moves of its ostensible friends as well as its obvious enemies. As in the previous years, the state had to meet four types of attack directed at its independence or its territorial integrity. First, it had to defend itself against the powers who wished to conquer and annex definite parts of its lands as, for example, France had previously taken Algeria and Russia Bessarabia. Second, it had to guard against a power or a group of powers exploiting the discontent of a subject people to gain control over Ottoman territory. French activity in Syria and Egypt and Russian actions in the Principalities were directed toward this end. Third, it had

to prevent other powers, principally Britain and Russia, fr
dominating the central government itself. Fourth, the nati
ments, particularly those originating in the Balkan peninsul
those in the Asian and African territories, had to be either s ppressed or appeased to prevent the empire from simply disintegrating into its national parts. The establishment of an independent Greece had already occurred. In the second half of the century a fifth danger, that of economic domination of the empire by outside interests, also arose. This process had in fact already begun through abuses of the rights gained in the capitulations.[1]

A complete lack of unity existed among the powers in their attitude toward the Ottoman Empire. In eastern affairs any combination was possible and any state might at one time or another support one of these five threats to the Ottoman government. The Porte had in fact no natural enemies and no real allies. Moreover, each power tended to extract a high price from the Ottoman government in return for support on an individual issue. As shall be shown at the period of the Congress of Berlin, the empire was in the end forced to surrender more to the powers who were in theory defending its interests, Britain and Austria, than to Russia, who had defeated the Ottoman armies in a major war. In addition, as the century progressed, the internal policy of each of the major states came to influence the attitude of that government toward the empire to an increasing degree. The changes within Britain and the Habsburg Monarchy were to have a particularly detrimental effect on the Ottoman future.

For all of the major powers the years between the Crimean War and the Franco-Prussian War, when this narrative properly begins, were a period of radical change in the international balance. At this time not the Eastern Question, but the events in central Europe, the unification of Germany and Italy and the reconstruction of the Habsburg Monarchy in the *Ausgleich* of 1867, dominated the stage. Because of the importance of both domestic and external events on the policy of the

1. In order to encourage trade the sultans after the middle of the sixteenth century made with other governments a series of treaties, called capitulations, which granted special privileges, exemptions and rights of extraterritoriality. For the misuse of these agreements see Davison, *Reform in the Ottoman Empire, 1856-1876*, pp. 73-74.

powers toward the Ottoman Empire, a short review of the attitude of each in 1871 should be made.

The greatest gain in influence by any power between 1856 and 1871 was that made by France. After the Crimean War the most energetic and active statesman in Europe was certainly Napoleon III. Although he at first showed himself the patron of national movements, such as the Rumanian, which were detrimental to Ottoman interests, after 1860 his representatives in Constantinople tended to work for the strengthening of the empire and were certainly influential in the Turkish government.[2] One of the major sources of French strength lay in the fact that the leaders of the Ottoman reform movement admired French civilization and preferred to adopt French models for the reorganization of the Turkish administration and government. Throughout the sixties French policy was often confused and contradictory, but certainly at the beginning of the year 1870 France held the most favored diplomatic position in Constantinople. The change was to be most sudden. On July 15 France declared war on Prussia; on August 31 at Sedan the army of Napoleon III was crushed. For the next ten years French influence was to remain slight in eastern affairs. As shall be shown, one of the major problems facing the Ottoman government in the fall of 1870 was the replacement of their former major source of foreign support.

In the years immediately preceding and for a period following the Crimean War, Britain was the principal friend and ally of the Ottoman Empire. Even such statesmen as Palmerston, who in other parts of Europe stood for national ideas, did not apply them in the Near East, preferring to uphold the rights of a reformed Turkey. The value of British support, however, depended on the readiness and willingness of

2. The Ottoman statesmen nevertheless recognized the continuing dangerous tendencies of the Second Empire. Âli Pasha, who will play such an important role in this narrative, wrote in a report of 1866 to the sultan Abdülaziz: ". . .il [Napoleon III] tendait à se mêler de nos affaires, et, comme s'il n'existait aucune convention à cet égard, il visait à nous nuire dans les questions de Roumanie, de Serbie, de Syrie et de Crète, en se proclamant pour le principe dissolvant que chaque peuple a le droit de choisir son propre gouvernement et son souverain, tandis qu'aucune nation n'a celui d'en gouverner une autre. Il a, de cette façon, troublé les esprits chez divers peuples et notamment chez nos chrétiens." Quoted in General M. Moukhtar Pasha, *La Turquie, l'Allemagne et l'Europe* (Paris, 1924), p. 13.

that power to maintain its active, interested role in the east. It was in this aspect that British influence waned, particularly after the death of Palmerston in 1865. Thereafter, as one British historian writes: "The natural reaction against excessive habits of interference practised by Palmerston the bully and Russell the busybody, made of Non-Intervention the fundamental creed. . ."[3] of both the Liberal and the Conservative parties. Public attention now centered more on internal issues, such as electoral reform and the Irish question. Moreover, British concern was naturally more involved in the great events on the continent in these years. Here she was conscious that, lacking a strong army, she was in fact powerless to influence decisively the course of events.

Of great importance for future relations with the Porte was also the increase in the numbers and influence of those people in Britain who were totally unsympathetic to the Ottoman Empire and its social and political system. Applying the standards of British liberalism to the empire, they could find little which met their approval. They blamed these conditions almost completely on the Ottoman administrative system and on Ottoman officials. Most influential among this group was certainly William E. Gladstone, who will play such a prominent part in this narrative, and who was able to make great political capital out of Balkan atrocities. Viewing the entire question often in simple terms of black and white, and with the complete and utter assurance that he was quite capable of deciding who represented the right and who the wrong, he was to play a role in international relations adverse to Ottoman interests, but favorable to those of Russia. The generally negative attitude of all Liberal party statesmen toward Turkish rights and interests will be fully documented in the following pages.

Unfortunately for the Porte, not only the Liberals, but also many members of the Conservative party came to hold opinions detrimental

3. R. W. Seton-Watson, *Britain in Europe, 1789-1914* (Cambridge: 1955), p. 474. In the report cited above, Âli commented on British policy: "Depuis quelque temps, l'Angleterre a complètement modifié sa politique mondiale et observe une réserve remarquable dans tout ce qui ne touche pas de près ses intérêts commerciaux. Son gouvernement, obéissant lui-même à des principes libéraux, est incapable de se mettre en contradiction avec les principes de nationalités. . .Tout espoir d'avoir un appui quelconque de sa part est donc exclu." Mouktar Pasha, *La Turquie, l'Angleterre et l'Europe,* p. 14.

to the empire. These varied from the belief that the Crimean policy had been a mistake and that the establishment of independent or autonomous Balkan countries would not necessarily lead to their total domination by Russia to the even more dangerous conviction that Britain should join with other powers in what was in fact the partition of Turkey into spheres of influence. British policy was to shift in particular in the 1880s after the acquisition of control in Egypt, the Sudan, and the Suez Canal.

From the beginning of the nineteenth century perhaps the most consistent supporter of the maintenance of the Ottoman Empire was the Habsburg Monarchy. Both states had a basic common interest as multinational empires with minorities susceptible to outside intrigue. For each Russia was the chief menace, both as a great power and as the source of internal disunion. However, the position of the Habsburg Monarchy was gravely damaged by her military defeats in 1859 by France and in 1866 by Prussia. Thereafter in the *Ausgleich* of 1867 she was forced to make an arrangement with the Hungarians of the empire which was to have a decisive effect on foreign policy. After this date Budapest exercised often an even greater influence on the course of foreign relations than Vienna. Dominated by a hatred and fear of Russia, the Hungarian statesmen in general favored an active eastern policy and usually opposition to St. Petersburg. In one sense the reorganization of the Habsburg state was of benefit to Constantinople. At times the Magyar leaders did stress their common "Turanian" ancestry with the Turks. On the negative side, however, was the Hungarian desire for an active and aggressive policy in the Balkans, usually at Ottoman expense.

In 1870 moderate and traditional policies were still dominant in Vienna. After the humiliating military disasters in Italy and central Europe, Habsburg policy was cautious. Until the questions of Prussian hegemony in Germany and the fate of France were settled the empire could not assume an active and positive role in Near Eastern affairs. Moreover, after the 1860s Habsburg policy toward Russia became increasingly careful. The responsible leaders were convinced that they alone could not win a war against Russia, particularly if this power was supported by Prussia. In the Black Sea crisis of 1870 the monarchy was thus unwilling to take a decisive stand unless it were assured of strong

British support. Even with this assistance, it was fully realized that it would be the Habsburg armies, not the British navy, which would bear the full brunt of any war with Russia.

Undoubtedly at this time in the eyes of the Turkish statesmen the chief danger came from the north. Although in the past Russian policy had not consistently been directed toward weakening the Ottoman Empire or undermining its authority in its territories, certainly the Russian government had the best weapons should these aims be pursued. The Russian army could always be launched across the Pruth River; the Orthodox and Slavic peoples were indeed susceptible to Russian suggestions. Moreover, after 1856 Russian policy had openly and with a remarkable single-mindedness been directed toward the destruction of the Treaty of Paris, which Tsar Alexander II and most Russians regarded as a national dishonor. The neutralization of the Black Sea and the cession of southern Bessarabia were the two sections of the treaty which were regarded as most humiliating. Since both of these measures had been designed as a protection for the Ottoman Empire, there was little chance that the Porte would willingly cooperate in a revision of these sections of the treaty.

Moreover, in Russia as in Britain in this period a current of popular opinion developed which was to become harmful to Ottoman interests. The 1860s marked the beginning of the Panslav movement and its involvement in international affairs. Although the term was used to designate many different ideas, most Panslavs looked to the destruction of both the Ottoman and Habsburg empires, their division into national states, and the predominance of Russia over the entire east and southeast European area. Like the British liberal, the Russian Panslav saw Ottoman rule over Balkan Christian peoples in the darkest colors. His doctrines were not only sentimental and romantic, based on a genuine concern for the welfare of the Balkan peoples, but also practical. The carrying into effect of this program would extend Russian national power far into Europe.

The Russian ambassador at Constantinople after 1864, N. P. Ignatiev, was one of the most prominent Panslavs. He was quite determined to use his position to carry out an active policy along the lines of Panslav doctrines. He sought first a revision of the Treaty of Paris; he then wished to proceed toward a program of securing Russian control over the Straits and Constantinople and of aiding the Slavic subject people. During his period at Constantinople he remained a source of dismay and disquiet, not only to the Ottoman government but also to the representatives of the other powers. He was, in his way, a highly effective diplomat.[4]

Nevertheless, in 1870 Ignatiev, despite his influential post, was not representative of prevailing Russian opinion on foreign policy. The great majority of Russian diplomats and statesmen wished to follow a traditional and not a revolutionary course in foreign policy. Like the Ottoman Empire, Russia in the 1860s was in a period of great and fundamental reform. Until these changes were completed it was recognized that an adventurous policy could not be followed and that it would be better if the Eastern Question remained in abeyance. In addition, the Russian government in its foreign relations was conservative; Balkan revolutionary movements, based on liberal and national ideologies, usually represented theories of government which were abhorrent and suspect in St. Petersburg. Although all currents of Russian opinion were united in the desire to overthrow the Treaty of Paris, the majority of Russian statesmen sought to attain this goal by traditional diplomatic methods. They wished no major crisis and they feared involvement in a European war.

In early 1870 the fate of the Ottoman Empire lay in the hands of four powers, Russia, Britain, Austria-Hungary, and France. By the fall of that year France had been eliminated from this number. Of the remaining three states, Russia sought actively certain goals which were detrimental to Ottoman interests; Britain, although in theory a supporter of the empire, was in a period of virtual isolation as far as continental affairs were concerned and under the direction of a government unsympathetic to the policy of the Crimean War. The Habsburg Empire was also in a process of internal reorganization and was faced with an as yet uncertain situation in the German lands. The future course of Ottoman relations with the two newly united

4. Two recent studies of Ignatiev's ambassadorship at Constantinople are: Gisela Hünigen, *Nikolaj Pavlovič Ignat'ev und die russische Balkanpolitik, 1875-1878* (Göttingen, 1968); and Thomas A. Meininger, *Ignatiev and the Establishment of the Bulgarian Exarchate, 1864-1872* (Madison, Wisconsin, 1970).

states – Italy and the North German Confederation (soon to become the German Empire) – could not be foretold. Neither the Porte nor the powers traditionally concerned with the Eastern Question could judge the effect on international relations of the changes in central Europe.

Certainly throughout the century the Ottoman leaders were acutely aware of the dangers facing their state, both from the great powers and from their own subjects. From the end of the eighteenth century repeated attempts were made to remedy the obvious failings in the military establishment. The reforms of the Tanzimat period were designed to strengthen and modernize the state so that it could survive in the competitive struggle among the great powers. The process of reform was not easy. The empire suffered particularly from the fact that it had been in the past one of the great military powers of history; it was hard to discard institutions that had once functioned efficiently. It was similarly difficult for those Ottoman citizens who regarded Islam as the basis of the state to accept Christians as equals. Yet these reforms were obviously essential for the survival of the empire.

In addition, in its dealings with the outside world and with its own internal problems, the Ottoman government was harmed by the dark picture which most of the people of Europe held of it, an attitude which was in a sense a carry-over of the old crusading spirit of the past. In sharp contrast to the subject nationalities, Ottoman statesmen could look to no major group or peoples, with the possible exception of the Hungarians, who would naturally tend to favor their position. Moreover, although the former religious antagonism had to an extent subsided, the empire faced continual opposition from a relatively new ideological grouping – from those who were convinced believers in the doctrines associated with the French revolution and with European liberalism in general. Many of the leaders of this body of opinion, as, for example, Gladstone, were not only convinced that the principles in which they believed could be immediately applied to all peoples and places, but tended to feel that it was in fact the duty of their governments to campaign actively to introduce these ideas throughout the world. The Ottoman Empire – which was not based on national equality and which did not have a representative government – was a natural target of attack. In foreign relations the Porte was caught between the outright imperial drives of the European powers and the desire of some of their leaders to undermine the Ottoman government in a quite different direction. In some instances, again best exemplified by Gladstone's period in control in Britain, the two conflicting pressures were applied simultaneously.

To combat foreign encroachment and internal subversion the Ottoman government had few effective means of defense. The military establishment was never reformed or strengthened sufficiently to meet the external threat. In the field of religious and political ideology, the weapons which the empire possessed in the common faith of most of its African and Asian citizens were never really used effectively. The sultans, for instance, could not in this age of nationalism mobilize the Turkic people of Central Asia threatened by Russian expansion, or the Moslems of British India. Although efforts were to be made, attempts to use the sultan's position as caliph to organize Moslems of Asia and Africa against European penetration and exploitation were largely unsuccessful. Thus despite the fact that the Russian tsars made good use of their role as titular heads of the Slavs and Orthodox Christians, their Moslem counterparts were never able to summon general Turk and Moslem support for the aid of the state.

Occupying an inferior position, in both a material and an ideological sense, the Ottoman statesmen found that their only real means of defense was the exploitation of the rivalry and conflicting interests among the powers. Being the weaker party in most disputes, they also usually remained the firm defenders of legality in international relations and of the sanctity of treaties. With its existence and integrity recognized by a series of international agreements, the empire naturally supported the maintenance of these stipulations. Unfortunately, as shall be shown, the other European powers did not regard their agreements with the Porte in a similar manner. Each placed its relations with Constantinople in a different category than those with the European states. It would perhaps be an exaggeration to say that their attitude resembled that of the United States government toward the Indian tribes, but nevertheless obligations toward the Ottoman Empire were not looked on in the same manner as those between European governments. The continued existence of the capitulations witnessed the European judgment that the Ottoman state occupied a different level of cultural development.

In 1870, when this study commences, the Ottoman administration was in the hands of as effective a leadership as was to be found throughout the century. From 1858 to 1871, the government was headed by two extremely competent statesmen, Âli Pasha and Fuad Pasha, who alternated throughout these years in the position of grand vezir. Until the death of Âli in September 1871, the sultan Abdülaziz interfered relatively little with the policies of his statesmen. The power in the government thus lay with the administration, the Porte, rather than in the Palace. After February 1869, when Fuad died, Âli held a dominant position in the domestic and foreign affairs of the country. In the crisis of 1870 he was ably seconded in foreign relations by Kostaki Musurus Pasha, the ambassador in London. A Phanariote Greek, Musurus was to hold the position of Ottoman ambassador in London for a period of more than thirty years. The relative Ottoman success at the Black Sea Conference was due to the ability of these diplomats and to their experience in foreign relations.

The Straits Question in International Diplomacy In the preceding pages an attempt has been made to describe briefly the attitude of the powers to the empire and its very difficult international position. In the next chapters the complexities of the problems facing the Porte will be studied in relation to the question of the Straits and certain closely connected episodes. The regulation of the passage of warships through the Straits was one of the most important issues in the diplomatic relations of the empire for the last century of its existence. In a very real sense its fate depended on the control of the passageway from the Black Sea to the Mediterranean. Throughout the nineteenth century it was assumed that if a foreign power gained domination of the Straits, with the inevitably associated hold on the city of Constantinople, it would also have in its hands the government and thus the vast lands of the Ottoman Empire. A withdrawal of the Ottoman government from Constantinople to, let us say, Ankara was not deemed possible or practical at this time. Constantinople was, of course, open to conquest from both the land and the sea. However, in the second half of the nineteenth century, with the improvement of naval armaments, the chief threat to the city was believed to come from a possible enemy sea attack. It was thus to the direct interest of the Ottoman state that no foreign fleets should pass through or stop in the entire area of the Straits.

Unfortunately for the Ottoman Empire, the Straits was a vital geographic area not only for her national security, but also for that of both Russia and the British Empire. Over the entire span of the nineteenth century perhaps the most enduring and interesting diplomatic antagonism was that between Britain and Russia. Having no contiguous territories until 1885, when they met in Afghanistan, the centers of their rivalry lay at those points where Russian expansion and military power appeared to threaten British imperial interests. The chief area in conflict became in fact the Straits, where both powers had interests at stake which they believed essential for their state and for which they were willing to go to war. In the first place, as has been mentioned, command of the Straits was believed to mean domination of the Ottoman Empire, a prize which neither power would concede to the other. In the second place, the Straits involved part of or access to the major commercial and naval sea-lanes of both states. For Russia the Straits was "the key to her house." Not only was this the commercial outlet for the grain of the Ukraine, but it was also a point of weakness from a military standpoint. As was demonstrated during the Crimean War, free access through the Straits would allow naval powers to attack Russian southern shores. For Britain a similar danger existed in a reverse sense. Her chief concern lay in the safety of her lines of communication with her empire, in particular with India. She feared a situation in which a Russian Black Sea fleet could freely enter the eastern Mediterranean and, in a time of crisis, endanger the British fleet.

Under these circumstances, for the three powers most directly concerned – Britain, Russia, and the Ottoman Empire – the best solution was the closure of the Straits to ships of war in time of peace with the maintenance of the sultan as the "guardian of the Straits." This rule did indeed limit the actions of each of the powers, but it was the best of the possible alternatives. The closure was limited to peacetime, since obviously should the Ottoman Empire be at war, she could summon the support of allied navies in defense of its possessions.

The closure of the Straits, it should be emphasized, was a compromise solution; for each of the three powers other arrangements were possible which better served their individual interests. For the

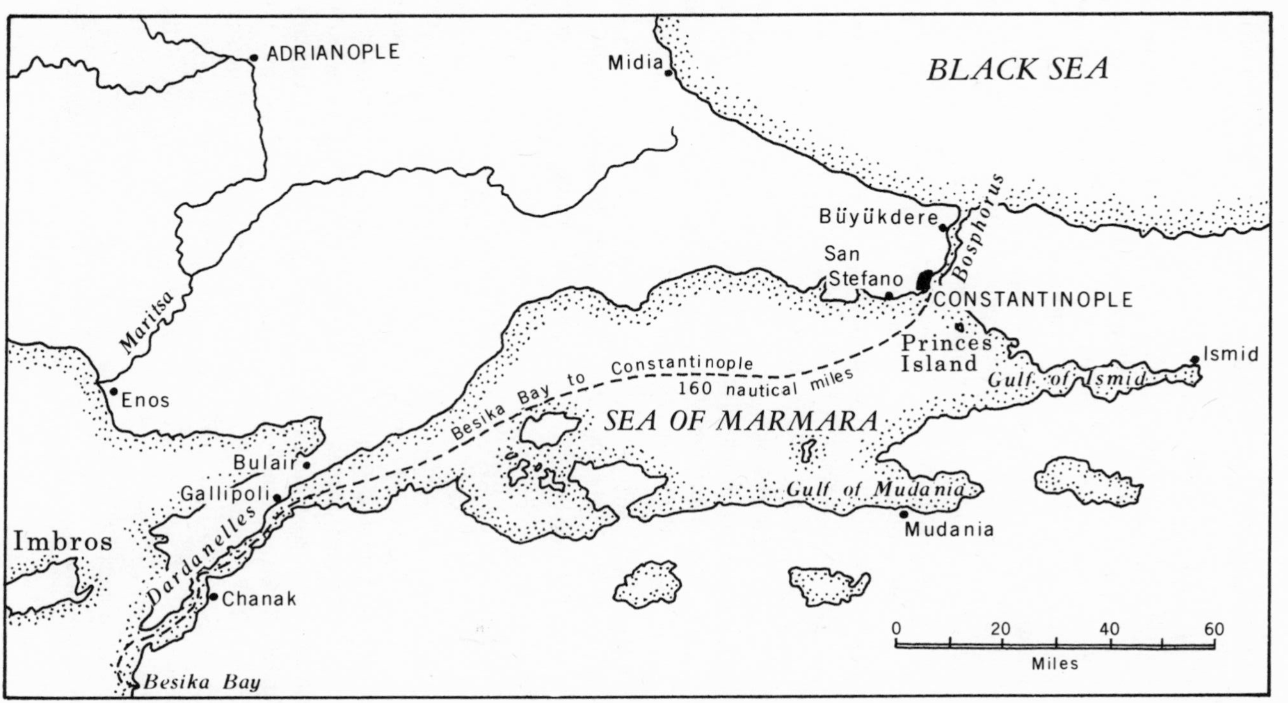
ADRIANOPLE
Midia
BLACK SEA
Maritsa
Enos
Büyükdere
Bosphorus
San Stefano
CONSTANTINOPLE
Princes Island
Ismid
Gulf of Ismid
Besika Bay to Constantinople 160 nautical miles
SEA OF MARMARA
Bulair
Gallipoli
Imbros
Dardanelles
Chanak
Gulf of Mudania
Mudania
0 20 40 60
Miles
Besika Bay

The Straits

sultan a full control over the area, with no limitations on his power, had certain advantages. He could then open or close the Straits in war or peace at his convenience. For Britain during most of the nineteenth century a full opening, accompanied by an alliance with the Ottoman Empire, had great attraction. With the world's greatest naval power in its control, the British government could use free access to enter the Black Sea at will and thus threaten the Russian lands directly and the communications with Central Asia.

Undoubtedly for Russia the best regulation would have been an arrangement by which the Straits would have been open to "riverain" powers, which in practice meant Russia, but closed to all others. This solution not only protected Russia from the British naval threat, but it would allow units of any Russian fleet stationed in the Black Sea to make raids upon British ships in the Mediterranean and then to retreat behind the barrier of the Straits. Russia could not openly challenge British supremacy on the sea, but she could use these means to endanger British lines of imperial communication. During the nineteenth century even more ambitious plans, involving actions ranging from the seizure of the entire area of the Straits including Constantinople to the occupation of the Bosphorus alone, were formulated by various Russian diplomats and writers. In the period under discussion here the Russian government always retreated before such extreme solutions, because it feared that it could not attain these goals without the danger of war with a European coalition.

Although British interests in the area were indeed great, it should be emphasized that the status of the Straits held a much greater importance for Russia from both a military and an economic aspect. Russia could not directly menace the British homeland either by land or by sea. In contrast, should the Straits be open, Britain, the world's greatest seapower, had almost free access to a long and virtually undefended Russian shoreline. The Russian Black Sea fleet was no match for British squadrons stationed in the Mediterranean. Moreover, from 1856 to 1871 a Russian fleet did not exist in this sea. From the economic point of view too the Russian stake in the question of the Straits was higher. Despite the fact that Britain had significant commercial interests in the Black Sea and the Danube, which involved passage of the Straits, the Russian position was far more vulnerable. By

1913, 60 percent of Russia's maritime exports and 45 percent of her entire exports passed through the Straits.[5] Between 1901 and 1910, 87 percent of all exports of wheat went by this route.[6]

The regime of the closure of the Straits, because of its obvious practical value, was established in a series of treaties concluded throughout the nineteenth century. Complete Ottoman control over the Black Sea had been gained at the end of the fifteenth century with the taking of the Crimea. For three centuries, with the exception of certain privileges granted to the Venetians for a short period, that sea remained closed to all ships except those of the Ottoman Empire. The Treaty of Kuchuk Kainardji of 1774 opened this area and the Straits for Russian commercial vessels. In the next years the other powers received similar rights.[7]

In 1789/90 and 1805 the more delicate question of the passage of warships was first introduced in agreements between Russia and the Ottoman Empire which opened the Straits to Russian warships under certain specified conditions. It should be noted that according to the generally accepted principles of the time the Porte had full sovereignty over the Straits. No general right of passage through straits connecting two international seas was recognized.[8] The agreements which were to be made henceforth on this question thus placed the Straits in an exceptional position. The aim of the subsequent treaties was to maintain a free passage for all merchant ships and to balance the political and military interests of Britain, Russia, and the Ottoman Empire.

The principle of the closure of the Straits to ships of war, the chief point at issue in all subsequent settlements, was first recorded in 1809 in a treaty between Britain and the Ottoman Empire. Here it was stated that:

5. P. P. Graves, *The Question of the Straits* (London, 1931), p. 146.

6. B. A. Dranov, *Chernomorskie Prolivy* (Moscow, 1948), p. 140.

7. The passage of commercial ships, a matter which caused little controversy, will not be discussed in this study with the exception of those issues surrounding the Russian Volunteer Fleet.

8. The Danes, for instance, collected tolls until 1857 from vessels passing through the Danish sound and the two other narrow passages connecting the North Sea with the Baltic. Charles Dupuis, "Liberté des voies de communication: relations internationales," Académie de Droit International, *Recueil des cours,* 1924, II, pp. 184, 185.

> As ships of war have at all times been prohibited from entering the Canal of Constantinople viz., in the Straits of the Dardanelles and of the Black Sea, as this ancient regulation of the Ottoman Empire is in the future to be observed by every Power in time of peace, the Court of Great Britain promises on its part to conform to this principle.[9]

The question of closure became an international issue again in 1833 when Russia signed the Treaty of Unkiar Skelessi with the Porte. This agreement, which was a military alliance between the two powers, contained a secret article which declared that the Ottoman government would limit its aid to its ally in case of war "to closing the Straits of the Dardanelles, that is to say, to not allowing any foreign vessel of war to enter therein under any pretext whatsoever."

The significance of this agreement for the international relations of the period was principally that, because of the conditions of the time, the pact placed the Ottoman Empire in a position of political semi-dependency in relation to Russia. In the next years the question of exactly what rights the Russian government had received in the secret article was a matter of dispute. However, for this study the most important aspect of the treaty was that it dealt with the Straits issue not by a multilateral convention, but on a bilateral basis. It also established a master-vassal relationship between the two signatories. For the other powers at the time, particularly Britain, who learned of the secret clause almost at once, the chief anxiety was caused by the fear that the closure did not apply to Russian warships.[10]

Because of its apprehension in this regard, the British government in the next years attempted to secure the annulment of this treaty. Exploiting the Egyptian crisis of the 1830s Britain was able to obtain

9. J. C. Hurewitz, *Diplomacy in the Near and Middle East* (Princeton, 1956), I. p. 83.

10. On the question of the closure in the Treaty of Unkiar Skelessi see J. C. Hurewitz, "Russia and the Turkish Straits," *World Politics,* XIV, October-July, 1962, pp. 605-632, and Philip E. Mosely, *Russian Diplomacy and the Opening of the Eastern Question in 1838 and 1839* (Cambridge, 1934), pp. 7-30. It should, however, be noted that no matter what the correct interpretation of the treaty is, many Russian diplomats believed that the secret article did allow Russian passage through the Straits in time of war. The phrase "the policy of Unkiar Skelessi" when used in the future usually meant the establishment of a close Russian-Ottoman alliance and the opening of the Straits to the warships of Russia or the "riverain" states alone.

the replacement of the bilateral Unkiar Skelessi with the multilateral Convention of the Straits in 1841. In this new agreement Britain, Austria, France, Prussia, Russia, and the Ottoman Empire agreed upon the closure of the Straits in time of peace:

> Art. I. His Highness the Sultan, on the one part, declares that he is firmly resolved to maintain for the future the principle invariably established as the ancient rule of his Empire, and in virtue of which it has at all times been prohibited for the Ships of War of Foreign Powers to enter the Straits of the Dardanelles and of the Bosphorus; and that, so long as the Porte is at Peace, His Highness will admit no Foreign Ship of War into the said Straits.
>
> And their Majesties the Queen of the United Kingdom of Great Britain and Ireland, the Emperor of Austria, King of Hungary and Bohemia, the King of the French, the King of Prussia, and the Emperor of All the Russias, on the other part, engage to respect this determination of the Sultan, and to conform themselves to the principle above declared.

In this, the most important of the treaties concerning the Straits, the sultan reserved the right to "deliver Firmans of passage for light Vessels under Flag of War, which shall be employed as is usual in the service of the Missions of Foreign Powers."[11] With this agreement the Treaty of Unkiar Skelessi lapsed.

The principles of this pact were confirmed in the Treaty of Paris of 1856.[12] The neutralization of the Black Sea, provided for in this agreement, gave a further assurance that the closure would be observed – at least from the Russian side. The regulation, of course, in theory also shielded Russia from attack from the British and French navies at a time when the Russian southern coast was without protection. From the Ottoman point of view the entire structure of the Treaty of Paris, including the closure of the Straits and the neutralization of the Black Sea, offered real advantages to the empire. Although the sultan, like the tsar, was compelled to recognize a limitation on his sovereignty in his own territory, the Porte accepted this condition because of the benefits to be gained from the entire arrangement. Certainly in a period of reform the Ottoman government had no desire

11. Edward Hertslet, *The Map of Europe by Treaty* (London, 1875), II, pp. 1024-1026.

12. For the terms of the Treaty of Paris see *Ibid.*, II, pp. 1250-1265.

to see any major changes in the international situation until its own armed forces and financial structure were in a favorable condition. The terms of the treaty were designed to maintain the status quo and to prop up the Ottoman Empire.

In addition to the reconfirmation of the closure of the Straits, the Treaty of Paris contained other provisions important for the following narrative. Although each of the great powers at different times had offered a major threat to Ottoman integrity and independence, Russia, because of her geographic proximity and her ability to exploit her religious and national ties with the Balkan peoples, remained in the best position to gain predominance over the empire. The Crimean War had been waged on this issue. In the Treaty of Paris the victorious coalition attempted to impose terms which would offer protection to the Ottoman Empire against her strong neighbor. The principal provisions were drawn up with the aim of containing and blocking the expansion of Russian power in three major geographic areas – the Black Sea, the Straits, and the Danube River.

The most important section of the treaty was undoubtedly that which established the neutralization of the Black Sea (Articles XI, XIII). Here both Russia and the Ottoman Empire, with certain minor exceptions, were forbidden to maintain naval forces in the Black Sea or to build military or naval arsenals on its shores. Since these limitations did not cover the Straits, the Ottoman government remained free to maintain a fleet there. The closure of the Straits was confirmed in Article X. In articles XV-XIX the Danube River was put under international control and provision was made for the future regulation of its traffic. The delta was returned to the Ottoman Empire. As an additional protection to the mouth of the river, Russia was required to cede to Moldavia three districts of southern Bessarabia (Article XX). Russia was thus no longer a riverain power and could be excluded from the commission made up of these states. These provisions concerning the Danube were sponsored chiefly by the Habsburg Empire and laid the basis for her future predominance on the river.

In other clauses, in an attempt to weaken the link between Russia and the Balkan peoples, Moldavia, Wallachia, and Serbia were placed under the collective guarantee of the signatory powers of the treaty, as well as under the suzerainty of the sultan, thus breaking the previously exclusive relationship with Russia. At the same time a direct effort was made to strengthen the position of the Porte in relation to its subject nationalities. The Ottoman Empire was specifically admitted into the European state system; the other signatories in turn engaged themselves "to respect the Independence and Territorial Integrity of the Ottoman Empire" (Article VII). Article IX, recording the communication to the powers of the reform decree, the Hatti Hümayun, stated:

> His Imperial Majesty the Sultan having, in his constant solicitude for the welfare of his subjects, issued a Firman, which, while ameliorating their condition without distinction of Religion or of Race, records his generous intentions towards the Christian population of his Empire, and wishing to give a further proof of his sentiments in that respect, has resolved to communicate to the Contracting Parties the said Firman, emanating spontaneously from his Sovereign will.
>
> The Contracting Powers recognise the high value of this communication. It is clearly understood that it cannot, in any case, give to the said Powers the right to interfere, either collectively or separately, in the relations of His Majesty the Sultan with his subjects, nor in the Internal Administration of his Empire.

Three other conventions important to this text were concluded at this time. On March 30 the powers signed a supplementary agreement reconfirming the closure of the Straits, with the exception that the sultan could grant firmans of passage not only to vessels in the service of the missions at Constantinople, but also to those which according to the provisions of the treaty were to be stationed at the mouth of the Danube. A second document, also signed on this date, between the Ottoman Empire and Russia, recorded the agreement of the two powers not to maintain ships of war on the Black Sea with the exception of those specifically designated.

Even more important to the defense of the empire was the third pact. On April 15, France, Britain, and Austria assumed the following obligations:

> I. The High Contracting Parties Guarantee, jointly and severally, the Independence and the Integrity of the Ottoman Empire, recorded in the Treaty concluded at Paris on the 30th of March, 1856.

II. Any infraction of the stipulations of the said Treaty will be considered by the Powers signing the present Treaty as a *casus belli.* They will come to an understanding with the Sublime Porte as to the measures which have become necessary, and will without delay determine among themselves as to the employment of their Military and Naval Forces.[13]

The settlement at Paris in 1856 was thus on the surface extremely favorable to the Ottoman Empire. The powers had collectively agreed to respect the territorial integrity of the empire on the one hand, and not to interfere in her internal affairs on the other. Unilateral Russian protection of the Danubian Principalities and Serbia had been replaced by far less effective European sponsorship. Russian warships could no longer sail the Black Sea, but an Ottoman fleet could remain in the Straits. Russia was now defeated, pushed back from the Danube, and apparently humiliated in the eyes of the Balkan people. In the agreement of April 1856 the three great powers, Austria, Britain, and France, joined together to protect the settlement which in turn shielded the Ottoman Empire.

The Treaty of Paris represented the expression of British, French, and Austrian convictions at the time that the preservation of the Ottoman Empire was the best available solution for the problems of the area. In the British and French view this settlement was closely tied to the continuation in the empire of the era of reform known as the Tanzimat. During the reigns of sultans Abdülmecid (1839-1861) and Abdülaziz (1861-1876) the attempt was made to strengthen the Ottoman state both to resist outside pressure and to preserve inner unity by the adoption of certain western institutions and ideas. The first reform decree, the Hatti Sherif of Gülhane, was adopted in 1839; the second, the Hatti Hümayun, was issued at the time of the Congress of Paris.

Logically the powers who had gone to war with Russia to save the Ottoman Empire from Russian domination and who had thereafter strongly supported internal reform should have made some attempt in the succeeding years to maintain the prestige and position of the Porte during what was bound to be a difficult period of readjustment. In fact, quite the contrary situation followed. All the powers, despite the

13. *Ibid.*, p. 1281.

specific prohibition in Article IX of the Treaty of Paris, continued to meddle in Ottoman internal affairs. As before, each demanded special privileges for its own position and its own protégés, particularly in the Balkans. All continued the old practices of mutual antagonism and intrigue on the local level. Moreover, in the affairs of the Danubian Principalities the powers, although divided among themselves, ultimately approved repeated violations of the treaties.

Although Moldavia and Wallachia had always enjoyed a special position within the empire, Ottoman control was steadily diminished and curtailed after 1856 through illegal actions initiated in the provinces and subsequently approved by the powers. At the congress itself the disagreements between the representatives over the political status to be given the area were so sharp that a decision was postponed and it was felt that the wishes of the inhabitants should first be consulted. In the next years two disputed elections were held; in May 1858 the powers were again forced to meet on Rumanian problems. In August 1858 a new convention was signed which called for the establishment of two separate but parallel administrations under elected native governors. In the winter of 1858-59 the principalities violated the intention of this agreement by electing the same man, Alexander Cuza, as governor of both provinces. In 1861, with the consent of the Porte, the two administrative systems were amalgamated. In 1866 a further violation of treaties occurred when Cuza was overthrown and Charles of Hohenzollern-Sigmaringen became prince. Each of these steps was accompanied by conflict and protests between the powers; each further diminished the position of the Porte in relation to the vassal territories.

A similar situation existed in other areas. In Lebanon the Ottoman government was faced with the necessity of combating the activity of France, based on her protection of Catholic interests.[14] French involvement in the fate of the Ottoman lands was further increased with the inauguration of the construction of the Suez Canal in 1859. In 1860 a revolt in Lebanon led to international intervention and the landing of a French expeditionary force. As a consequence the Porte was compelled to grant the area an autonomous status. In a similar

14. The best general account of this and other episodes comprising "the Eastern Question" can be found in M. S. Anderson, *The Eastern Question* (London, 1966).

manner the powers pressed the Porte to abandon by the end of 1867 its last garrisons and fortresses in Serbia. Thus, while urging internal reform, the powers chiefly supporting the empire, France and Britain, condoned further moves toward its disintegration. Nevertheless, despite these exceptions, of which undoubtedly the most significant had been those pertaining to the Danubian Principalities, the provisions of the Treaty of Paris of chief importance to the protection of the Ottoman Empire were maintained. As long as the barrier erected at the Danube and the neutralization of the Black Sea remained, the Porte was protected from Russia, who at this time was still the single great power who most directly threatened Ottoman integrity. From 1856 to 1870 the Ottoman government thus enjoyed a period of relative respite from foreign dangers. This situation ended in the summer of 1870 with the outbreak of the Franco-Prussian War.

II

THE BLACK SEA CONFERENCE

At the end of October 1870, exploiting the opportunity provided by the international disarray caused by the Prussian defeat of France at Sedan, Alexander II decided that the moment had come to denounce the Black Sea clauses of the Treaty of Paris. A lengthy note, arguing the Russian case, was dispatched to the signatories of the pact in the first week of November 1870.[1] The Porte, like the other European governments, had in previous years received ample warning that Russia would when possible break the terms of the agreement. By the time the Russian message arrived in Constantinople the Ottoman premier, Âli Pasha, not only was expecting a Russian move, but he also knew that the Turkish government would receive little international assistance in resisting any Russian action. Already in August the Russian ambassador, Ignatiev, on his own initiative had brought up the question of both southern Bessarabia and the Black Sea.[2] At this time Âli showed himself chiefly concerned with Turkish possession of the delta of the Danube and the maintenance of international authority on the river. He was not in favor of a change in the status of the Black Sea and strongly opposed any action leading to the opening of the Straits. In his discussions with

1. For the books which have been used for the diplomatic background for this chapter see the "Bibliographic Note."

2. Serge Goriainow, *Le Bosphore et les Dardanelles* (Paris, 1910), pp. 149-153.

Âli, Ignatiev assured the Turkish minister that Russia had no designs against the integrity of the empire nor did she oppose the collective guarantee. Ignatiev's initiative was subsequently criticized by the Russian foreign minister, A. M. Gorchakov, who did not like his rival's interference in a question which he wished to regulate himself. Âli had, of course, no means of knowing of this conflict within the Russian Foreign Ministry.

The defeat of the armies of Napoleon III at Sedan had a tremendous effect in Constantinople. The Porte now lost at one blow the cooperation and support of the power who had previously held the major influence in its councils. An alternative was hard to obtain. Obviously it was only in London that assistance could be found should Russia move, but here the situation was not favorable. In 1868 Gladstone became prime minister with the Earl of Granville as foreign secretary. Not only was Gladstone not a friend of Turkey, but the British government too was paralyzed by the unexpected events on the continent. It was certainly highly unlikely to undertake any strong or positive action in the Near East. In October in a process of reviewing its position it requested from the ambassador in Constantinople, Sir Henry Elliot, an appreciation of the means by which the Porte could defend itself against Russia or Austria-Hungary. Because of his anxiety over the question of defense, Âli had already spoken with Elliot along the same lines. He wished to know at this time what assistance in money and arms he could receive from the British government. When Elliot gave a very discouraging reply, Âli reminded him of the territorial guarantee and expressed the hope that British sympathy for the Ottoman Empire "might again be calculated upon if the occasion called for it."[3]

A strong supporter of the policy of the maintenance of the empire, Elliot in his subsequent despatches to Granville argued always in favor of the interests of the Porte.[4] He believed that Turkey could resist

3. Elliot to Granville, F.O. 78/2125, no. 242 confidential, October 17, 1870.

4. Elliot's opinions were well expressed in a letter of November 4 to Granville. He first commented on the question of the reforms: "There is no doubt yet a great deal to be done in that direction, and it is not rendered easier by the undoubted fact of the Christians in the East being decidedly inferior to the Mohammedans in all the higher moral qualities, and more especially as regards the integrity which is required for men in public employment." On the maintenance of the empire he wrote: "However awkward, cumbersome, or inconvenient the

either Russia or Austria alone, but not the two in alliance. The shortage of money and arms was emphasized. He also called attention to the importance of the Black Sea clauses of the Treaty of Paris to the defense of the state: "The neutralization of the Black Sea is a bulwark as strong and more reliable than the signed guarantees of all the Great Powers of Europe. . . ."[5] The Porte could not surrender on this point; it was "the one thing which could not possibly be obtained from her."[6] Elliot's favorable attitude found little echo in London. Writing at this time to Granville, Gladstone commented: ". . .the whole policy of the Crimean War is now almost universally, and very unduly depreciated, and the idea of another armed intervention on behalf of Turkey, whether sole or with allies, is ridiculed."[7]

Although expecting some Russian action, Âli, like the other European statesmen, was surprised and disconcerted by the form of the move. For the Ottoman Empire two documents had been called in question: the Treaty of Paris and the special convention with Russia alone which had designated the few ships which both powers could station in the Black Sea. In a sense the Porte was relieved that Russia had chosen to attack the Black Sea clauses rather than to reannex southern Bessarabia. This latter question involved the territorial integrity of the empire and thus the honor and prestige of the sultan.[8]

---

existing Ottoman Empire may be, and supposing everything alleged against the Turks by their enemies to be true, were they driven away, there is no possible combination that would offer the slightest prospect of stability that I can see, and I hope it may be long before we have the experiment to try." Elliot to Granville, private letter, P.R.O. 30, 29/102, Therapia, November 4, 1870. Gladstone did not like Elliot's general attitude. In a letter to Granville he wrote: "I think Elliot ought not to pass judgment in his Dispatches on the cogency of the Ottoman Guarantee. His opinion may hinder, cannot help, and is wholly out of place, as anticipating in a public document, the judgment of those who are to instruct him." Gladstone to Granville, Hawarden Castle, November 19, 1870. Agatha Ramm, *The Political Correspondence of Mr. Gladstone and Lord Granville, 1868-1876* (London, 1952), I, p. 160.

5. Elliot to Granville, F.O. 78/2125, no. 254 confidential, Therapia, October 31, 1870.

6. Elliot to Granville, private letter, P.R.O. 30, 29/102, Therapia, November 4, 1870.

7. Quoted in W.E. Mosse, *The Rise and Fall of the Crimean System 1855-1871* (London, 1963), p. 164.

8. Elliot to Granville, F.O. 78/2125, no. 277 confidential, Therapia, November 17, 1870.

The Russian circular, which was communicated to the other courts around November 9, was not officially handed to the Ottoman government until November 15. The Porte thus learned of the Russian move through the other governments. The first reaction of the Ottoman diplomats was strong. In a conversation with Granville on November 14, Musurus declared that "Turkey would never submit to these pretentions, that if the Government of the Emperor of Russia thought fit to denounce any portion of the Treaties of 1856, Turkey on her part would at once denounce all of her engagements with Russia and that she was perfectly prepared for the consequences which might ensue." Granville in an attempt to calm the situation advised the Ottoman government not to "act precipitously" or without consultation with the other signatories of the Treaty of Paris.[9]

In Constantinople Âli spoke with Elliot in less strong terms and indeed with a note of relative caution. He hoped that the Porte would not be abandoned by her allies and that Austria and Britain would act in an energetic manner.[10] He saw three courses open for the powers: a declaration of war, the referral of the question to a congress, or the issuance of a protest against the action as a violation of treaties. A war would of necessity be offensive; the Porte would join her allies if this course were decided upon. However, Âli commented: "I think. . .I can guarantee that the Porte would not look upon itself as deserted in its emergency if the allied Governments considered the third alternative as the best and the safest for the interests of Turkey." Elliot, like Granville, urged that the Porte refrain from action and consult its allies.[11]

In his conversations with the Habsburg representative, Anton von Prokesch-Osten, Âli spoke in a similarly restrained and pessimistic manner, but he used those arguments that stressed the common Turkish-Habsburg concern over the national movements. He expressed the fear that the denunciation of the Black Sea clauses by Russia was only a first step. She would next support Prince Charles' desire for Rumanian independence and she would "kindle aspirations at Belgrade

9. Granville to Elliot, F.O. 195/959, no. 238, F.O., November 14, 1870.

10. Elliot to Granville, F.O. 78/2125, nos. 267 and 268, Therapia, November 14, 1870.

11. Elliot to Granville, F.O. 78/2125, no. 274, Therapia, November 17, 1870.

and favor ideas of nationality and aggression among the Rumanians and the Slavs."[12] In a later conversation he stressed in particular the community of Ottoman and Habsburg interests: "It is up to Austria to ascertain whether in working for the breakup of the Ottoman Empire, Russia is not undermining in the same way the Austrian Empire. She [Russia] will be supported by aspirations already existing in Rumania and Serbia and you will soon become aware of these in Bukovina and Transylvania as well as in Croatia and Dalmatia."[13]

In his conversations with Prokesch, Âli recognized that the British attitude would be decisive. He feared that Britain would not go beyond a counter-proposal suggesting the full opening of the Straits, a measure which the Ottoman government strongly opposed. The pessimistic attitude of the minister was to be reflected in his later conversations and instructions. The Ottoman government was from the beginning fully aware that no other state would be willing to go to war to preserve a stipulation of the Treaty of Paris which was of vital importance chiefly to the Ottoman Empire. Without a strong and united stand by all the powers, there was no hope that the Russian government would abandon its position.

The Porte, as has been mentioned, received the Russian circular after the other powers. Since Ignatiev was in Russia on leave, the chargé d'affaires, E. E. Staal, handed Âli the despatch. The Turkish minister received it with the words: "You bring us war".[14] He told the Russian representative that the Porte would have to consult its allies before

12. Prokesch to Beust, H.H.S. XII, 97, no no., Constantinople, November 12, 1870.

13. Prokesch to Beust, H.H.S. XII, 97, no. 82A, Constantinople, November 15, 1870. Âli and Prokesch had discussed this matter before. Ali had stated that it was a mistake to believe that the complaints of the Christians of the empire were due to their position, which was the same as the Moslems except that they did not serve in the army. He continued: "L'on chercherait donc en vain le motif des plaintes des Chrétiens de l'Empire Ottoman dans leur sort, mais on en trouverait plutôt la source là, où puisent leur sujet de désaffection les Tcheques, les Dalmates et d'autres fractions des nationalés, que peuplent la Monarchie Austro-Hongroise." Prokesch to Beust, H.H.S. XII/97, no. 80 AB, Constantinople, November 4,1870

14. Goriainow, *Le Bosphore et les Dardanelles,* p. 187. For the Russian attitude see Ismail Kemal Bey, *The Memoirs of Ismail Kemal Bey* (New York, n.d.) pp. 59-61.

replying.[15] In this conversation Staal made every effort to conciliate and calm Âli. In fact, thereafter in its dealing with Constantinople the Russian government, which wished to avoid a major crisis, did all it could to appease and reassure the Porte. The Russian diplomats preferred, and now attempted to obtain, a direct agreement on the Black Sea question between the Russian and Turkish governments without the participation of the other powers. Although at this time the Russian words were usually soft, the Russian government was always aware that it could use the weapon of the threat of a rising of the Balkan peoples in its dealing with Constantinople. This idea was clearly expressed in Gorchakov's instructions to Staal, which stated, as paraphrased by the Russian historian Serge Goriainow:

> The Christian populations in the East are far from being satisfied. They are perhaps waiting for the moment when an obvious disagreement arises between ourselves and the Porte and offers them the chance to realize their desires for emancipation. This opportunity can occur even without any participation on our part if the attitude of the Turkish government in the special question of the moment should be of a nature to offend Russia, if it carried the character of an outdated mistrust. In contrast, a calming down [of the situation] would be inevitable if the suppression of a clause impossible for a great nation and without practical value for Turkey would be allowed by her with good grace.[16]

When Ignatiev returned to Constantinople, he discussed the abrogation of the treaty with the Turkish minister in conciliatory terms. Âli then asked him why the Russian government had not first consulted the signatory powers. Ignatiev replied that it had not wished to put itself at the mercy of the good will of these states. He added the very true comment that the Porte should not object to the method because if such deliberations or a conference had been held, questions in regard to the east might have arisen which could have had unpleasant consequences for the Ottoman Empire. The Russian ambassador suggested that the Porte would be well advised to take the initiative of suggesting an entente with Russia on the question. At this time, however, and in

15. Elliot to Granville, F.O. 78/2125, no. 272, Therapia, November 16, 1870.
16. Goriainow, *Le Bosphore et les Dardanelles,* p. 188.

subsequent conversations, Âli did not encourage the idea of a direct understanding.[17]

At the end of the month Ignatiev was received in audience by the sultan. In this conversation Abdülaziz discussed the compensation which the Ottoman government desired in return for its assent to the Russian denunciation. The sultan, although depreciating the general value of the neutralization of the Black Sea, nevertheless declared that it contributed to the security of the state. He could accept the Russian action if the Porte in return received an equivalent guarantee which would aid it in dealing with internal unrest. Although the exact nature of this was not defined, Ignatiev in his report on the meeting wrote:

> They wish. . .perhaps to obtain a declaration having the effect of discouraging the aspirations of the Christians and guaranteeing Turkey against all interference of our part in cases similar to that of the Cretan insurrection. Such a demand would place us in a delicate position.[18]

In a conversation with the Ottoman representative, Rustem Pasha, Gorchakov at this time also used the opportunity to press for a Russian-Turkish rapprochement. On the question of the compensation which the sultan had indicated, he replied that it had already been the subject of Russian action.

> For a number of years. . .we have not ceased advising the Christian populations under the domination of the Porte patience and confidence in the intentions of their sovereign. These counsels have fundamentally contributed to maintain peace in the east. Moreover, we have proposed, more than a year ago, the principle of its [Ottoman] intervention in case of internal

17. *Ibid.*, pp. 189, 190.

18. *Ibid.*, p. 192. In 1866-68 a revolt had taken place in Crete which led to prolonged discussions between the powers.

At this time Ignatiev, who had a bad reputation in the diplomatic world for lying, evidently spread the rumor that the sultan had said that he could easily come to an agreement with Russia, but the other governments prevented this. In denying this statement to Elliot, Âli "groans over the impossibility of doing business with a man who, more or less, distorts almost every word that is said to him and we, his colleagues, have the uncomfortable feeling of never knowing what may be put into our mouths to go the round of half the governments of Europe." Elliot to Granville, P.R.O. 30, 29/102, Therapia, December 2, 1870.

troubles in Turkey, pledging our word if the other powers wish to accept the same obligation.[19]

The Russian government thus desired a separate agreement with the Porte. In return the assurance would be given that Russia would not use her new strength in the Black Sea to extend her power in the Balkans by supporting insurrectionary movements. Throughout these conversations the Russian statesmen emphasized that they had no desire to change the Straits settlement. The rule of the closure of the Straits was certainly to Russian advantage as long as a Black Sea fleet was not yet in existence.

The Porte also turned to Berlin. The advice which it received from Prussia was from the beginning clear and direct, qualities for which the Ottoman government was later to express appreciation. The timing of the Russian denunciation had been a rude surprise for Bismarck, although Prussian support for the action had already been assured. The Prussian government wished no further complications to arise on the European scene until the war with France was concluded. When queried on the Prussian attitude by Aristarchi Pasha, the Ottoman representative in Berlin, Bismarck first declared that he had to ascertain the opinion of the other German states in the North German Confederation. Aristarchi correctly commented that Bismarck was not in the habit of consulting these states on foreign policy and that he was obviously seeking to gain time. Bismarck also told Aristarchi that although Prussia had signed the Treaty of Paris, with its guarantee of the Ottoman Empire in Article VII, he believed that it was up to the signatories of the Treaty of April 15, Austria, Britain, and France, to decide if the Russian move was a *casus belli.* He did not consider that his government was obliged to fight over a matter of form rather than fact unless an infraction occurred which directly affected Prussian honor or interests.[20] The Ottoman government was made aware from

19. Goriainow, *Le Bosphore et les Dardanelles,* p. 217.

20. Aristarchi to Âli, M.N. 20/6, no. 3089/249 confidential, Berlin, December 7, 1870. Bismarck was determined that the Black Sea question should not trouble Prussian-Russian relations. He wrote Bernstorff: "Auf keinen Fall darf die Konferenz mit ihren Verhandlungen uns mit Russland verstimmen oder gar entzweien." Bismarck to Bernstorff, no. 79, vertraulich, Versailles, November 28, 1870. *Die Grosse Politik der Europäischen Kabinette, 1871-1914,* edited by J. Lepsius, A. M. Bartholdy, and F. Thimme (Berlin, 1922), II, pp. 18, 19. Cited hereafter as *G.P.*

the beginning that it could not count on any support from Berlin against Russia on the major issue of ending the neutralization of the Black Sea.

Meanwhile, despite the fact that the British government had told the Porte not to act without consulting its allies, Granville and Gladstone proceeded to settle the question through negotiation with Bismarck, and through him with the Russian government, with little reference to either the Turkish or Habsburg opinions. When the Russian circular was delivered, both the British government and the press reacted quite strongly but on different issues. To many in Britain the Russians had now rid themselves of the restriction which was the single major British gain of the Crimean War. Gladstone, who had never approved of the stipulation, was in contrast less concerned over the fact than over the form, that is, the unilateral denunciation of an international treaty.

In fact, the provisions of two agreements signed by Britain were now to be involved in the negotiations: the Treaty of Paris and the tripartite agreement of April 1856. Since Russia had not yet violated a treaty, but had only declared an intention, neither of these pacts was as yet affected. Nevertheless, the obvious assumption that the Russian government would indeed soon carry through some measures of rearmament in the Black Sea area made it imperative that the consequences of such acts should be considered. Moreover, since it was from the beginning of the crisis evident that Britain would not go to war over the issue, it was obviously to the interest of that government to find a peaceful solution to the crisis and one which would not violate the principles proclaimed by the Liberal cabinet concerning the unilateral breaking of treaties.

With this aim in mind Odo Russell, an under-secretary at the Foreign Office who was visiting the Prussian Headquarters at Versailles, spoke with Bismarck on November 21. Using stronger language than his instructions in fact justified, he tried to convince the German leader "that unless he would get Russia to withdraw the circular, we should be compelled, with or without allies, to go to war."[21] Even before this meeting, Bismarck had taken steps to arrange a conference. Acting as an intermediary, he was able to gain an acceptance from both Russia and

21. Quoted in Mosse, *Crimean System,* p. 171.

Britain for the submission of the question to a conference composed of representatives of the signatories of the Treaty of Paris. British objections to the Russian circular were met by simply ignoring its existence. It was not withdrawn, but it did not form part of the subsequent negotiations. Britain accepted participation in a conference "for the consideration of an adequate statement of the grounds on which Russia may put forward a proposal for the revision of the special Convention annexed to, and embodied in, the Treaty of 1856." To further emphasize its attitude, the British government insisted that all of the representatives should go to the meeting without previous agreements, and:

> It must be understood, that such a Conference could be subject to no previous assumption as to its results; but Her Majesty's Government would feel themselves bound to weigh with fairness, and without bias, any claims which Russia might advance, and any proposals which she might make.[22]

Britain did not wish it to appear that the powers would automatically approve the Russian action. Russia had already indicated that she would agree to some alteration of the Straits agreements.[23]

It is interesting to note that although Gladstone and Granville now placed their entire emphasis on the sanctity of international treaties, they were in fact themselves preparing the ground to disentangle their government from the obligations of the tripartite treaty of April 1856. This agreement was quite clear: "Any infraction of the stipulations of the said Treaty will be considered by the Powers signing the present Treaty as a *casus belli.*" Gladstone had no intention of ever honoring this obligation. To justify this end he summoned a great number of arguments. Since the Russian government had only declared an intention to act:

22. Granville to Russell, P.R.O. 30/29/254, tel., F.O., November 25, 1870.

23. On December 17 an official in the Russian foreign ministry told the Prussian representative that: "um England gefällig zu sein" Russia would agree "bei Fortdauer der Schliessung der Meerengen für alle, Möglichkeit für Sultan, wenn er sich bedroht glaubt, auch ohne Kriegszustand verbündete Flotten zu rufen." Prince Henry VII Reuss to Bismarck, St. Petersburg, December 17, 1870. Kurt Rheindorf, *Die Schwarze Meer (Pontus) Frage, 1856-1871* (Berlin, 1925), p. 163.

> . . .there had as yet been no infraction of the Treaty. – This being the case, and one of the three co-signatories being in a position in which it might be difficult to require an exact execution of the stipulations of the second Treaty, it was better to postpone discussion of it for the present.[24]

Later he produced an even more artful excuse for avoiding British obligations:

> . . .stringent as it is in its terms, it does not appear to me to have much force as a covenant at present, when Turkey declares her own incapacity to fight except with (virtually) our money. Guarantees as such seem to me to presuppose the capacity of any guaranteed State to fight for herself; and then to supply a further auxiliary defense. At least I think it must be so in the case where nothing is expressed to give a different construction to the guarantee.[25]

Granville felt similarly. On December 10 he wrote to Gladstone: "But what sticks in my gizzard is the Tripartite Treaty. How very foolish it was of us to have concocted it. But there it is, with obligations as binding as were ever contracted."[26]

As has been mentioned, Austria-Hungary, like the Porte, was largely left out of the negotiations which led to the calling of a conference. Although the monarchy had if anything an even stronger interest in checking Russian expansion than did Britain, this state was in November in a difficult and dangerous position. Until the issues brought up by the Franco-Prussian War were settled, Austrian attention had to be primarily concerned with events in central Europe. The monarchy had also in previous years recognized the fact that the neutralization could not be retained permanently. In this question, Vienna could not afford to antagonize Russia. It had been made abundantly clear that Prussia and Russia were giving full support to

24. Quoted in Mosse, *Crimean System,* p. 189.

25. Gladstone to Granville, no. 2, Hawarden Castle, December 12, 1870. Ramm, *Political Correspondence,* I, p. 185.

26. Granville also wanted Prussia to join the treaty to form a strong front should Russia denounce the rest of the Treaty of Paris. In this case: "If Prussia played false to us, it would diminish the necessity of our putting ourselves forward alone, or with only half the other cosignatories." Granville to Gladstone, private letter, Walmer Castle, December 10, 1870. Ramm, *Political Correspondence,* I, pp. 181, 182.

each other; opposition to either might lead to war with both.[27] Moreover, the consequences for Habsburg foreign policy from the *Ausgleich* were being felt. The foreign minister, Frederick Ferdinand von Beust, a former Saxon official with a prime interest in the events in western and central Europe, had now come into severe conflict with Magyar opinion, led by Count Julius Andrassy.[28] The Hungarian minister-president felt that the Habsburg government should adopt a strong position against the Russian action.[29] Later the Hungarian government was to support a policy of the exaction of a high level of compensation. The question of the Russian circular was discussed at an Imperial Council on November 14. It was here decided that because of the general circumstances of the time the Habsburg government would have to follow Britain.[30]

The instructions which Beust sent to the Austrian ambassador in London, Count Rudolf Apponyi, on November 23 were thus to adopt a moderate policy and above all to follow the British lead: "we shall be ready to follow England wherever she wishes to go."[31] The monarchy

27. In discussing the Russian note the German ambassador in Vienna, Schweinitz, made this point quite clear to Andrassy: ". . .ich sage ihm ganz offen, dass wir, sobald wir gezwungen werden, zwischen Russland und Osterreich-Ungarn zu optieren, uns fürs ersteres entscheiden müssen. . . ." Lothar von Schweinitz, *Denkwürdigkeiten des Botschafters General von Schweinitz* (Berlin, 1927), I, p. 282.

28. Granville wrote: "Beust who can never keep his tongue or his pen quiet for a moment is mounted on his high horse and Apponyi tells me that Hungary very French, and anti-Russian will exert much pressure to keep him there." Granville to Gladstone, private letter, F.O., November 16, 1870. Ramm, *Political Correspondence,* I, p. 157. Also Bloomfield to Granville, F.O. 7/769, no. 201 confidential, Vienna, November 23, 1870.

29. Bloomfield reported that Andrassy expected war sooner or later because of the Russian action and that he spoke also of Russian intrigues among the Slavs of the monarchy. Bloomfield to Granville, F.O. 7/769, no no., November 23, 1870. The Ottoman representative in Vienna, Halil Pasha, wrote that when the news of the Gorchakov circular reached Austria-Hungary, the Hungarian press was unanimous in preaching "résistance à outrance." Halil to Âlil, M.N. 20/6, no. 3303/384, Vienna, November 24, 1870.

30. Mosse *Crimean System,* pp. 168, 169.

31. Beust to Apponyi, H.H.S. VIII/75, no no., Vienna, November 23, 1870. On November 28 Apponyi delivered this message to Granville. He emphasized that the Habsburg Monarchy wished to follow moderate policies, but added that ". . .if the British Cabinet was inclined to display energy, it might reckon entirely upon Austria, whose concurrence was in any case to be relied upon." Granville to Bloomfield, F.O. 7/763, no. 130, F.O., November 30, 1870. Also Bloomfield to Granville, F.O. 7/769, no. 208, Vienna, November 27, 1870.

did not want a war nor did it desire to press other powers to extreme steps, but if the British government decided to adopt a firm policy, it could count on Habsburg support. Like the Porte, the Habsburg government was most concerned about the effect of the Russian action on the national minorities. In this same despatch Beust wrote: "In declaring that her will alone is law, and that she has only her interests or her requirements to consult, Russia obviously intends to recapture in the eyes of the populations of the east her former reputation of power and grandeur."

In one regard the Habsburg government was willing to take a more firm position than the British. On November 29 Beust telegraphed Apponyi that in order to remove any doubt about its attitude, the Habsburg government declared: "We consider ourselves bound by the special treaty of April 1856 and we are ready to fulfill the obligations that it imposes on us in regard to Turkey." The Ottoman government was given a similar notification.[32] The British reaction was along the lines previously discussed; no treaty had yet been broken and the third signatory, France, was in no position to assist in carrying out the terms of the agreement.[33]

Despite the similarity of their general interests, the British and Habsburg governments did not cooperate without friction. Initially Beust was not in favor of a conference. When it was agreed upon, he believed that the four powers signatory to the Treaty of Paris – Britain, Austria, Turkey, and Italy – should hold preliminary discussions through their representatives in Constantinople with the aim of framing a common policy.[34] Granville refused this suggestion because of his previous stand that the powers should enter the conference without preliminary specific engagements. He did not, however, preclude "a general agreement as to the objects which we should keep steadily in view."[35] Under this elastic heading the British government did in fact

32. Beust to Prokesch, H.H.S. XII/96, no. 20 B, November 29, 1870.

33. Apponyi to Beust, H.H.S. VIII/74, tel. no. 52, London, November 30, 1870; Apponyi to Beust, *Ibid.,* no. 66a, London, November 30, 1870; Granville to Bloomfield, F.O. 7/763, no. 137, F.O., December 2, 1870.

34. Beust to Apponyi, H.H.S. VIII/75, no no., Vienna, December 4, 1870; Beust to Apponyi, *Ibid.,* tel. no. 999E, Vienna, November 28, 1870.

35. Granville to Bloomfield, F.O. 7/763, no. 143, F.O., December 7, 1870; Apponyi to Beust, H.H.S. VIII/74, tel. no. 54, London, December 6, 1870.

discuss most of the issues which were to arise in the congress with the other powers before the opening session.

Neither Britain nor the Habsburg government was satisfied with the other's attitude; each accused the other of weakness before Russia. When Granville reproached Apponyi on the Habsburg hesitation, the ambassador replied: "Situated as we are between Russia and Germany, with very inflammable Slavic elements on our southern frontiers, we are forced to be very careful and we are able to take a firm stand only if we are certain of being strongly seconded and supported."[36]

Like the Habsburg Empire the Porte was dissatisfied with the British attitude. In particular the Turkish government did not want the matter handled through a congress; it feared that any such meeting might also discuss the demands of the subject nationalities. In his conversations with Granville, Musurus "dwelt particularly on this last point: and urged that a Congress would only end to the disadvantage of Turkey and that there was no compromise possible."[37] In a meeting on November 26 in which the chief topic of discussion was Russell's report on his talks with Bismarck, Musurus expressed his regret that Britain had admitted in principle the idea of a conference. He argued that his government could not accept a revision of the Treaty of Paris and that the powers could not act without Ottoman acquiescence. The ambassador felt that the Porte would be in a most difficult position in any conference, since it would not command the support of the majority. He felt that if ever Russia should maintain a fleet in the Black Sea, it would be better that it be by "a crime odious to the sanctity of treaties, of which she is guilty, than with our concurrence and as a result of a legal sanction."[38]

The position of the Porte in the first phase of the negotiations was thus certainly logical and based on a clear understanding of the

36. Apponyi to Beust, H.H.S. VIII/75, private letter, London, November 25, 1870.

37. Granville to Elliot, F.O. 195/959, no. 249, F.O., November 23, 1870.

38. Musurus to Âli, M.N. 20/6, no. 4280/141, London, November 24, 1870, Musurus to Âli, *ibid.,* no. 4278/139 confidential, London, November 26, 1870. Granville wrote to Elliot: "His Excellency expressed his regret at what had been done: he had already, he said, informed me of the objection which Turkey would feel to a Congress, which would result in loss to her, as there was no possible middle course with regard to the neutralization of the Black Sea." Granville to Elliot, F.O. 195/959, no. 256B, F.O., November 28, 1870.

weakness of its own position. It was recognized that Russia would not withdraw the circular and that the Ottoman allies were not about to go to war over the issue. A conference would be perhaps the most dangerous solution of all for the interests of the empire. Since the Ottoman Empire could not fight Russia alone, an acceptance of the Russian circular and bilateral negotiations offered perhaps a preferable course of action.[39]

However, despite its strong aversion to the event, when it became clear that a conference would be held, the Porte could not well hold out alone. In a circular despatch to its representatives dated November 29, the Ottoman government agreed to the meeting, but made this acceptance dependent on an understanding that the discussions would be limited to the single question at issue. The other parts of the Treaty of Paris were not to come under discussion.[40] Granville, in accordance with his previous insistance that the powers should make no prior agreements, would not accept this condition either.[41]

In the negotiations preceding the conference it was recognized that the three powers injured by the Russian denunciation would be entitled to some sort of compensation. The British wished some action which would reinforce the idea of the sanctity of treaties. The Habsburg government drew up a list of measures connected with the Danube River which they wished accepted by the powers. The state most affected by the Russian move was, of course, the Ottoman Empire. The question of what compensation the Porte should ask was difficult to decide. The Ottoman leaders wanted to make no changes in their general international relations which would make their position worse. If they had been allowed a really free choice, they would undoubtedly have asked the kind of compensation indicated in the sultan's conversation with Ignatiev – that is, some measure which would

39. Cemal Tukin, *Osmanli Imparatorluğu devrinde Boğazlar Meselesi* (Istanbul, 1947), pp. 298, 299.

40. Circular despatch, M.N. 20/6, no. 29026/29, November 29, 1870; Musurus to Âli, *ibid.*, no. 4211/142, November 29, 1870.

41. Musurus to Âli, M.N. 20/6, no. 4286/46, confidential, London, November 30, 1870; Musurus to Âli, *ibid.*, no. 4291/150, London, December 8, 1870; Granville to Elliot, F.O. 195/959, no. 258A. F.O., November 28, 1870; Granville to Elliot, *ibid.*, no. 259A, F.O., November 30, 1870; Granville to Elliot, *ibid.*, no. 266, F.O., December 8, 1870.

strengthen their position in regard to the Balkan Christians. Since, however, they were now forced to follow a policy of reliance on Britain, they could not hope to obtain much in this line. In fact, they came to adopt as their major demand an alteration in the Straits settlement which appears to have been suggested by Elliot and subsequently approved by Gladstone and Granville.

When the question of compensation was first discussed, a change in the Straits settlement was an obvious possibility. Since the tsar now wished to assume sovereignty over his territory, the sultan could in answer reassert his full control over the Straits. He could then allow his friends to enter and he could exclude his enemies. The dangers of this policy were obvious to both the British and the Turkish statesmen. Such a move would mean in practice a full opening of the Straits, since it would be difficult at this time for the sultan to exclude the ships of any power without bitterly antagonizing that government. Elliot, however, on his own initiative suggested a variation on this idea to Âli. He proposed that the Porte should consider if "while maintaining the principle of keeping the Straits closed, some additional security might not be afforded to the Porte by allowing the Sultan to invite the Fleets of his Allies, when an exceptional emergency might seem to make their presence desirable." Under the regulations in force the sultan had no protection against a sudden attack on his capital. With these new arrangements he would be able to call in the help of other powers in a moment of danger. This suggestion had the advantage of allowing the sultan in actual practice more freedom of choice in that it established the closure of the Straits as the normal condition; the sultan would be able to act only in exceptional circumstances. He would thus not be under constant pressure to allow the passage of warships. Elliot reported that Âli's first reaction to this suggestion had not been very favorable; he felt that it would weaken too much the rule that the Straits should as a normal condition remain closed.[42]

42. Elliot to Granville, P.R.O. 30, 29/102, Therapia, November 18, 1870; Elliot to Granville, F.O. 78/2125, no. 293, Therapia, November 21, 1870. Also Elliot to Granville, P.R.O. 30, 29/102, private letter, Therapia, November 21, 1870. Elliot to Granville, *ibid.*, private letter, Therapia, November 28, 1870. Gladstone approved the idea; he wrote: "I think Elliot hits the point in his suggestion that the Sultan should not resume an unbounded discretion but one to

When Granville spoke of this change, that is, that the sultan should be allowed to open the Straits to foreign warships in case of need, Musurus was also not enthusiastic. He argued that if the Porte exercised the right in favor of France or Britain, then Russia would also expect similar treatment. Ottoman relations with St. Petersburg would be severely compromised by a refusal. Granville replied that his government would avoid establishing a precedent unless it were absolutely necessary; British and allied fleets would only enter the Straits and the Black Sea in exceptional circumstances and in the interest of the Ottoman Empire.[43]

Gladstone and Granville were both most concerned over the British obligations in the April 1856 treaty. Musurus was willing to see the treaty annulled.[44] When, however, Elliot spoke with Âli about the possibility of the cancellation of the treaty and reliance only on Article VII of the Treaty of Paris as a guarantee of the independence and integrity of the Ottoman Empire, Âli strongly objected. He emphasized the drastic effect which such a move would have in the Near East, where it would be regarded as proof that Britain no longer attached as much importance as before to the maintenance of the Ottoman Empire. The Porte had seen one of the supports to its security taken away; it would not be understood if it lost yet another guarantee.[45] The

---

be exercised in case of menace, or to use our word in the Naval Reserve Act in case of 'emergency.'" Gladstone to Granville, Hawarden Castle, December 3, 1870. Ramm, *Political Correspondence,* I, p. 170.

43. Musurus to Âli, M.N. 20/6, no. 4278/146, London, December 2, 1870; Granville to Elliot, F.O. 195/959, no. 261, F.O., December 1, 1870. In this same conversation Musurus mentioned as compensation the abolition of Article IX of the Treaty of Paris so that no power could interpret this falsely and intervene directly or indirectly in the internal affairs of the Ottoman Empire. In contrast to the Russian government, which had not discouraged the Porte from seeking compensation in the general area of its relations with its subject people, this approach did not satisfy Granville at all. He claimed to see in it no connection with the Russian action and the questions at issue.

44. Granville to Elliot, F.O. 195/959, no. 277 confidential, F.O., December 17, 1870.

45. Granville to Elliot, F.O. 195/959, tel. no. 26, F.O., December 24, 1870; Elliot to Granville, F.O. 78/2126, no. 380 confidential, Pera, December 27, 1870; Elliot to Granville, *ibid.,* no 381, Pera, December 27, 1870; Elliot to Granville, private letter, P.R.O. 30, 29/102, Constantinople, December 30, 1870. On

Ottoman government, in fact, would have liked to have enlarged the April treaty to include all of the great powers.

By the middle of December the Porte was able to inform both Elliot and Prokesch of the two guarantees which it was most interested in obtaining. The first was the assurance that the stipulations of the Treaty of Paris, other than those concerning the Black Sea, would be maintained; the second was the proposal that the sultan should regain his sovereign rights over the Straits. The Porte also favored the conversion of the tripartite pact into a general agreement protecting the remaining treaty obligations and to be signed by all the powers. Prokesch reported to Beust that the Ottoman government would have liked to have proposed amendments to the Treaty of Paris, but it feared to put in jeopardy those sections which guaranteed:

> . . .the conditions indispensable to its existence, namely, independence and territorial integrity, admission to public law and to the European concert, the right to appeal to the arbitration of the cosignatories and the prohibition imposed on the powers to intervene in the relations of the sultan with his subjects and in the internal administration of the empire.[46]

On December 21 the Porte sent very detailed instructions to Musurus, who, as the Ottoman ambassador in London, would represent his government at the coming conference.[47] This document is of great interest because of the clearness of its exposition of the Ottoman viewpoint. It first stated that the best solution for the Porte would be maintenance of the status quo, that is, the neutralization of the Black

---

January 3, 1871 Granville informed Elliot that Britain did not insist on the abolition of the tripartite agreement; the move had been taken on Musurus' suggestion. Granville to Elliot, F.O. 195/971, no. 1 confidential, F.O., January 3, 1871.

46. Prokesch to Beust, H.H.S. XII/97, no. 56, Constantinople, December 12, 1870; Prokesch to Beust, *ibid.,* no. 89 A-C, Constantinople, December 13, 1870; Prokesch to Beust, *ibid.,* no. 90 A-D, Constantinople, December 16, 1870.

47. See Appendices I and II for the complete text of the instructions. Although Elliot's influence was undoubtedly strong in the drawing up of this document, Ignatiev wrote that the instructions "furent rédigées en dehors de toute pression étrangère. Je fut même le premier des Représentants à en avoir connaissance." Ignatiev, "Zapisky Grafa N.P. Ignatieva (1864-1874)," *Izvestiia Ministerstva Inostrannykh Diel,* V, 1914, p. 133.

Sea. There was, however, little hope that this desire could be achieved. Russia could not be expected to retire voluntarily. If the Ottoman Empire wished to keep conditions as they were, she would have to be prepared to fight. Although Ottoman defenses were deemed to be in satisfactory order, an offensive war could not be undertaken without allies. Only participation in a coalition would give hope for success, but even if one could be formed, the results of the venture could prove unfortunate: "Can we be sure of coming out of it without losing anything either morally or materially?" Because of these considerations the Council of Ministers had decided that a war could not be undertaken, either alone or in an alliance. The empire needed a dozen years of peace and tranquility: "In addition, experience has shown us that more powerful allies become semi-protectors and are obliged to demand from those for whom they have shed their blood and spent their money sacrifices that one cannot refuse them without showing ingratitude."

The Porte would thus have to accept the Russian action, but it could seek compensation in other fields, in particular in connection with its sovereign rights over the Rumanian principalities and Serbia, in regard to the capitulations, and, most important, concerning the Straits. In the question of the vassal states the Porte sought an alteration in the international treaties, in particular Article XXVII of the Treaty of Paris which prevented the empire from using military force at once when agreements were broken. Musurus was instructed to discuss this matter with Granville, but the question was to be brought up in "an intimate and very personal conversation." A similar hesitancy and awareness that little could probably be gained are shown in the section on the abolition of the capitulations. The expectation was clearly expressed that the Porte would be faced either with an outright refusal or with impossible conditions should this question be brought before the powers. It was believed better to remain under the present treaties than to "subordinate the justice of the land to international restrictions."

With little expectation that compensation could be gained in the question of the vassal states or the capitulations, the Porte put the emphasis in the instructions on the section on the Straits. It now desired that the sultan gain full control over this part of his territory. Musurus was directed to declare to the conference that the Porte,

> . . .while determined to maintain the principle of the closure of the two straits, a principle sanctioned by its ancient legislation, demands to be freed from any international engagement relative to it and reserves the right to open them or to close them to warships of other powers as its interests and security demand and excluding that this change authorizes any foreign government to demand any exception whatsoever in its favor.

The Porte thus wished to rid itself of the great power tutelage which had commenced with the Treaty of Unkiar Skelessi and had continued through the Straits Convention of 1841 and the Treaty of Paris. In no case, however, did the Porte wish the Straits open. Musurus was instructed to oppose "formally and categorically" any such proposition.

In addition, the instructions expressed approval of any action which served to confirm the other stipulations of the Treaty of Paris or to block future actions similar to the Russian unilateral denunciation. The Porte also favored the incorporation of the provisions of the April 1856 treaty into any new act which might be made by the congress. It was hoped that the conference would succeed: "I do not speak of another arrangement which would consist of protesting officially and letting matters follow their own course. That is the worst that one can imagine that is bad and dangerous."

A summary of these instructions was communicated to both London and Vienna at the end of December.[48] Meanwhile, the Habsburg government had decided on its demands for compensation. It now desired (1) that the Porte be given the right to open the Straits to a certain number of foreign warships; (2) that a Turkish port be

48. Prokesch to Beust, H.H.S. XII/97, no. 93A, Constantinople, December 27, 1870. Granville commented on them: "The Turk's instructions are moderate concession of non neutralization, return of Sovereign Rights to the Sultan, and confirmation of treaty of 1856. But he would like to add the particular condition of the Treaty of April, into the general Treaty. This would be worse than all parties entering into the Treaty of April. – And Prussia would not consent, but Musurus thought there might be means of leaving out the fighting clause which appears to be the essential point. I will ask him to show me something in writing. He would like to get [rid] of the Capitulations, and he wishes to bring the Principalities before the Conference, which I told him was impossible, that I had said so to Prussia and Austria, in conformity with what Turkey had said to me." Granville to Gladstone, F.O., January 5, 1871. Ramm, *Political Correspondence,* I, p. 206.

designated as an international naval station; the number of ships which could be stationed here were to be in proportion to the maritime forces of Russia in the Black Sea; (3) that the number of ships which the powers could have at the mouth of the Danube be raised; (4) that Austria be delegated the leading and directing role in undertaking the improvement of the navigation of the Danube, in particular at the Iron Gates. Other suggestions in regard to the river were also made. The renewal or extension of the April agreement was not approved unless all of the signatories of the Treaty of Paris supported such a move.[49]

These ambitious proposals were not received with favor either in London or in Constantinople. When Apponyi communicated them to Granville, the British minister made several obvious objections. He believed that the best compensation to give the sultan would be to allow him to exercise his right of sovereignty over the waters of the Straits. He did not think that this measure should be accompanied by conditions which determined in advance how many ships each state could send through the Straits. He considered it better simply to give the Porte the right to call in foreign warships in case of real need. If passage was always open to a certain number of warships, it would be difficult to control this movement or limit it to time of need. Granville wished no stipulation introduced which would allow Russia access to the eastern Mediterranean. On the Danube issues Granville preferred that the conference concentrate on the Black Sea. However, when this question was settled, he saw no reason why the Habsburg delegates should not make suggestions regarding the river.[50]

Needless to say, Âli viewed these proposals with even less approval. He strongly opposed both the assignment of a Turkish port in which the western powers could station ships and an increase of the number of ships to be allowed each state at the mouth of the Danube. The assignment of a Turkish port as a maritime arsenal for foreign fleets was obviously incompatible with the idea of the maintenance of the territorial integrity of the empire and the dignity of the sultan. The Ottoman minister also observed that: "A few more steamships at Sulina

49. Beust to Apponyi, H.H.S. VIII/75, no. 1., Vienna, December 22, 1870.

50. Apponyi to Beust, H.H.S. VIII/74, no. 74 AB, London, December 28, 1870; also Granville to Bloomfield, F.O. 7/763, no. 164 confidential, F.O., December 28, 1870.

cannot avert the danger which the creation of a considerable Russian naval force in the neighborhood offers the Danube."[51] The attitude of the Porte toward the general question of the Danube and the Austrian proposals relative thereto will be discussed in detail in a succeeding section.

As can be seen, although the British government stood firmly by its desire that the powers go to the conference without prior commitments, an exchange of views on the question of compensation had taken place between the three governments chiefly concerned. Two other matters were also discussed thoroughly before the opening of the congress: first, the wording of the declaration required by Britain in particular which would in effect, although indirectly, condemn the unilateral method of denunciation, and, second, the statements which the Russian representative, F. I. Brunnow, and Musurus would make at the first meeting giving the positions of their governments. The Porte was little concerned in the negotiations on the first question, although it too supported the British and Austrian attitude in the matter. The Ottoman government had certainly every interest in reconfirming the principle that treaties could not be changed without the unanimous consent of all the signatories. The final formula for this statement was worked out by Granville, Brunnow, and the Prussian ambassador, Albrecht von Bernstorff.

On the second question Musurus received instructions that he should reply to any Russian statement in a manner which would not produce "sharp discussions." Âli believed that: "In the matter before us, I think that moderation would be in good form."[52] Musurus had planned to give a "fairly complete" refutation of Brunnow's arguments, but upon the receipt of these instructions he agreed to limit himself to a short reply and to attribute the Porte's consent to any changes to the Ottoman desire to maintain good relations with Russia. Only if Brunnow showed himself hostile, or if he did not take the dignity of the Porte into account, would Musurus use his stronger arguments.[53] This concilatory attitude was approved by the council, but Âli wrote Musurus: ". . .do not base our adherence exclusively on our desire to

51. Âli to Musurus, M.N. 20/6, no. 29256/11 confidential, January 8, 1871.
52. Âli to Musurus, M.N. 20/6, no. 29200/4, January 5, 1870.
53. Musurus to Âli, M.N. 20/6, [defective no.], January 7, 1870.

maintain the best relations of friendship with Russia. . .you should emphasize above all our spirit of conciliation and the respect that we have for the counsel of friends."[54] Before the first meeting Granville gave Musurus a copy of the remarks which were to be made by Brunnow; the Ottoman ambassador in turn allowed Granville to read his arguments. Granville requested that certain negative sections be omitted.[55]

The Conference The first meeting of the conference was held on January 17, 1871. The powers were represented by their ambassadors in London – Musurus, Apponyi, Brunnow, Bernstorff, and Carlo Cadorna for Italy. Granville attended for Britain. Count Anton Szechen was sent to assist Apponyi on matters connected with the Danube. A French representative attended only the final session. As president of the conference Granville opened the first meeting with the statement that the representatives were assembling without a prior understanding and that they were to discuss in perfect freedom the propositions which the Russian delegate wished to make concerning the Black Sea. The main accomplishment of the first session was the acceptance, recorded in the protocol of the declaration that the powers "recognize that it is an essential principle of international law that none of them can release themselves from the engagements of a treaty, or modify the stipulations without the consent of the contracting parties [reached] by means of a friendly agreement."[56] The British government thus had the statement it wished.[57]

In the second meeting, held on January 24, Brunnow presented the Russian case for a change in the Black Sea clauses of the Treaty of Paris; in reply Musurus gave a "mild rebuttal" but declared that the Porte would accept the alterations in return for new guarantees. Musurus was well satisfied with the Ottoman position at this time. He

54. Âli to Musurus, M.N. 20/6, no. 29261/12, January 9, 1871.

55. Musurus to Âli, M.N. 20/6, no. 4328/5 confidential, London, January 11, 1871.

56. The protocols for the conference are to be found in *British and Foreign State Papers* (London, 1877), LXI, pp. 1193-1227.

57. Âli also approved the statement. He felt that Granville had obtained a great success in winning Russian approval. Elliot to Granville, F.O. 78/2173, Constantinople, January 13, 1871.

also reported to Âli that "... everything that I did in the meeting today had also been determined by a preliminary understanding with Lord Granville."[58] The question of compensations was to be presented at the next session.

The most interesting and lengthy meeting of the conference was held on February 3. At this time a draft of four articles for a future treaty, which had been prepared by Granville, Cadorna, and Bernstorff, was presented. It covered the Straits question and included an article reconfirming the Treaty of Paris. The Habsburg government at the same time introduced the measures which it wished in relation to the Danube. Britain then proposed an article providing for the extension of the jurisdiction of the International Commission of the Danube to Braila. All of these questions were discussed simultaneously in detail over the next month. Because of the complexity of these issues, they will here be dealt with topically – first, the question of the Straits, second, the Danube, and third, the attempt of the Porte to gain further compensation by a change in the regulations regarding its right of intervention in the Principalities. It will be noted that under all three headings the desires of the Porte were opposed usually not by Russia but by supposed friends and allies of the Ottoman government.

The Straits Question In the instructions sent to Musurus, it will be remembered, the Porte expressed the desire to change the Straits settlement so that the sultan would regain his full sovereignty over the area not only in form but also in substance. This solution, however, did not satisfy the Habsburg government; it wished no agreement made which could be used to allow Russian ships into the eastern Mediterranean and from there into the Adriatic. Since this was also essentially the British position, this view was accepted in drawing up the four points previously mentioned. The second of these stated:

> His Imperial Majesty the Sultan, in virtue of the right of sovereignty which he exercises over the Straits of the Bosphorus and the Dardanelles, reserves the right in time of peace to open them by way of a temporary exception in the sole case where the

58. Musurus to Âli, M.N. 20/6, no. 4348/19 confidential, London, January 24, 1871; Musurus to Âli, *ibid.*, no. 4346/25 personal and confidential, London, January 28, 1871.

> interest and the security of his empire lead him to recognize the necessity of the presence of ships of war of non-riverain powers.[59]

This proposal had been communicated to the Ottoman government at the beginning of January and was discussed by the Council of Ministers. On January 7 Âli informed Prokesch that the council preferred its own form, but that it would accept this project with the single condition that the words "friendly or allied" be substituted for "non-riverain." The Porte wished to reestablish the sovereign rights of the sultan over the Straits in compensation for the losses to Ottoman security resulting from the rearming of the Black Sea. The words suggested were a restriction which in fact limited the sultan's rights and took from him the means of acting according to the needs of the empire.[60] This position on the Straits question was maintained by the Porte throughout the conference.

At this early date Musurus was optimistic about the probable results of the conference. He felt that not only would the Porte gain the right to open and close the Straits, but that something more could be obtained. He requested Âli to let him handle the matter. If Elliot spoke to him of other compensations, he should be told that Musurus would deal with the question, but that "we would be very sorry if the conference, convened to abolish purely and simply the only real advantage that we won by the Crimean War, should only substitute for it an ancient sovereign right that was exercised without any dispute before 1841."[61]

On January 22 Âli telegraphed Musurus the terms of the settlement which the Porte preferred:

> Here is the solution that we wish to see given to the question of the Straits: you will make a declaration at the conference in which you will express the wish of the S. [Sublime] Porte to be released from the obligations of the convention of the Straits,

59. Of the other three articles, the first confirmed the closure of the Straits in time of peace; the third declared that Article II replaced articles XI, XIII, and XIV of the Treaty of Paris and the special convention between Russia and the Porte; the fourth renewed and confirmed the rest of the stipulations of the Treaty of Paris.

60. Âli to Prokesch-Osten, M.N. 20/6, private letter, January 7, 1871.

61. Musurus to Âli, M.N. 20/6, no. 4326/5, January 9, 1870.

> adding that it [the Porte] expressly promises to maintain its ancient legislation on the closure of the Straits of the Dardanelles and the Bosphorus to foreign ships of war without any exception, except light vessels employed in the services of the embassies and the Danube, and that it reserves the right to open them in the sole case where its security and interests demand it. The conference will record this declaration and it will be stated textually in the protocol: a protocol which will also contain the adherence and the acknowledgement of the powers.[62]

The Porte was not, however, to obtain its aim. The British desire was, and remained, Article II of the four points. In a meeting with Musurus on January 22 Granville urged that the Porte accept the wording "non-riverain." In return, he argued, the Habsburg Monarchy would abandon its demand for an international port on the Black Sea. The British foreign secretary wished to "be agreeable to" Vienna and he also thought that the proposal was in the Ottoman interest. Musurus saw in the paragraph the single advantage that with this clause the Porte was free to refuse should Russia ask that the Straits be opened.[63] In his conversations with Musurus, Granville continued to argue along these lines. By January 26 he could report that all of the powers except the Ottoman Empire supported the four articles.[64] The Porte, however, remained firm. On January 30 Âli informed Musurus that the sultan

62. Âli to Musurus, M.N. 20/6, no. 29355/27, S. Porte, January 22, 1870.

63. Musurus to Âli, M.N. 20/6, no. 4345/16 very confidential, London, January 22, 1871. Granville was himself not too enthusiastic about the paragraph, but he agreed in the interest of cooperation with Vienna to try to obtain the assent of the other powers. He wrote to Bloomfield that Musurus approved, a statement which is certainly not confirmed by the Turkish reports. Granville to Bloomfield, F.O. 7/786, no. 21 confidential, F.O., January 23, 1871. There was also confusion whether the term "non-riverain" could refer only to the Straits – an interpretation which made nonsense out of the provision. Goriainow, *Le Bosphore et les Dardanelles,* pp. 254-258.

64. Musurus to Âli, M.N. 20/6, no. 4351/22, London, January 26, 1871. During this period Elliot also tried to persuade Âli to accept the British point of view, but he was a bad advocate. He told Granville that at the time of the drawing up of the instructions to Musurus, he had discussed with Âli the forms possible on the Straits question. It had been agreed to avoid terms such as *friendly, allied,* etc. Elliot to Granville, P.R.O. 30, 29/102, Constantinople, January 27, 1871. Elliot later told the Italian minister Barbolini that the instructions had been drawn up by Âli "in my presence and with my full concurrence in its terms, without the possible instigation of any Foreign Power. It did not seem desirable either to Âli

shared the opinion of the council and that he charged Musurus "to request Lord Granville to spare him the very great unpleasantness of leaving the conference with the limitation of a part of his independence."[65]

Similar arguments were used with the Habsburg representatives. Âli told Prokesch that his government could not accept a phrase that put it in a worse position than it had been in before.[66] On February 1 he wrote to the Ottoman representative in Vienna, Halil Pasha:

> Certainly, we prefer the status quo to a modification which in effect would mutilate the independence of our August Master. It will be impossible for us to be able to justify this restrictive stipulation before public opinion, which would consider it a dangerous and humiliating concession made in place of a compensation that we have a right to ask. . . .We would be distressed to see the conference fail. The situation would become excessively dangerous if it adjourned without deciding anything.[67]

Throughout these discussions Musurus strongly approved the attitude of resistance adopted by his government. On January 25 he commented that his instructions caused him "a certain satisfaction for our friends have become accustomed to expect everything from us without giving us anything in return."[68] He agreed that the Porte should remain firm or "public opinion would find it illogical and unjust if after

---

Pasha or myself to divide the European governments into two camps by the insertion of words which would seem to record a standing suspicion of the intentions of Russia, and, when the apparent acquiescence of the Russian Government in the form of the words diminished that objection, there remained the unwillingness of the Porte to consent to a form which would limit the freedom of action of the sultan in a possible contingency." Elliot to Granville, F.O. 78/2173, no. 68, Pera, February 3, 1871.

65. Âli to Musurus, M.N. 20/6, no. 29401/38, January 30, 1871.

66. Âli to Halil, M.N. 20/6, no. 29392/31, January 28, 1871.

67. Âli to Halil, M.N. 20/6, no. 29438/39, February 1, 1871. Bloomfield reported that he judged from Halil's language that the Porte felt that at some time the aid of Russia might prove useful also against the monarchy. Bloomfield to Granville, F.O. 7/787, no. 55 confidential, Vienna, February 1, 1871.

68. Musurus to Âli, M.N. 20/6, no. 4350/21, London, January 25, 1871. Gladstone also commented on the change in the Turkish attitude toward Britain. Gladstone to Granville, private letter, P.R.O. 30, 29/59, London, February 8, 1871.

having given the S. Porte its rights of sovereignty, they persist in imposing sacrifices on us under the heading of compensation."[69]

In addition to the argument that the words "non-riverain" restricted the sultan's authority, the Porte quite correctly argued that the terms were unnecessarily provocative and wounding to the Russian government.[70] On February 1 Granville and Musurus had a long discussion on the matter. When Granville commented that the Porte should not object to the proposal since Russia had accepted it, Musurus replied that the Russian government could agree because it did not involve a restriction of Russian sovereign rights. He then repeated the argument which had been used before, that Russia would certainly take the first occasion to insist on the abrogation of this clause because of "its offensive character" in the same manner that she now sought to change the restrictive clauses accepted in 1856. If the British government had wished guarantees against Russia, it should have opposed any change in the status of the Black Sea. The previous condition had imposed equal restrictions on both riverain powers; the new plan was a provocation to Russia as well as a limitation on the independence and the sovereignty of the sultan. Moreover:

> The proposed arrangement keeps Turkey in an attitude of mistrust vis-à-vis Russia, who, nevertheless, is herself according to the treaty one of the guarantors of the integrity and the independence of the Ottoman Empire, and it is destined to remain a cause of irritation in Russia.

The Habsburg Empire, Musurus continued, whose relations with Russia were at present bad, supported the arrangement now. However, in a few years, in order to win Russian friendship, Beust or his successor might be the first to propose a change. In the future also the Russian chancellor might make a new protest and "Turkey will be thus condemned to fill the role of an instrument which Russia and her adversaries make use of by turns to show mutually their ill-will, a role incompatible with the dignity of a great power."[71]

69. Musurus to Âli, M.N. 20/6, no. 4362/27 personal and confidential, London, January 30, 1871.

70. Elliot to Granville, F.O. 78/2173, no. 44, Pera, January 24, 1871. Gladstone agreed that Russia would probably resent the article and would try to change it later. Gladstone to Granville, P.R.O. 30, 29/59, January 22, 1871.

71. Musurus to Âli, M.N. 20/6, no. 4366/29, London, February 1, 1871.

On February 3, the third meeting of the conference was held, despite the fact that the Ottoman Empire had not agreed to the controversial article. Although Musurus requested an adjournment, Granville insisted on proceeding with the meeting. He opened the session by proposing the adoption of the four articles.[72] Musurus answered, opposing the section on the Straits on the basis that it restricted the sovereignty of the sultan and that it had the appearance of being directed against Russia. Apponyi and Cadorna gave their support to all four articles. Brunnow then spoke and stated his appreciation of the Turkish attitude, but he also gave his assent. The Russian delegate's position throughout the conference was determined by his strong desire to secure approval of the Russian remilitarization of the Black Sea without a major crisis. Musurus wrote to Âli on this session:

> Your excellency has no idea of the profound distress that I feel in seeing myself suddenly in complete isolation before the unanimous agreement of all the plenipoteniairies. However the protocol which reports the meeting will establish that justice, reason, and legality are on our side.[73]

Despite the strong pressure exerted upon it, the Ottoman government held to its firm position. On February 6 Âli told Prokesch: "the Ottoman Empire has its own conditions of existence, and there are limits beyond which it cannot subordinate them to the convenience of the friendly powers. . . ."[74]

Faced with a deadlock in the conference, Âli on February 6 telegraphed Musurus a final suggestion. Although the council of ministers still refused to accept the paragraph proposed, in order not to delay the conference, "we renounce our demand for a change in the status quo of the Straits. You are therefore authorized to withdraw our proposition and to declare at the conference the desire of the S. Porte to conserve intact the Convention of 1856." The Ottoman government

72. Musurus to Âli, M.N. 20/6, no. 4367 confidential, London, February 3, 1871.

73. Musurus to Âli, M.N. 20/6, no. 4345/31 confidential, London, February 4, 1871.

74. Prokesch to Beust, H.H.S. XII/98, no. 8 AB, Constantinople, February 10, 1871.

was thus willing to give up any claim to compensation in regard to the Straits. Once this question was disposed of Musurus would only have to deal with questions directly relating to the Russian denunciation of the Black Sea clauses and the confirmation of the rest of the Treaty of Paris. Musurus was instructed to avoid bringing up himself, or agreeing to, the discussion of any questions except the prolongation of the powers of the International Commission of the Danube for a fixed period.[75]

During the entire period of discussion over the wording of the Straits clause, the position of Russia was most interesting to follow. Although directly involved, and the real target of the proposal, the Russian statesmen, Brunnow in particular, showed their greatest concern over obtaining European recognition of the remilitarization of the Black Sea.[76] Brunnow was anxious to obtain a settlement of the major question even at the price of an alteration of the Straits settlement unfavorable to Russian interests.

The Russian position, however, changed during the negotiations. In the first part of January Rustem, after a conversation with Gorchakov, reported that he believed that Russia would not oppose the Ottoman right to open the Straits "at our convenience alone" while maintaining the principle of closure. The confirmation of the other clauses of the Treaty of Paris would also be accepted. Gorchakov even appeared inclined to allow the Ottoman government the right to intervene in Moldavia and Wallachia should disorders arise there.[77] When the question of the modification of Article II of the four points arose, Gorchakov at first approved of the Ottoman objection and he told Rustem that Brunnow had "received instructions to support our [the Ottoman] proposition energetically. The desire expressed by the S. Porte to treat all the powers on a basis of complete equality seemed to

75. Âli to Musurus, M.N. 20/6, no. 29450/45, February 6, 1871.

76. Brunnow was not happy about his position at the conference. In December he had proposed that Gorchakov be the Russian delegate, but the chancellor had refused. Brunnow commented to Granville: "In short. . .Prince Gorchakoff wishes to gain in Russia applause for the boldness of his Circular & to put upon me the dirt of getting out of it in England. I do not like being between the hammer of public opinion in Russia and anvil which England presents." Granville to Gladstone, P.R.O. 30, 29/58, London, December 5, 1870.

77. Rustem to Âli, M.N. 20/6, private letter, St. Petersburg, December 31, 1870/ January 12, 1871.

him to compel us to insist on that request which is entirely in the recognized interest of H.I.M. [His Imperial Majesty] the sultan."[78]

However, only a few days later, undoubtedly influenced by Brunnow's reports, Gorchakov changed his mind. He now argued with Rustem that the efforts of the Porte to alter the wording of the article would not succeed, and that if the Russian and Ottoman representatives continued to oppose it, "that could lead to serious complications." Desiring that the conference succeed, Gorchakov thus advised Brunnow to accept the original draft; he suggested that Âli send the same instructions to Musurus in the interest of not breaking off the negotiations.[79] In a later conversation Gorchakov again expressed the desire that Âli accede to the wishes of the others:

> Everything would be finished if that adherence were obtained and a prompt solution is more than ever desirable in the interest of all. The emperor of Russia acknowledges that the objection of H.I.M. the sultan has to do with a feeling of tact (*delicatesse*) toward himself, which he appreciates highly and whose purpose is thus attained. Now he would be extremely obliged to H.I.M. the sultan if by his adherence our August Master could conclude the negotiations.[80]

In London Brunnow spoke to Musurus in the same tone. The Ottoman delegate, however, remained strongly in favor of the position adopted by his government. He felt that Brunnow took the stand he did because of anxiety over the fate of the Russian action. Musurus did not see how the powers could impose on the Porte the words "non-riverain" if his government remained firm.[81]

The deadlock on the question of the Straits was broken finally when the Italian government submitted a new wording which the Porte could accept. In this draft the phrase "non-riverain" was omitted; the right of the sultan to open the Straits was limited to the necessity of

78. Rustem to Âli, M.N. 20/6, no. 193/126, January 29, 1871.

79. Rustem to Âli, M.N. 20/6, No. 209/139 confidential, St. Petersburg, February 2, 1871. Ignatiev did not approve of the Russian attitude. He felt that it had "un effet très regrettable sur les Turcs se voyant abandonnés la première fois qu'ils avaient tenté de montrer quelqu'indépendance à l'égard de l'Occident et de marcher de concert avec nous. . . ." Ignatiev, "Zapiski," V (1914), p. 136.

80. Rustem to Âli, M.N. 20/6, no. 213/142, St. Petersburg, February 4, 1871.

81. Musurus to Âli, M.N. 20/6, no. 4370/33 personal and confidential, London, February 5, 1871.

safeguarding the Treaty of Paris. Since it was assumed that the danger to this treaty would come only from the Russian side, the western powers had in theory the guarantee they needed. The first Italian proposal, which was the basis for the final form, stated:

> The Sublime Porte assumes the formal engagement to maintain its ancient legislation on the closure of the straits of the Dardanelles and the Bosphorus to foreign ships of war without any exception except for light vessels in the service of foreign missions and the Danube and at the same time reserves the right to open them in the sole case where it judges that this measure is necessary to safeguard the execution of the clauses contained in the Treaty of Paris of March 30, 1856.[82]

The final acceptance of a version of this proposal was not registered until the fifth meeting on March 13. The delay was caused by further discussions on the wording, the Danube controversies, and the delay in the arrival of the French delegate. Shortly before this final meeting Musurus learned that Cadorna proposed to introduce a form differing from that originally sent to Constantinople. In the subsequent negotiations changes were made to meet the Ottoman desires.[83] In the session of March 13 Musurus, as had been agreed upon among the powers, proposed, as instructed, a return to the status quo. The Italian version was then introduced and the Porte adhered. The Ottoman government thus gained its desire that the wording not be directed against Russia; the qualification that the Straits could be opened only to protect the Paris settlement seemed, however, to preclude that the clause could be used to give Russia access to the Mediterranean.

Granville was not pleased with the results of the deliberations. Speaking with Apponyi on February 8, he appeared, in the opinion of

82. Âli to Musurus, M.N. 20/6, no. 29452/47, February 6, 1871. Âli explained to Elliot why the Porte could accept the Italian proposal: "The disputed words were omitted from this project, the only change from the form proposed by the Porte being the substitution of an expression stating that the Straits were only to be opened when the Sultan's government judged it necessary to protect the execution of the objects of the Treaty of 1856, in lieu of the Turkish form which merely alluded to the interests and security of the empire." Elliot to Granville, F.O. 78/2173, no. 72, Constantinople, February 6, 1871.

83. Musurus to Âli, M.N. 20/6, no. 29685/83 very confidential, London, March 11, 1871; Musurus to Âli, *ibid.,* no. 4429/74, London, March 12, 1871; Apponyi to Beust, H.H.S. VIII/76, no. 23 AB, London, March 14, 1871.

the ambassador, "in a state of perplexity and despondency difficult to describe." He declared at this time that he had always believed the original wording was the best solution to the problem and the only form which, "in forbidding the access through the Straits to Russia, offered a counterbalance to the concession which that power would receive." He did not like the Italian draft; it appeared to him "ambiguous and unsatisfactory." He complained also strongly of the attitude of the powers in their relations with the Porte. He did not like the fact that the Habsburg government had made it clear during these negotiations that it was willing to bargain on this point in return for Turkish acceptance of certain concessions in regard to the Danube. He felt that if Italy, Austria, and Britain had stayed together and insisted upon the first form, the Porte would have given in. In commenting upon Granville's displeasure, Apponyi wrote that he felt the blame should lie on the British statesman because of his refusal to take part in negotiations leading to a firm agreement before the opening of the conference.[84]

In the question of the Straits the Porte had to meet the combined pressure of Britain and the Habsburg Monarchy, although undoubtedly British influence was more important. The Danube, in contrast, was principally a Habsburg sphere of interest. Here the British government, while cooperating with Vienna on some issues, nevertheless joined the Porte in opposing the more extensive Austrian demands.

The Danube Like the neutralization of the Black Sea, the international status of the Danube River had been established in the Treaty of Paris.[85] The regulation of the traffic of the river had not been included in the decisions of the Congress of Vienna, which had dealt with Europe's other great international waterway, the Rhine and some of its tributaries, because the middle and lower courses of the Danube were under the territorial control of the Ottoman Empire, who was not a participant in that congress. After 1815 the question of the navigation of the river became acute. Russia had become a riverain power in 1812

84. Apponyi to Beust, H.H.S. VIII/76, no. 12 A-C, secret, London, February 8, 1871.

85. For books concerning the question of the Danube River see the "Bibliographical Note."

with the acquisition of Bessarabia; in 1829 in the Treaty of Adrianople she acquired the delta. In the next years traffic on the river increased greatly. Although the Habsburg Empire remained the main power concerned, British trade interests were also important. Both Austrian and British commerce were injured in this period by the apparently deliberate Russian policy of allowing the mouths of the river to silt up so that passage was not possible for large ships. This condition gave an advantage to the port of Odessa and to the grain-producers of the Ukraine, since with the blockage or partial blockage of the Sulina and St. George channels, produce for the Danube ports had to be transshipped. Because of these difficulties, the question of the Danube became a major subject of negotiation at the time of the Crimean War.

In the Treaty of Paris the regulation of the Danube was dealt with in articles XV through XIX. In Article XV the general principles for the navigation of rivers that separated or crossed several states, which had been previously adopted at the Congress of Vienna, were applied to the Danube.[86] In the same article it was agreed that no special toll "founded solely upon the fact of the Navigation of the River, nor any Duty upon the Goods which may be on board the Vessels" should be levied. In articles XVI and XVII two commissions were established. The first, the European Commission, composed of the signatories of the treaty – Austria, France, Britain, Prussia, Russia, Sardinia, and the Ottoman Empire – was responsible for making the mouths of the river navigable with a jurisdiction extending to Isaccea. This body was allowed to collect dues to pay for the work. At the end of two years the commission was to dissolve and its functions were to be taken over by a second group. The Riverain Commission, a permanent body with jurisdiction over the whole course of the river, was formed with delegates from the Habsburg Monarchy, the Ottoman Empire, Bavaria, and Württemberg, with commissioners from the three vassal principalities of Moldavia, Wallachia, and Serbia. It was to draw up regulations for the navigation and policing of the river, to remove impediments to navigation, and to carry out any necessary works. In Article XIX each of the powers on the International Commission was to be allowed to maintain two "stationaries," i.e. light naval vessels, at the

86. Hertslet, *Map of Europe,* III, pp. 1257-1259.

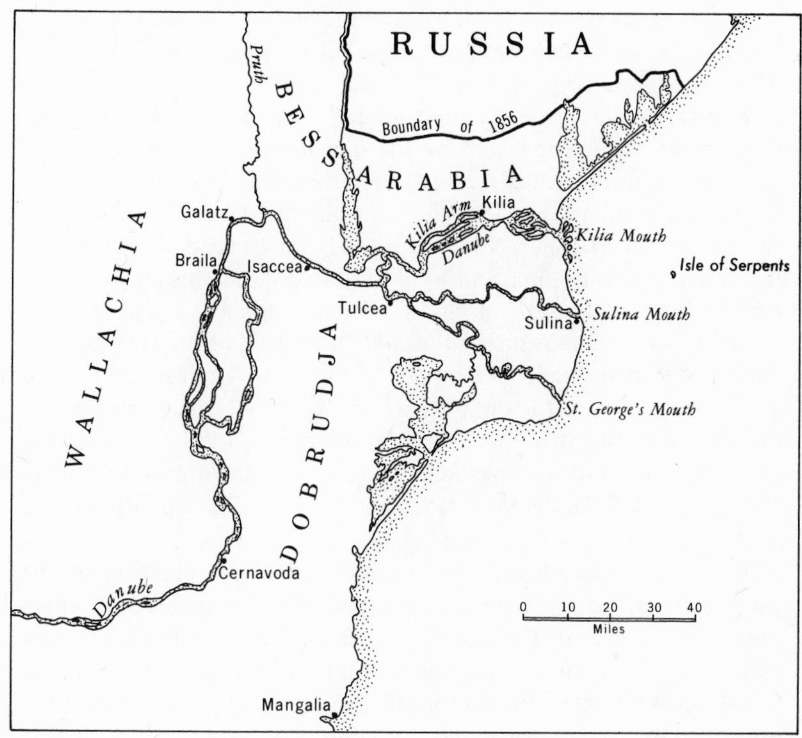

The Danube Delta

mouth of the Danube. These, as we have seen, could pass through the Straits.

In the next years the work of the European Commission proceeded smoothly. Since its task was not completed in the designated two years, its duration was prolonged in 1857 and again in 1866, but this later date was to form the "utmost limit." The task of the Riverain Commission was complicated by the disagreement among the powers over the measures it should propose for the regulation of the river and the conflict within it between the Porte and the vassal principalities. In this period the Habsburg Empire showed a constant desire to replace the International Commission by the Riverain Commission, where she held the predominant position. Britain usually supported the International Commission and would have liked its jurisdiction extended at least to Braila. Despite the fact that the Ottoman Empire was the territorial power for the part of the river chiefly under discussion, the Habsburg Monarchy held the predominant political influence over the entire course of the river, a position she was determined to defend. The Black Sea Conference gave her the apparent opportunity to strengthen and widen this authority.

It will be remembered that in addition to the question of the Danube the Habsburg Empire had hoped at the conference to obtain two other measures: the assignment of a Turkish port as an international naval station and permission for passage through the Straits of a designated number of naval vessels. Because of the opposition of the other powers, these questions were not pressed by the Habsburg representatives. In contrast, the three demands concerning the Danube became major issues in the negotiations: these were (1) the prolongation of the term of the International Commission, (2) an increase in the number of warships which the powers could station at the mouth of the Danube, and (3) the formulation of new provisions which would name the Habsburg Empire as the power responsible for the works on the Danube in the area in particular of the Iron Gates. These issues will be discussed separately in the following pages. It should be noted that the Porte was not enthusiastic about the introduction into the conference of problems such as that of the International Commission or the Iron Gates, since it felt that these were out of the original jurisdiction of the conference, which was supposed to be limited to issues arising out of the Russian denunciation.[87] It could not, however, prevail against Britain and the Habsburg Empire, who wished to use the opportunity to settle Danubian affairs in their own interest.

The first question, that of the prolongation of the term of the International Commission, caused the least controversy. The financial and technical functions of the committee had not yet been completed. With the remilitarization of the Black Sea, both the Habsburg Empire and the Porte now regarded the continued existence of this commission, where they had the majority of votes with them, as a protection against Russia. Moreover, the Riverain Commission was in no condition to take complete control. The rights of the vassal states in the body were still uncertain and a new problem had arisen as a result of the Franco-Prussian War. It could be assumed that Prussia would control the two votes of Bavaria and Württemberg. The Habsburg Monarchy wished to settle this issue later and by direct negotiation with Berlin.

The major disagreement on this stipulation arose over who should propose it in the congress. The Habsburg Monarchy, who had previously opposed such an action, did not wish to do so. They wanted either Britain, a supporter of the international authority, or the Ottoman Empire, the territorial power, to present the proposal. The monarchy could then accept it as a concession; on this basis they could urge its adoption on the powers and even claim in return the changes they wished in regard to the Iron Gates.[88] Both the British and the Habsburg governments thus turned to Constantinople. Âli refused to take such an action, but he "had no objection to the prolongation of the present powers of the European Commission for a *determined and definite* time on the express condition that its powers and the limits of its action remain the same as they are designated in the Treaty of Paris."[89]

In the meeting of February 3, Granville thus introduced the measure. He proposed first an extension of twenty-six years, stating that the British government in fact would prefer an indefinite limit.

87. Elliot to Granville, F.O. 78/2173, tel., February 17, 1871.

88. Beust to Apponyi, H.H.S. 34/48, Vienna, n.d., 1870; Beust to Apponyi, *ibid.,* Budapest, January 19, 1871; Beust to Prokesch, *ibid.,* Vienna, January 21, 1870; Musurus to Âli, M.N. 20/6, no. 4353/24, London, January 27, 1871.

89. Âli to Rustem, M.N. 20/6, no. 29436/28, February 2, 1871.

Apponyi then answered with a proposal for a twelve year term, a move which the majority supported. Granville next suggested that the representatives refer the issue back to their governments. The Porte regarded the period of twelve years as more than sufficient; it would have chosen a shorter span. In the final treaty the limit was extended to 1883.

The proposal to increase the number of ships at the mouth of the Danube caused more controversy. In a meeting with Halil on February 2, Beust explained that he wished the wording of Article XIX of the Treaty of Paris changed from "two light vessels" to "vessels without determining the number." The sultan, Beust argued, would control the situation because, although the ships from the western states would obviously have to pass the Straits, the Turkish government would still have the power to grant or refuse firmans of passage according to its pleasure.[90]

In discussing this proposal, and in fact the Danube problems in general, Beust made it quite clear to the Ottoman representative that he was chiefly concerned with satisfying the Hungarians. Although he had been willing not to insist on this proposal, he had met such opposition in Pest that he was forced to support it.[91] The negative Turkish response could be expected. As Âli wrote Halil, if the powers could station an unlimited number of warships at the mouth of the Danube, the closure of the Straits was an illusion. The sultan could not in fact stop the passage of any ships of war destined ostensibly for the Danube. If he refused any one, each occasion would be the cause of disagreeable discussions and conflicts. Moreover, Russia, with a fleet in the Black Sea, would be in the best position to use the right.[92] As Âli explained

90. Halil to Âli, M.N. 20/6, Pest, February 2, 1871.

91. Halil to Âli, M.N. 20/6, no. 3468/33, Pest, February 1, 1871. Beust also later explained to Bloomfield that ". . .most of the opposition which had been raised in the Conference. . .was the result of Hungarian Inspiration, and the necessity he was then under of conciliating various recalcitrant parties. . . ." Beust did not approve of Andrassy's ideas on the Danube and he wished to cooperate with Britain ". . .and any apparent deviation from this course, he repeated, was attributable to Influences which for the moment were not easily controlled." Bloomfield to Granville, F.O. 7/787, no. 85 confidential, Vienna, February 15, 1871.

92. Âli to Halil, M.N. 20/6, no. 29456/41 confidential, February 7, 1871. Elliot wrote: "Among other objections Âli Pasha says that whenever Russia

to Prokesch, the best defense against Russia as far as the Danube was concerned was the Treaty of Paris: "she [Russia] cannot use force against the stationaries without attacking Europe. The real guarantee is in the treaty, not in a few more light vessels which do not even constitute a defense."[93]

Despite the attempts of both Apponyi in London and Prokesch in Constantinople, the Habsburg government failed to win support for its stand. It was even willing to agree to the Turkish proposal for the Straits in return for the Porte's acceptance of this measure. On February 8 Beust admitted to Halil that his efforts would probably fail, but that Apponyi would nevertheless bring the question before the congress, because: "It is only thus. . .that I can get rid of the Hungarians." The strong opposition of the powers, however, prevented even this; the issue was never formally presented at the conference.[94]

The third question relating to the Danube which the Habsburg government wished discussed concerned its desire to undertake the improvement of navigation on the river, in particular at the Iron Gates. This approximately eighty-mile series of gorges was a serious hindrance to river traffic. The authority of the Riverain Commission was to be used chiefly for this purpose. Since the monarchy wanted to collect a toll to compensate itself for the expenses incurred in works on the river, Article XV of the Treaty of Paris, which prohibited such a levy, had to be amended. In addition, Austria-Hungary wished changes in Article XVII in relation to the duties of the Riverain Commission. The Habsburg proposals would have strengthened the position of this power on the Danube, but would have reduced the influence of the Porte in relative terms. Apponyi did not expect much opposition on these changes from the European powers; he correctly expected the main objections to come from the Porte.[95]

On January 27 Granville, Musurus, and Szechen discussed together the question of allowing the Habsburg Empire, with the cooperation of

---

wished to introduce vessels into the Black Sea she would be entitled to demand their Passage through the Straits, on the Pretext of their being destined for the Danube Service." Elliot to Granville, F.O. 78/2173, tel. no no., February 6, 1871.

93. Prokesch to Beust, H.H.S. XII/99, tel. no. 3, Constantinople, January 30, 1871.

94. Halil to Âli, M.N. 20/6, no. 3478/38, Vienna, February 8, 1871.

95. Apponyi to Beust, H.H.S. 34/48, tel. no. 22, London, February 1, 1871.

the riverain states, the exclusive right to undertake works to improve the navigation of the Danube, in particular around the Iron Gates.[96] When Âli received his ambassador's report on the meeting, he first replied: "As for the works to be undertaken at the Iron Gates, we are in no manner prepared at this moment to express any opinion whatsoever in this regard and we are obliged to reserve our judgment."[97] On February 5 Musurus sent to Constantinople the text of the articles proposed in regard to the question of works and on the problem of future meetings of the Riverain Commission.[98] The Turkish answer was negative. The proposals were yet another alteration of the Treaty of Paris, which the Porte wished to preserve, and the whole question seemed outside the limits of discussion set for the conference. Moreover, the Serbian government now became involved in the controversy and it appealed to its suzerain for support against the Habsburg actions.[99] Unwilling to concede its exclusive rights to the monarchy in an area on its own borders, Serbia argued that the work on the Iron Gates should not enter the competence of the London Conference, but should be discussed and settled through an entente among the riverain states. A Serbian representative, Mijatović, was in London during the conference to defend the Serbian views.[100]

The Porte retained its strongly opposing stand. Âli instructed Musurus to avoid the acceptance of the Habsburg proposals. He felt that the question could better be handled by the Riverain Commission, which he believed could on its own authority levy a toll and simply declare Article XV not applicable. Although the Porte preferred that the entire subject be dropped, Âli sent to Musurus on February 13 the drafts which he could accept if necessary. Here the monarchy was not designated as having the chief responsibility, and Article XV was simply considered suspended during the period necessary for the repayment of

96. Musurus to Âli, M.N. 20/6, no. 4353/24, London, January 27, 1871.

97. Âli to Rustem, M.N. 20/6, no. 29436/28, February 2, 1871.

98. Musurus to Âli, M.N. 20/6, no. 4371/34, London, February 5, 1871.

99. Âli to Musurus, M.N. 20/6, no. 29440/44, S. Porte, February 4, 1871; Âli to Musurus, *ibid.*, no. 29458/48, S. Porte, February 7, 1871.

100. Szechen to Beust, H.H.S. 34/48, tel. no. 36, London, February 10, 1871; Kallay to Beust, *ibid.*, no no., Belgrade, February 18, 1871; Apponyi to Beust, *ibid.*, no. 16, February 22, 1871; Kallay to Beust, no no., February 24, 1871; Granville to Elliot, F.O. 195/971, no. 54, F.O., February 23, 1871.

the debt incurred by the improvements. In transmitting this article to Musurus, Âli told him to introduce it only in case of absolute necessity. He thought also that this version would satisfy the Serbs and leave Article XV intact.[101]

In discussing this question with Prokesch, Âli continued to press his objections. He particularly did not like the Austrian proposals, which appeared "to assure Austria-Hungary *by treaty* full control in the projected enterprise and to substitute for the equality of rights of the riverain powers the supremacy of Austria-Hungary on the river on which the principal obstacles whose removal is in question lie exactly in the part crossing the Ottoman Empire." Prokesch attempted to justify the Habsburg position by arguing that the empire was going to carry the main financial responsibility for the improvements on the river. Âli replied that it was the duty of the riverain states, not the other powers, to regulate internal questions of precedence and direction. The Porte would also probably not refuse to pay at least a share in the costs. Âli strongly insisted on the Turkish draft; he felt this did not alter the Treaty of Paris and it would "shut up" (*fermer la bouche*) the Serbs.[102] Despite this strong opposition, Beust, largely because of Hungarian pressure, continued to instruct Prokesch to urge the Habsburg proposals, in particular "to have our government mentioned as offering itself as entrepreneur."[103]

Although the Ottoman government could not prevent the introduction of the Austrian proposals at the conference, it was largely successful in gaining the adoption of its own draft proposals. The final version accepted in the treaty was based on the Turkish suggestions. Most important, the Habsburg Empire was not designated as entrepreneur and the position of the vassal states received some protection in the wording of Article V of the final treaty.[104] The Porte also gained its aim of leaving Article XV of the Treaty of Paris intact. As will be discussed later, it was the failure to achieve their goals in this section of

101. Âli to Musurus, M.N. 20/6, no. 29488/53, February 13, 1871.

102. Prokesch to Beust, H.H.S. 34/48, no. 9 AB, Constantinople, February 17, 1871.

103. Beust to Prokesch, H.H.S. 34/48, tel. no. 123, Vienna, February 20, 1871; also Beust to Chotek, Vienna, February 22, 1871.

104. Musurus to Âli, M.N. 20/6, no. 4400/51, London, February 21, 1871; Âli to Musurus, *ibid.*, no. 29516/59, London, February 21, 1871.

the treaty which left the bitterest feelings among the Habsburg diplomats.

The Porte was thus, as can be seen, successful in resisting changes in relation to the Danube which were sponsored chiefly by the Habsburg Empire. A similar victory was gained in relation to a proposal which Britain supported. In the interest of protecting its own commerce, the British government now attempted to gain the agreement of the powers to an extension of the jurisdiction of the International Commission from Isaccea to Braila.[105] When informed of this threat to Ottoman interests, Âli replied to Musurus that not only was it a new break in the Treaty of Paris, but it was "an attack" on the right of suzerainty of the sultan in a part of his empire which had never been in question. The aim of the Porte at the conference was to preserve intact those sections of the Treaty which remained valid after the Russian denunciation of the Black Sea clauses. In addition:

> Experience has sufficiently demonstrated to us that these pernicious examples are authorized in order to take away from us one by one the guarantees that the international act in question offers us. Besides it is very difficult to see foreign jurisdiction extended over another part of the empire. We are also obliged to take into account the reasonable objections of the principalities. They ask us to defend their legitimate rights; it is impossible for us to refuse them our assistance.[106]

Despite the fact that the British government did not receive Habsburg support on this issue,[107] Granville made a great effort to

105. Musurus to Âli, M.N. 20/6, no. 4395/48, London, February 16, 1871.

106. Âli to Musurus, M.N. 20/6, no. 29513/57, February 20, 1871, also Musurus to Âli, *ibid.*, no. 4378/37 confidential, London, February 8, 1871; Elliot to Granville, F.O. 78/2173, no. 90, Constantinople, February 20, 1871.

107. The Habsburg apprehension was well expressed in an instruction to Prokesch: "De même nous ne voyons pas de raisons majeures pour étendre en amont d'Isaktchah l'autorité de la commission. Nous avons au contraire un intérêt marqué et bien fondé à tenir éloignés les pouvoirs de cette commission de la partie supérieure du Danube, surtout s'il s'agissait de les étendre jusqu'à Orsova, voire même jusqu'à Belgrade. Il ne saurait nous être indifférent de voir la commission dans laquelle siègera toujours un commissaire russe, établir ses opérations jusqu'aux confins de nos provinces de la Save, où nos populations Slaves, de même que celle de l'Empire Ottoman dans ces parages, seraient exposées à une influence pernicieuse venant de ce côté." Beust to Prokesch, H.H.S., A.R. 34/48 Vienna, January 21, 1871.

convince the Porte.[108] Musurus again favored the resistance shown by his government to outside pressure. He reported to Âli that in a meeting on February 20 Granville had pressed hard for Turkish acceptance of the proposal, arguing that:

> . . .in consideration of the trouble to which he had gone for us, he hoped that we would not refuse him such a little thing and he begged me to telegraph once again to Y.E. [Your Excellency]. I answered him that it was not we, in my opinion, who were the cause of so many preoccupations, since we were not asking for any favors; that on the contrary it was we who were making all the concessions to satisfy Russia, Austria and everyone. . . .[109]

In this issue also the firm Ottoman stand was successful. The British government, too, had to wait until a later date to achieve its desires.

In addition to the provisions on the Danube already discussed, the final agreement also contained a stipulation concerning the neutrality of the works and the personnel under the jurisdiction of the European Commission of the Danube. It was further stated that the "benefits of the immunities which result therefrom shall extend to the whole administrative and engineering staff of the Commission," a provision which incidentally was a milestone in the extension of diplomatic immunities and privileges to international organizations and which later was to cause considerable friction between Rumania and the powers. In the same article at the insistence of the Ottoman government the sentence was included stating that: "It is, however, understood that the dispositions of this article affect in no way the right of the Sublime Porte as the territorial power to send as always its ships of war into the Danube."[110] This provision was designed to meet Ottoman fears that the article would be used in the future to prevent the empire from dealing with unrest in the Bulgarian lands. A proposal that a majority vote should be sufficient for decisions on the commission was defeated with Ottoman approval.[111]

108. Granville to Elliott, F.O. 195/971, no. 62, F.O., March 10, 1871.

109. Musurus to Âli, M.N. 20/6, no. 4399/50 confidential, February 20, 1871.

110. Musurus to Âli, M.N. 20/6, no. 4403/54 confidential, London, February 24, 1871; Musurus to Âli, *ibid.*, no. 4406/57, London, February 25, 1871; Musurus to Âli, *ibid.*, no. 4407/58, London, February 27, 1871.

111. Âli was strongly against this measure, which he believed would "rendre la commission souveraine absolue. La Puissance territoriale n'aura plus la faculté

As has been shown, in the questions relating to the Danube the Ottoman Empire was chiefly in conflict with her supposed friends and allies, Britain and the Habsburg Empire, who should also have had an interest in preserving the Treaty of Paris and the integrity of the Ottoman Empire against Russian encroachment. In contrast, the Russian government used the opportunity to extend repeated courtesies to Constantinople. Since during the conference Prussia consistently followed the Russian lead, this attitude was very valuable. On January 26 Gorchakov asked Rustem the attitude of the Porte on the Danubian questions. He had not yet sent Brunnow instructions on these and he wished to know first the Turkish point of view so that the two powers could agree. He wanted to give the Porte "a proof of good will" by supporting the Ottoman position.[112] Gorchakov similarly backed the Turkish resistance to the increase of the number of ships at the mouth of the Danube,[113] and he sought the opinion of the Porte on the question of the extension of the jurisdiction of the International Commission to Braila.[114] On the issue of the Iron Gates, he told Rustem that he believed that negotiations on this question should take place at Constantinople, "in view above all of the delicate issues which can cause questions to arise concerning the suzerainty of the Sublime Porte and the vassalage of the Danubian provinces and the presence of their delegates." Of course, the Russian government had an equal interest in blocking the extension of either Habsburg or British influence on the Danube.[115]

In the conference the Ottoman government had succeeded in gaining

---

de refuser l'exécution de tout ce qu'il plaira à la majorité de décreter." Âli to Musurus, M.N. 20/6, no. 29586/68, London, February 28, 1871. The British had argued that the measure would prevent Russia from obstructing work on the St. George Channel of the Danube. Musurus to Âli, *ibid.*, no. 4403/54 confidential, London, February 24, 1871.

112. Rustem to Âli, M.N. 20/6, no. 188/124, St. Petersburg, January 26, 1871.

113. Rustem to Âli, M.N. 20/6, no. 211/140, St. Petersburg, February 4, 1871; also Chotek to Beust, H.H.S., A.R. 34/48, St. Petersburg, January 30/February 11, 1871.

114. Rustem to Âli, M.N. 20/6, no. 264/169, St. Petersburg, February 24, 1871.

115. Rustem to Âli, M.N. 20/6, no. 272/177, St. Petersburg, February 16/28, 1871.

what was in fact a compromise on the Straits question, and it had blocked the attempt of other powers to extend their control on the Danube. The main Ottoman achievements had been largely negative. In theory the Porte should have received some compensation to balance the gains made by Russia in relative strength with the denunciation of the Black Sea clauses; the major achievement of the Ottoman delegates had been to preserve their government from further losses on the side of their allies. Concurrently with the discussions on the Straits and the Danube, the Porte did attempt to gain a better position in relation to the Danubian Principalities in line with the instructions of December 21. Although the question of the provinces never became an issue in the sessions of the conference itself, the relations of the Porte with Wallachia and Moldavia and the status of Prince Charles was in this period the subject of an active international diplomatic correspondence. This issue became involved and intertwined with the questions discussed at the congress.

The Rumanian Question In addition to the compensations already discussed, the instructions sent to Musurus on December 21 covered at length measures to be taken to strengthen the position of the Porte in regard to the Danubian Principalities. The Ottoman government wished to obtain from the powers a change in Article XXVII of the Treaty of Paris. This stipulation stated that there was to be no armed intervention in Rumania without a prior agreement among the powers. The Porte now wanted itself named as the state which would intervene, although it was willing to keep the limitation that no such action could be taken without the assent of the others and also that commissioners from these governments would accompany the Ottoman troops. The Porte's concern over the Principalities was not academic; a very serious situation existed at this time in Bucharest.

Although Prince Charles was to face many difficulties as ruler of Rumania, the real crisis of his reign occurred in the winter of 1870-71. His chief problems were the inherent instability of the Rumanian political scene, his mistakes in the problems connected with finance and railroad construction, and, of great importance at this time, his obvious espousal as a Prussian prince of a German victory in a Latin and intensely pro-French country. In September and October 1870, convinced that he could not govern with the extremely liberal Rumanian constitution, he felt that he would have to abdicate. He decided, however, that he would first appeal to the protecting powers and inform them of his difficulties in trying to govern with "too liberal" institutions. He had sworn to obey the constitution; he intended to abide by his oath. But he wished to assure that his successor would have a better political framework for his reign.[116] At the beginning of November he put his plan into action. Without consulting the members of his own government or any of the foreign representatives, he despatched a personal letter to the rulers of Russia, Austria, Britain, Prussia, and Italy. Here he attempted to "show clearly to the Guarantor Powers the state of affairs in Rumania in order to know the future of the country was assured before leaving."[117] Most important was also his request that the Rumanian question be discussed at a future European conference. The time for this appeal could not have been worse chosen. Bismarck's negative reception to the idea was known before the letter reached Berlin. The Prussian statesman wanted no more disturbances on the international scene until the war with France was over; the Russian denunciation had been bad enough.[118] Moreover, the letter was largely misunderstood. It was generally interpreted as an attempt by the prince to strengthen his personal power and prestige and to change the constitution with the assistance of the protecting powers. As such the British government tended to be wholly unsympathetic; Prussia, Russia, and the Habsburg Empire showed more understanding.

Of the powers, the Porte was the most disturbed by Charles' initiative. The prince had not sent a letter to his sovereign. In contradiction to his obligations to the Porte as a vassal prince he had addressed other monarchs directly. When pressed by the representatives of the powers, Charles finally did write the sultan, but the letter arrived about three weeks after the date on which the previous communications had been delivered in the other capitals. The Ottoman government

116. *Aus dem Leben König Karls von Rumänien* (Stuttgart, 1894), II, pp. 127-129. For an excellent collection of documents covering this period of Rumanian internal crisis see D. A. Sturdza, *Charles Ier. Roi de Roumanie* (Bucharest, 1899), I, pp. 609-683.

117. *Aus dem Leben König Karls,* p. 134.

118. *Ibid.,* p. 135.

immediately saw dangers in the wording of the message; it was particularly disturbed by the section in which the prince wished to be delivered "from the obstacles which impede the present regime both at home and abroad."[119] The Porte now viewed the prince's move as nothing more than an attempt by Charles to use the coming conference to gain recognition of Rumanian independence, an action which would, of course, strengthen his position in Bucharest. In other words, the Ottoman government feared that the congress would result not in the gaining of compensation for the Russian action, but in a further erosion of the Turkish position in the Balkans. Strong opposition was thus shown to the introduction in the conference of the issues raised by the prince's letter; Musurus was instructed to leave if Charles' *démarche* succeeded.[120] The Porte was not against a discussion of the Rumanian problem, but it was to be along the lines indicated in Musurus' instructions.

In dealing with the problem of the Rumanian principalities the Porte was faced with the major obstacle that the guaranteeing powers stood between it and the vassal principality. Two separate issues had now arisen: first, Charles' difficulties in ruling and his request for assistance, and second, the relation of the Principalities to the suzerain state. There was little disagreement between the powers on Charles personally. All of the representatives felt that his position was hopeless; no political party supported him and he did not control an army on which he could base his rule. The Habsburg government under Beust did not like a Hohenzollern prince in Bucharest.[121] Napoleon III, Charles' original sponsor, was in exile and France was powerless to aid him. The Russian government was not against a return to the regime of the Treaty of Paris, with a separation of the two principalities and with native governors. Bismarck, in a difficult international situation, was certainly not prepared to compromise Prussian interests over Rumanian affairs. Gladstone and the Liberal government disliked Charles, who was regarded as a despotic German princeling.

119. *Ibid.*, p. 136.

120. Prokesch to Beust, H.H.S. XII/97, no. 93 B, Constantinople, December 27, 1870.

121. Schweinitz tried to reassure Beust on this matter: ". . .wir haben ihn [Charles] nicht dorthin geschickt, um als Torpedo gegen Österreich zu wirken. . . ." Schweinitz, *Denkwürdigkeiten*, I, p. 286.

Although the powers were in agreement that Charles would probably be forced to abdicate, they were divided on what course should be pursued after the prince left the country. What the Porte wished to do was clearly shown in the instructions.[122] Since it was convinced that the fall of the prince would be followed either by a condition of complete anarchy or by the establishment of a regime which would be too radical for it to accept, the Ottoman government felt that a military force would have to be sent into the country to establish order and to lay the foundations for a new regime. It wished the guarantor states to agree before Charles' fall that the Porte would provide the necessary army, although it would be accompanied by commissioners representing the other powers. A new government would then be established on what the Porte considered the legal basis – the separation of the principalities and native governors. Âli emphasized to Prokesch that the Porte could not allow the establishment of a "Red Republic" or:

> . . .a hot bed of anarchy on the other side of the Danube, because of the proximity of Bulgaria and Serbia and because of the intrigues and enticements from which our Christian populations would not be spared. Our own defense forces us to put out the fire and there is only one way to do it, a military occupation.[123]

In this issue the Ottoman government found the chief resistance to its arguments in London. The difficulty lay not so much with the British representatives on the scene. The consul in Bucharest, John Green, wrote at this time in a most critical fashion both of the prince and of the Rumanian government. Charles' position, he commented, ". . .was that of a complete nonentity, a mere ornamental expression of

122. See Appendix II.

123. Prokesch to Beust, H.H.S. XII/98, no. 5 A-F, Constantinople, January 20, 1871. Âli spoke in this sense to Elliot. The Porte could not tolerate a socialist republic or anarchy in Rumania and "as it would be vain to expect that these could be avoided excepting through the presence of an armed force, he trusted that the guaranteeing Governments would interpose no difficulties to an occupation of the Provinces by sufficient Turkish troops to ensure the maintenance of order." Elliot to Granville, F.O. 78/2173, no. 24, Pera, January 14, 1871. Âli told Prokesch that Russia would not oppose a Turkish occupation. Ignatiev spoke with the Habsburg representative in the same sense. A Turkish intervention would mean Russia would not have to act. If Russia moved, Austria-Hungary would also. A. von Prokesch-Osten, "Erinnerungen aus den Jahren 1870 und 1871" *Deutsche Revue,* IV:3 (1880), pp. 11-21.

mock sovereignty, in a country which had never been accustomed to view their Princes in any other light than that of irresponsible Governors invested with sufficient power to cause their decisions to be respected." Green agreed that the constitution of the country was bad: it "seemed framed with the principal object of rendering all Government impossible."[124] In his despatches Elliot also showed himself well aware of the sensitive position of the Porte.[125] The British Liberal government, in contrast, was frankly hostile both to the prince and to the Porte's desire to intervene. Granville expressed to Apponyi his conviction that the prince's action had been motivated by dangerous absolutist tendencies.[126] At the same time, Gladstone wrote Granville: "What scandalizes me in P. [Prince] Charles' letter is its shabby intriguing clandestine character. I hope it may be found proper & practicable to snub him. . . ."[127] In another letter to Granville Gladstone roundly condemned both the prince and the Porte:

> The Turk does not & never will either understand or value freedom for its own sake, but will, at his best, keep faith in tolerating it as a necessary evil until he can get a fair or plausible excuse for evading it. That the position of a man like Prince Charles should be untenable, is no reproach to the Roumanian people. I know of no fact yet shown against them except their persecution of the Jews, i.e. their having much the same feelings as the people of England had about one hundred thirty years ago. What right can the Porte have to send in troops on a supposition that there will be a disorder? What right has it to say the people shall not govern themselves as they please so long as they respect the Suzerain Power?[128]

124. Green to Granville, F.O. 195/967, no. 88 confidential, Bucharest, October 16, 1870. Later Granville found it necessary to advise Green not to express any opinion on the events and to desist from "encouraging any dispositions which Prince Charles or his advisers may show, to set aside the existing Constitution of the Principalities. It is not for a British Agent to take any part in these internal affairs." Granville to Green, F.O. 78/2132, no. 30 confidential, F.O., December 9, 1870.

125. Elliot to Granville, F.O. 78/2126, no. 370 confidential, Constantinople, December 21, 1870; Elliot to Granville, *ibid.*, no. 394, Pera, December 30, 1870.

126. Apponyi to Beust, H.H.S. VIII/76, no. 1., London, January 2, 1871.

127. Gladstone to Granville, Hawarden Castle, January 5, 1871. Ramm, *Political Correspondence,* I, p. 205.

128. Gladstone to Granville, private letter, Hawarden Castle, January 12, 1871. *Ibid.,* I, p. 209.

Joined to these questions of sentiment was also that of practical policy. Britain, like Prussia, wanted to avoid another eastern crisis which might accompany any attempt at foreign intervention in the Principalities. In January Granville sent instructions to Bucharest which were wise and moderate in character. He advised Green to tell Charles that if he intended to abdicate he should first inform the influential persons in Rumania so that some plan could be worked out to avoid anarchy. The local leaders in the Principalities could then prepare their own plans for the government of the country. After they had done this, the powers could decide if their decisions were in accordance with the treaties. Granville commented: "If the Powers take a contrary course and assume the initiative of giving a government to the Principalities, they will in some degree be responsible for its proper working."[129] The British government, along with the other powers, feared also that any intervention would result in a renewal of the Russian-Austrian antagonism over influence in the area.

With this attitude in London there was little chance that the Porte could receive any kind of compensation in the field of its relations with the Principalities. On January 11 Âli instructed Musurus to speak with Granville in the sense of the instructions.[130] On January 27 the Ottoman ambassador reported his complete failure. He had communicated the portion of his instructions dealing with the Principalities and "Granville met all my requests with a formal refusal."[131] Granville also would not allow the question to be introduced in the congress.

In the question of the Principalities the British and Habsburg governments did follow a policy of mutual consultation and cooperation. Both felt that Charles was making a move toward gaining Rumanian independence; both opposed Turkish intervention. The Habsburg government wished the Austrian and British agents to cooperate in Bucharest to advise together moderation on all parties, but not to support any particular side, a policy which Granville also favored.[132] On the question of Ottoman intervention, the monarchy

129. Granville to Elliot, F.O. 195/971, no. 24, F.O., January 23, 1871.

130. See Appendix II.

131. Musurus to Âli, M.N. 20/6, no. 4356/15 confidential, London, January 27, 1871.

132. Granville to Bloomfield, F.O. 120/487, no. 3 confidential, F.O., January 2, 1871.

agreed with British opposition to the move, but it showed itself more favorable to eventual changes in the administration of the Principalities which the Porte desired – in particular a dissolution of the union. On February 8 Apponyi told Granville that the Habsburg government was not against the separation, but that "we should positively insist that such an important change not be imposed by foreign pressure, doing violence to the feelings of the country, but that it should be the spontaneous product of the wishes of the people."[133] Beust instructed Prokesch in a similar vein: "We have nothing to object to and we even find that arrangement satisfactory, but we do not think that it should be the task of the powers to impose it on the populations of the Principalities."[134]

Despite this lack of success in convincing the powers, the Porte continued to press its views through the month of February. In a circular despatch dated February 1, but delivered in London on February 23, it restated its position.[135] Here once again the condition of the Principalities was considered in most critical terms. The constitution was judged impossible; it "is made to favor their [Rumanian] anarchical tendency, to give free reign to the intrigues of the parties and to assure impunity to all kinds of misdeeds." The Porte agreed with the prince that the document should be changed. Such an act could only be carried out through a *coup d'état.* Charles, however, had neither a party nor the army behind him; he was "alone and unfortunately hated by all the parties." An intervention of the protecting powers was needed, since only in this way could events in Rumania be influenced: "It is thus necessary to occupy the Principalities militarily and institute the necessary changes under the bayonettes of the soldiers." The program of the Porte was thus to allow Charles the

133. Apponyi to Beust, H.H.S. VIII/76, no. 12C, London, February 8, 1871; also Granville to Bloomfield, F.O. 7/786, no. 38, F.O., February 12, 1871; Bloomfield to Granville, F.O. 78/787, no. 84 confidential, Vienna, February 15, 1871.

134. Beust to Prokesch, H.H.S. XII/99, tel. no. 51, Budapest, January 26, 1871. Beust thought that the Porte's policy of seeking the separation of the Principalities was shortsighted. Moldavia was "more Russian than ever." The provinces united formed some sort of a barrier against Russia. Bloomfield to Granville, F.O. 7/788, no. 121 confidential, Vienna, March 16, 1871.

135. Âli to Musurus, S. Porte, February 1, 1871 to be found in F.O. 78/2202; Granville to Bloomfield, F.O. 195/971, no. 51 confidential, F.O., March 3, 1871.

opportunity to solve his political problems. If he failed, as was obviously expected, and left the country, the powers should take the responsibility of giving the Principalities a new government. Such a move was believed absolutely necessary. Another foreign prince would not be available; the "Rumanian demagogues" would wish to proclaim the "Red Republic." The Porte could not allow this, since it would result in the breaking of the bonds of suzerainty and the land would become a center of anarchy and intrigue. Intervention would then be necessary. The Porte proposed under such circumstances to send in an army which would allow the reestablishment of the old political order of two separate principalities with native governors. The powers were to impose the solution; no mention was made of consulting the wishes of the population.

In this message the Ottoman government went too far; both Vienna and London were disturbed. The two states now cooperated to calm the situation.[136] On March 13 Granville instructed Elliot that he should make this statement of the attitude of the Porte toward the Principalities the subject of special representations. He should inform the Porte that its views tended in the direction of interference in the internal affairs of the state and that it assumed a right to control the character of the government which would be set up should the prince leave. Elliot was to remind the Porte that it could not deal with Rumania "according to her good pleasure"; any interference was contingent on the consent of all the guarantor powers. Moreover, even if Charles abdicated, it was possible that an acceptable government would be set up after his departure.[137]

When this reprimand was delivered to Âli, the Ottoman minister protested that his original despatch had been misunderstood. The Porte did not want to intervene in the Principalities, but it was bound to accept there only the form of government established by the treaties.

136. Granville to Bloomfield, F.O. 7/786, no. 51 confidential, F.O., March 3, 1871. Gladstone wrote to Granville: "I own it appears to me that the time has come, upon the receipt of these most unsatisfactory papers from Musurus, for admonishing the Porte as to its language and attitude with respect to the Principalities." Gladstone to Granville, Carlton House, March 10, 1871. Ramm, *Political Correspondence,* I, p. 226.

137. Granville to Elliot, F.O. 195/971, no. 70, F.O., March 13, 1871; Granville to Elliot, F.O. 78/2127, no. 65, F.O., March 13, 1871.

Elliot replied that Âli's despatch had shown a "readiness, if not an anxiety" for a military occupation of the country, a move which could not be taken without the approval of the powers. The ending of the union of Moldavia and Wallachia without the consent of the population was also not favored.[138]

The reaction of the Habsburg government was much the same. In his conversations with Prokesch, Âli in vain attempted to convince the Habsburg government of the immediate danger of the establishment of a revolutionary government. What should the Porte do if a "Red Republic" were proclaimed and

> . . .if it was sanctioned in the country by the regular means of revolutionary action? Can we let ourselves be fooled by these maneuvers? Can we abandon the populations to the good will of the demagogues? Is it necessary for us to wait until the fire, prepared by criminal hands, breaks out in our neighboring provinces? I do not think that a government which respects itself can in such a manner bow its head to the will of the conspirators and their allies of the inflammatory press.

Âli further pointed out that the international agreements on the Principalities had been overturned by *faits accomplis* carried out by "a small but daring party composed of men affiliated with the revolutionary committees of Europe, doctrinaires or ambitious men, the same ones who today again make government almost impossible in Rumania."[139]

Meanwhile, the Rumanian question gradually died down. In Bucharest, after a critical stage was reached at the end of March, the political situation became calmer. The Rumanian politicians themselves became aware of the dangers which their country faced should Charles abdicate. A government was finally formed with which the prince could cooperate. The Porte assured the powers that it would not break the treaties or resort to military measures without the consent of the guarantor states.

Neither Russia nor Prussia played a major role in the discussions over

138. Elliot to Granville, F.O. 78/2174, no. 136, Constantinople, March 30, 1871.

139. Prokesch to Beust, H.H.S. XII/98, no. 13 A-C, Constantinople, March 17, 1871.

the Principalities. The German government wished the Prussian prince to remain, but it had more important matters on its hands. Russia had never been in favor of the appointment of a foreign prince, but the fact that he was a Hohenzollern, a family with which the Russian court was in close relations, was important. At first, Gorchakov had thought that Charles would abdicate, an event which he feared would lead to disorders. In that case Rustem believed "that the Russian government would not oppose an Ottoman intervention, but if Austria made any kind of an attempt to intervene," Russia would "oppose it by every means."[140] Gorchakov now had no objection to the idea of the separation of the Principalities and a return to the basis of the Treaty of Paris. Conservative, autocratic Russia did not like the Rumanian Liberal party, which had been responsible for the past political changes. Gorchakov also expressed the opinion that if a republic were proclaimed in Bucharest, the Porte could ask for the right to intervene, and that in doing so it would be acting "on the basis of the treaties."[141] However, the Russian government shared the desire of all the powers in this period that events in Rumania would not require the intervention of the guaranteeing powers or the Porte.

The Signature of the Treaty: The Reaction of the Powers The treaty was not signed until March 13. By that time the French representative, the Duc de Broglie, had arrived so that representatives from all of the signatories of the Treaty of Paris were present. Bernstorff now attended for the German Empire, a change in title which occurred during the conference.

In addition to the questions already discussed, one of the major concerns of the Porte, as we have seen, had been to secure the confirmation of the rest of the Treaty of Paris. This objective was attained in Article VIII, although the wording was not as exact as the

140. Rustem to Âli, M.N. 20/6, private letter, St. Petersburg, December 31/January 12, 1871.

141. Rumbold to Granville, F.O. 120/487, no. 48 confidential, St. Petersburg, April 4, 1871. Prokesch-Osten in his memoirs wrote that Ignatiev supported the division of the Principalities and the restoration of the separate governors. Prokesch-Osten, "Erinnerungen" *Deutsche Revue,* IV, 3 (1880), pp. 13, 18. See also Ignatiev, "Zapiski," V (1914), pp. 147, 148.

empire desired. It stated simply: "The High Contracting Parties renew and confirm all the stipulations of the Treaty of March 30, 1856, as well as its annexes, which are not annulled or modified by the present Treaty."[142] The special Russian-Turkish agreement of 1856 on the Black Sea was annulled by a simple mutual understanding.

As much as can be judged by the Ottoman material, the Porte was not dissatisfied with the results of the conference. The original instructions and Âli's subsequent despatches show the Ottoman government had a very clear view of the weaknesses and limitations of its position. Musurus also seems to have been content with his role. On March 15 he wrote in a letter to Âli that he had indeed been faced with many difficulties and had "always to regulate my actions and words so as to meet the demands of public opinion in general and in particular that of England and the Ottoman Empire."[143] In thanking the sultan for a letter commending his work at the conference, Musurus commented in approval of the attitude of his ruler, who in devoting ". . .all his solicitude to the organization of his army and navy and to the improvement of the administration of his vast estates has shown how much he is aware that the maintenance of his rights of sovereignty and the integrity of his empire is more firmly assured when it is based on his own power and on the devotion of his people than when it rests basically on international guarantees."[144]

It has been shown in the previous pages how the Ottoman statesmen tried to maintain an independent position on the major issues. They attempted also to cooperate with Britain and the Habsburg Empire, but

142. Âli and Musurus wished a far more elaborate wording to be adopted. Their version was: "les hautes parties contractantes confirment et consolident toutes les stipulations du Traité de 30 Mars 1856 et des ses accessoires qui n'ont pas été annulés ou modifiés par le présent Traité. Il est bien entendu qu'aucune infraction à ces stipulations et à celles qui en découlent, ne sera désormais permise; que toute interpretation de ces stipulations incompatible avec la dignité et les droits souverains d'une Puissance indépendente sera inadmissible et que si à l'avenir il est jugé nécessaire d'y apporter une modification, ce ne sera que dans les formes de la légalité et à la suite d'un accord entre les Puissances contractantes." Musurus to Âli, M.N. 20/6, no. 4346/18 confidential, London, January 23, 1871; Âli to Musurus, *ibid.*, no. 29385/32, London, January 25, 1871; Musurus to Âli, *ibid.*, no. 4351/23, London, January 26, 1871.

143. Musurus to Âli, M.N. 20/6, no. 4433/40, London, March 15, 1871.

144. Musurus to Âli, M.N. 20/6, no. 4473/61, London, May 2, 1871.

their first concern was naturally the defense of their own national interests. As a result their chief controversies in the conference had been with the powers who were in theory their friends and allies; their relations with Russia had been relatively smoother. After the congress the sultan received Ignatiev in a special audience; here the ambassador expressed the tsar's satisfaction with the "friendly and moderate attitude" of the Porte on the question of the Black Sea.[145] Gorchakov, as we have seen, went out of his way to consult the Porte's interests. As a result, the Ottoman government received repeated complaints on its "pro-Russian" attitude; throughout the entire period of the conference rumors spread of the existence of a secret Russian-Turkish agreement.

The Italian representatives appear to have been particularly active in circulating reports in this regard. On February 24 Emilio Visconti-Venosta, the Italian premier, told Photiades, the Ottoman ambassador in Florence, that "several governments" were convinced that a secret entente existed between Russia and Turkey on the question of Prince Charles.[146] Later he reported that the British government was suspicious because of Musurus' attitude during the conference and his overtures to Granville on an eventual intervention in the Danubian Principalities.[147] Âli answered these reports with the strong denial: "As for our supposed entente with Russia, it does not exist, it has never existed."[148] Fears that the Porte wished to force the congress to fail came also from Berlin.[149] The British concern was probably best summarized in a speech given by the Conservative leader Lord Salisbury in the House of Lords on May 15.

> It is a singular feature in these proceedings that Turkey is to be seen eagerly struggling for that which would be beneficial and agreeable to Russia alone. . . .I cannot help noticing the sundry reports I have heard of the sudden pacific attitude of Russia towards Turkey, and I confess I cannot help suspecting that the noble Earl knows also that Turkey has come to the conviction

145. Âli to Halil, M.N. 20/6, no. 29888/85, April 8, 1871.

146. Photiades to Âli, M.N. 20/6, no. 6883/50 personal, Florence, February 24, 1871.

147. Photiades to Musurus, M.N. 20/6, private letter, Florence, March 3, 1871.

148. Âli to Photiades, M.N. 20/6, no. 29700/38, March 15, 1871.

149. Aristarchi to Âli, M.N. 20/6, no. 3155/38, February 20, 1871.

> that the assistance of the Western Powers is a broken reed that will pierce her hand – for what with the impotency of France, and the irresolution of England, Turkey has come to the conviction that it is cheaper to purchase the good will of Russia, and that it will be safer for her to become a feudatory of Russia, and more honourable than to become a despised and rejected suppliant for Western assistance.[150]

The greatest dissatisfaction with Ottoman independence and the strongest suspicions concerning her relations with Russia were to be found, as could be expected, in Vienna and Budapest. The chief opposition to the Habsburg proposals came not from Russia, but from the Porte. Except for Ottoman opposition the other powers would have accepted the term "non-riverain" and at least some of the Austrian desires for the Danube. Halil reported repeatedly throughout the conference the suspicions that existed in Vienna of the existence of a secret agreement between the Porte and Russia and the belief that Ignatiev dominated the councils of the Ottoman Empire.[151] At a dinner on February 2 Franz Joseph himself expressed these sentiments to Halil. The Ottoman representative reported: "He began the conversation by saying to me in an agreeable tone: You wish then to make common cause with the Russians and you show yourself more Russian than they."[152] Âli naturally reacted with indignation against these charges; in his reply to Halil he denied that Ignatiev was "all powerful here. We protest with all our might against such an accusation." There was no secret agreement with Russia. "It is very difficult to see oneself accused in this manner when one is only seeking to defend one's rights." The basis of the Turkish action at the congress lay in the instructions. "If the Cabinet of St. Petersburg puts a certain ostentation in the marks of friendship which it has lavished on us for some time, we do not know the reasons for it. I believe that no one would advise us to respond to these actions by rudeness or by manifestations of a *too marked mistrust.*"[153]

The bitterest reproaches from Vienna were, however, reserved for later and in particular for after the signature of the convention. At the

150. Hansard, *Parliamentary Debates,* 3rd series, CCVI, pp. 798, 799.
151. Halil to Âli, M.N. 20/6, no. 3470/35, Pest, February 2, 1871.
152. Halil to Âli, M.N. 20/6, no. 3409/34, Pest, February 2, 1871.
153. Âli to Halil, M.N. 20/6, no. 29441/40, February 5, 1871.

beginning of March, Esad Bey, the Turkish consul-general in Pest, met Andrassy, who expressed his surprise at the Ottoman attitude. The Habsburg minister had favored the proposal for the creation of an international naval station in the Black Sea; to him the question of the integrity of the empire was less important than the assuring of its peace and tranquility. He could not understand why the Porte "...gave herself up to Russia.... In fact what I understand even less in all this, he said, is the influence of General Ignatiev and the absence of a full understanding between the Sublime Porte and Austria-Hungary, whose interests are almost identical in the questions which are at present under discussion."[154]

At the end of March the Habsburg government through Prokesch formally communicated its objections to the Turkish attitude.[155] It was noted that the Porte had been chiefly injured by the Russian denunciation. The form of the announcement could cause agitation among both the Turkish and the Habsburg national groups. The monarchy had taken a firm stand; it had gone so far as to invoke the application of the April 1856 treaty. Instead of cooperating, the Ottoman government had taken a position in opposition to that of the Habsburg Empire. The apparent harmony between Serbia and the Porte had also been a surprise. In conclusion, the message warned against trust in Russia and recalled her attitude toward the Slavic subjects of the two empires.

In reply, in April Âli sent a long despatch to Halil, which is reproduced in full because of the summary which it gives of the Turkish position at the conference.[156] When Halil read this message to him, Beust answered with the previous arguments. The monarchy's prime concern had been to maintain the Treaty of Paris and the integrity of the Ottoman Empire; in addition, "the propositions that we believed we had to make had above all the aim of inflicting a humiliation on Russia in order to reduce the disastrous effect of her insolence." Beust had presented the proposal on the Iron Gates because the Hungarians considered it important. Halil noted in his despatch that he had here

154. Esad to Âli, M.N. 20/6, no. 204/1, Pest, March 9, 1871 in Âli to Halil, no. 29814/82, March 29, 1871.

155. Beust to Prokesch, H.H.S. XII, 99, no no., Vienna, March 24, 1871.

156. See Appendix IV for the complete text.

refrained from commenting that this was not an important consideration for the Porte.[157]

Musurus, who was informed of this interchange of opinions, was also disturbed by the Austrian attitude. He noted that the more the Porte tried to cooperate with Vienna, whose position in regard to Russia was similar, the more Beust expressed doubts on these dispositions to the conference. He pointed out that both Britain and the Ottoman Empire had rejected the proposal of a naval port and the increase in the number of ships at the mouth of the Danube; this had been done before the opening of the conference. On the question of the Iron Gates and the Riverain Commission, although it was true that the Porte had made certain changes which Serbia desired, there was no reason why the Habsburg Empire should object to this relationship between a vassal province and its suzerain. It would perhaps have been better if the Habsburg government had first discussed the matter with Belgrade. It could then have made the necessary changes in the proposal and have been the recipient of the Serbian gratitude.[158]

In the conference the Ottoman government was thus able to maintain a strong and independent stand. It remained on friendly terms with Russia, the power that appeared to pose the chief threat to its territories. It was successful in resisting measures which, although introduced by its theoretical friends, would be detrimental to its interests. The Black Sea was now no longer neutralized, but the rest of the Treaty of Paris remained intact. The Straits settlement was changed in a manner which could benefit the Ottoman government if the state in fact maintained its national prestige and power in the next years. The international position of the Porte reflected the relative stability of the internal regime. The leading Ottoman diplomats were obviously on good terms with each other; the ambassadors, especially Musurus, were allowed considerable freedom of action. Âli certainly handled the very sensitive and difficult problem of his relations with the other powers

157. Halil to Âli, M.N. 20/6, no. 3602/126 confidential, Vienna, April 30, 1871.

158. Musurus to Âli, M.N. 20/6, no. 4482/67 confidential, London, May 16, 1871. In July before the Delegations Beust defended the Austrian attitude as correct and energetic, but, he added: "La Sublime Porte a, il est vrai, en cette matière, inauguré une nouvelle politique qui consisterait à faire preuve d'indépendence. . . ." Halil to Âli, M.N. 20/6, no. 3668/166, Vienna, July 3, 1871.

with considerable skill. Unfortunately, the next decade was to witness a complete reversal of these conditions. It seems safe to say that the Conference of London marks the last time when the Ottoman Empire appears on the diplomatic stage in such a dignified and independent role.

The events of the conference not only reflected relatively favorably on the Ottoman position in Europe, but they also showed a basic interest on the part of all of the powers for the protection of at least the outward forms of "legality" in international relations. Although the Russian government unilaterally denounced a clause of the Treaty of Paris, thus declaring its intention to violate an engagement, it finally consented to present its position at an international conference. Here it signed a declaration on the validity of treaties which constituted in fact a reprimand for its previous action. In the same manner the British government, while contemplating means of evading obligations to the Ottoman government, remained concerned that changes in international treaties should be accomplished by peaceful means and through the proper procedures.

The provisions concerning the Straits stated at this time remained in effect until the signing of the Treaty of Lausanne in 1923. In the years between 1871 and 1887, which are the chief concern of the remainder of this study, the controversies over the Straits involved more a clash of opinion over the interpretation of the stipulations of the Treaty of London than an attempt to formulate new rules. In this period the swift decline of Ottoman prestige and influence is sharply indicated. The competing policies of Russia and Britain, not the concerns of the Porte, hold the center of the stage. Thus in the next pages it will be observed that the policies of the powers, rather than the position of the Porte, will receive the major emphasis.

III

THE STRAITS SETTLEMENT APPLIED AND INTERPRETED

At the London conference the Porte had, as we have seen, lost the protection afforded by the neutralization of the Black Sea. Important safeguards, based on international treaties, nevertheless remained. The Danube barrier was intact; Russia was still excluded from the ranks of the riverain states. The reconfirmation of the remaining clauses of the Treaty of Paris gave, at least on paper, the assurance that the signatories respected the territorial integrity of the empire and recognized that they should not interfere in its internal affairs. The Straits agreement had been strengthened to allow the Porte to call in outside aid if the empire were in danger. The three power pact of April 1856 was still in effect. Moreover, in the declaration in the protocol of the first meeting of the conference the powers had recognized the obligation not to abrogate unilaterally treaties to which they were signatories. The paper fortress constructed around the Ottoman Empire by the mutual jealousies of the powers thus still appeared formidable.

Unfortunately for the Porte the next decade was to show the feebleness of these obstacles to foreign penetration and imperial appetites. The new Straits clause in particular was to prove not a protection for the empire, but the cause of major, continual diplomatic controversies until the outbreak of the First World War. Granville's apprehensions over the nebulous nature of the wording were to be fully justified. The greatest controversy was to center over the definition of the obligations undertaken by the signatories to the agreement – whether they were unilateral between the individual powers and the Porte or multilateral among all the states concerned. This question became a major international dispute at and after the Congress of Berlin in 1878. In addition, almost every word and phrase of the clause proved open to varied and twisted interpretations. The powers were to disagree, for instance, on what constituted a "ship of war" and on the definition of "in time of peace."[1] If the sultan were to open the Straits to one of the "friendly and allied powers," they did not know whether he would have to allow the fleets of the others in also. It was not clear how far the phrase "to safeguard the execution of the treaty of 1856" could be stretched to cover cases not clearly relevant to this agreement.[2]

In its continued attempt to maintain the integrity of the empire, the Ottoman government still had, of course, the weapons of its own resources and the rivalries of the great powers. In the next decade, however, changes in domestic politics and in the international scene were to take place which were to have most disastrous consequences for the empire. The reforms of the Tanzimat era did not strengthen the internal fiber of the state sufficiently to allow it to maintain its role as a great power on its own resources. In its foreign relations, the Porte was to see its former allies, Britain and Austria-Hungary, become partitioning powers. The new era in international relations which was to come after 1870 was to prove particularly unfortunate for the Ottoman Empire.

In the 1870s two of the great powers, France and Italy, were to play a relatively minor role in eastern affairs because of their own internal problems. The fate of the Ottoman Empire thus depended upon Britain, Russia, Austria-Hungary, and to a lesser extent, on the new Germany. In the years after 1871 in dealing with these powers the Porte continued to follow a policy of balance – of using the interests of one state against the others. Both Ignatiev and Elliot still exerted a

1. In the treaties of 1841 and 1856 it was specifically stated that the phrase "time of peace" referred to the Porte; this is omitted in the 1871 agreement.

2. Memorandum on the "Right of the Sultan of Turkey to exclude Foreign Ships of War from, and to restrict the passage of Foreign Merchant-Vessels through the Dardanelles and Bosphorus." by E. Hertslet, the Foreign Office librarian. F.O. 78/4271.

major influence on the decisions of the Ottoman government. Changes which were to have a strongly negative effect in Constantinople, however, now occurred in the internal and foreign policies of the governments chiefly concerned with the fate of the empire. Most important for European politics were the consequences of German unification and the inauguration of new programs of imperial expansion in Asia and Africa by Britain, France, and Russia in particular. Because of their decisive influence on the Porte, the alterations in policy and the conflicts within the European states will be briefly reviewed.

With France and Austria-Hungary both in a temporarily weakened state due to past military defeats and domestic reorganization, Britain should in theory have emerged as the principal prop to the Ottoman Empire in international politics. With its increasing imperial entanglements, the British government had certainly every interest in the maintenance of Ottoman authority at the Straits. In the 1870s the major conflict with Russia stemmed from this power's steady advance in Central Asia and its involvement in Afghan affairs. Since the most effective way that Britain could counter Russian superiority in ground troops was still the threat of a naval attack in the Black Sea region, the independence of the Ottoman government and the status of the Straits remained a major issue in British foreign policy. However, an important change occurred whose full effects were to be felt only in the 1890s. In 1869 the Suez Canal was opened; in the next years this route was to become the main British commercial artery and imperial line of communication. It was also, incidentally, the shortest and most convenient link between Russia proper and her Far Eastern possessions. In 1875 the British government purchased the shares in the canal which had belonged to the khedive of Egypt, thus giving Britain a direct voice, but not a predominant one, in the affairs of the Suez Canal Company. In 1876, in cooperation with France, Britain established a system of financial supervision in Egypt. Although the opening of the canal made naval predominance in the eastern Mediterranean even more important to Britain, it also marked the beginning of a subtle shift in emphasis from the Straits and Constantinople to Suez and Egypt. This move was to signify eventually a tendency by the British government to acquire more direct political control over the Ottoman vassal Egypt and to lessen its interest in defending the Ottoman position at the Straits and Constantinople.

A change also occurred in the stand of both the Liberal and Conservative political parties on the whole question of the maintenance of the territorial integrity of the Ottoman Empire. The highly negative attitude of Gladstone has already been described. In 1874 the Conservative Party under Disraeli won a major electoral victory; they were to hold power until 1880. Although the new leadership undoubtedly placed much more emphasis on international relations and on Britain's imperial position, Disraeli was always willing to compromise the integrity and prestige of the Ottoman Empire when it served British purposes. Certainly neither party now placed a major emphasis on the preservation of Ottoman interests. Moreover, Conservative policy was undoubtedly affected by the swing in public opinion occasioned by the events in the Balkans at this time.

In April 1876 an uprising in Bulgaria was suppressed by Turkish irregulars who, in the process, committed widespread atrocities.[3] In this same year Gladstone, who had virtually retired from politics, returned to the political scene with a pamphlet, *Bulgarian Horrors,* which described in impassioned terms the massacres which had taken place. The Bulgarian episode not only swayed Liberal public opinion, but it appears to have affected many of the leaders of the Conservative Party. Despite evidence of similar behavior on the part of Christians, the number of those who felt that the Ottoman Empire was simply not worth preserving was thus increased.[4] Even among those who believed that the creation of national states was not the solution to the problem, there was now less feeling that the Porte should be treated as were the governments of other European nations. The Ottoman Empire was now equated more with the states of Africa and Asia, which were to be the

3. See the "Bibliographical Note" for books on the eastern crisis of 1875-78.

4. One author has commented on this episode: "Many of us were in that old Puritan frame of mind, which could be satisfied with little less than the hewing piecemeal of the abominable Turk before the Lord. Not only had every humane feeling been hurt, but we felt a sense of national dishonour. But for England, Turkey would long ago, in all probability, have been free of pashas and Bashi-Bazouks." Andrew Lang, *Life, Letters and Diaries of Sir Stafford Northcote, First Earl of Iddesleigh* (London, 1891), p. 296. See also R. W. Seton-Watson, *Disraeli, Gladstone and the Eastern Question* (London, 1935), pp. 277-287. An opposite picture of Christian atrocities against Moslems is given in the Blue Book, *Accounts and Papers,* LXXXI (1878), Further Correspondence respecting the Affairs of Turkey, C. 1905.

targets of imperial conquest. By 1878 there was little opposition in either party to the acquisition of outright domination over Ottoman lands, although different excuses and justifications were used.

The attitude of the Habsburg Empire toward the eastern problems suffered from a similar division of ideas and principles. In the wider view, because of its own national problems and its relations with Russia, the monarchy continued to have every interest in preserving the Ottoman Empire. However, in the preceding years the state and, in particular, the Habsburg dynasty had suffered a series of humiliating military defeats; it had lost the rich provinces of Lombardy and Venetia and had surrendered its leading position among the German states. Without seapower or a tradition of overseas colonial expansion the monarchy could not recoup these losses by imperial conquest overseas. While Russia, Britain, France, and Italy could envisage the partition of Asia and Africa, the Habsburg Monarchy could only move forward in the Balkans. The acquisition of territory there was certainly appealing; Bosnia and Hercegovina might replace Venetia and Lombardy. The temptation to return to the policy of the eighteenth century, when Russia and Austria advanced into Ottoman lands together, was thus great. Austrian interest in the furtherance of its economic position in the area similarly increased.

German policy after 1870 also contributed to the Habsburg decision. After the victory over France and after German national unification, Bismarck in the next years concentrated on the construction of a European diplomatic system which would protect his great accomplishments. In the 1870s he strongly encouraged a policy of cooperation between Vienna, St. Petersburg, and Berlin. This alignment, the Three Emperors' Alliance, was designed to preserve peace and stability on the continent. The weakness in this partnership was the Russian and Austrian antagonism in the Balkans. Although Bismarck repeatedly claimed that Germany had no interest in Balkan affairs, German influence did play indirectly a major role in events in that area. Bismarck's solution for the tension here was the division of the peninsula into Austrian and Russian spheres of influence. This program naturally involved the virtual exclusion of Ottoman control over the majority of its Balkan lands. It was also to be the basis of the Treaty of Berlin.

Despite the interest of other nations in the Ottoman possessions, Russia was still in the 1870s regarded as the chief menace to the empire. Certainly, after the goal of ending the neutralization of the Black Sea had been achieved, it appeared that the Russians were doing exactly what they had assured the Porte they would not do – that is, encourage the revolt of the Balkan Christians. It was also obvious that in this period both Panslav and Russian national sentiments were increasing. The Crimean War had been a national humiliation. After its conclusion the Russian government had concentrated on internal reform and had played a generally negative role in European affairs. During this period the great events of the unifications of Germany and Italy had been accomplished. In the 1870s in Russia there occurred a reaction against the inactive policy of the previous decade. The reforms had not brought the social and political results which had been expected; the enormous increase of German power and prestige caused in some resentment and dismay. The desire to play a more direct, decisive, and glorious role in world affairs was a natural reaction to a period of relative passivity.

The obvious field for Russian action at this time was the Balkan peninsula. As in the past, the Balkan people looked to Russia first for aid against the Ottoman Empire. Within Russia Panslav sentiment assured that appeals to the Russian government would receive attention. On this issue there was, however, a decided division of opinion. Most of the responsible officials, particularly in the Foreign Ministry, were well aware of the dangers to Russia, in regard to both internal and foreign policy, of the Balkan revolutionary movements. During the Russo-Turkish War of 1877 a split developed between those who opposed extreme solutions and believed that peace could not be made without consultation with other European governments and those who wished to solve the eastern question according to the Panslav program by negotiation with the Ottoman Empire to the exclusion of other powers. The Porte could expect little sympathy from either faction; both contemplated the further partition of the empire.

To counter this aggressive attitude on the part of the powers, the Porte had few resources. The reforms of the Tanzimat period had not fully attained their goals. Although it was to be doubted if any internal changes would have made loyal Ottoman citizens out of the Balkan

Christians, it could have been expected that the central administration would have been strengthened. However, it was precisely at the center that the state showed its weakest side. Âli died in 1871; no statesman of his ability or stature succeeded him. In contrast to the earlier years Abdülaziz now exerted more direct power in the government. A grave crisis occurred in 1876, the year of the three sultans, when the capital itself was prey to revolt and disorder. In May 1876 Abdülaziz was replaced by Murad V. At the end of August this sultan, who suffered from mental and nervous disorders, was overthrown. Abdülhamid II, who next succeeded to the throne, came to power with a program of reform. In December 1876 a constitution was in fact issued which was based on the equality of all Ottoman citizens and which closely resembled western constitutional forms. A Chamber of Deputies was subsequently chosen. It met from March to June 1877 and from December to February 1878 when it was prorogued. Until 1908, Abdülhamid exercised his powers as an autocratic ruler. His policies in these years have been strongly criticized. It must be remembered, however, that he was under constant strong foreign pressure in all sections of his empire.

Parallel with this condition of political instability was the concurrent decline of the economic position of the empire. To pay for reforms, military and naval improvements, and the building of a costly railroad network, the Porte had contracted large loans from European financial institutions. By the middle of the 1870s the government paid in interest 14 million Turkish pounds out of a total revenue of 17 to 18 million.[5] A similar situation had developed in Egypt, leading in 1876 to the assumption of joint financial control by France and Britain. In the next years the powers were to use this financial breakdown as another weapon against the empire. From the viewpoint of internal political stability and economic balance the Porte was thus in the 1870s in a worse position than in the period immediately after the Crimean War.

When a revolt broke out in Bosnia and Hercegovina in 1875, the

5. Rafii-Sukru Suvla, "Debts during the Tanzimat Period," in Charles Issawi, editor, *The Economic History of the Middle East,* (Chicago, 1966), p. 101. European financial and economic penetration in the Ottoman Empire will not be discussed in detail. See Donald C. Blaisdell, *European Financial Control in the Ottoman Empire* (New York, 1929).

empire was therefore in no position to meet the problems associated with it. The period of reform had not resulted in the conciliation of the nationalities, nor had it provided the basis for the building of strong military power so that solutions of force could be resorted to. The situation became worse when in 1876 the vassal states, Serbia and Montenegro, declared war on the Porte. Although the empire was able to defeat the Balkan armies, it could not withstand a Russian invasion launched in April 1877. Despite a heroic Turkish resistance at Plevna, the Russian armies by the new year were encamped at Adrianople, within easy striking distance of Constantinople. Thus in 1877-78 exactly the situation had arisen which the treaties of March and April 1856 and March 1871 had been designed to prevent. The Russian armies had marched down the Balkan peninsula, crossed the Balkan mountains, and were now encamped outside of Constantinople. It was obvious that the Porte would now be forced to accept harsh terms in what would be a dictated peace. The powers, especially the old defenders of the empire, Britain and the Habsburg Empire, had not moved. What then had happened to the treaties and agreements which had been designed to protect the Ottoman Empire from Russian control?

No attempt will be made here to review the complicated diplomatic situation surrounding the eastern crisis of 1875-78, except as it concerns the status of the Straits as regulated by the Treaty of London. Suffice it to say that the Habsburg Empire under German persuasion returned to the pattern of the eighteenth century and adopted a policy of the partition of Ottoman lands, rather than that of opposition to any Russian advance. In the Reichstadt Agreement of 1876 and the Budapest agreements of 1877 the monarchy in effect agreed to allow Russia to go to war against the Ottoman Empire in return for Bosnia and Hercegovina. Britain, on whom the Porte had principally relied, was neutralized by a strong internal debate over the question of the support of the empire and by the fact that she would obviously obtain no military aid from her former Crimean allies. In these circumstances all of the powers simply ignored their treaty obligations in regard to the Ottoman Empire.

Specific guarantees of Ottoman independence and integrity were, as we have seen, contained in Article VII of the Treaty of Paris and in the tripartite treaty of April 1856. Article VII need not concern us; as far as the interests of the Porte were involved, it remained from the beginning a dead letter. The treaty of April did, in contrast, receive some attention from the signatories.[6] It must be remembered that the Porte was not a party to this pact and could therefore not call it into force. In addition, one signatory, France, as in 1870 remained in no condition to observe its terms. The other two proceeded to reduce its obligations to nothing. The most direct method of dealing with the treaty was adopted by the Habsburg Empire. The Budapest agreement with Russia of January 1877 contained the following clause:

> If the government of the emperor [of Austria-Hungary] is invited to cooperate in the putting into effect of the treaty of April 15, 1856, it will decline to cooperate in the case provided for in the present convention and, without contesting the validity of the said treaty, will proclaim its neutrality.[7]

The third party, Britain, on other occasions the vocal defender of the sanctity of treaties, handled the matter in another manner. The question was discussed in the House of Lords in February, April, and May 1877. The chief argument used was the dubious claim that Britain was not obligated to act under the treaty unless her cosignatories invited her to. It is interesting to note that the foreign secretary, Lord Derby, in a debate with a Liberal member, the Earl of Rosebery, while not supporting the unilateral abrogation of agreements, argued that no treaties

> . . .can or are intended to be eternal. They are framed with reference to existing circumstances, and though I do not say whether that is so or is not the case in regard to the treaty of 1856, yet nothing has been more common in European diplomacy than the recognition of the fact that treaties do by the lapse of time and the force of events become obsolete.[8]

This was one of the arguments which Gorchakov had used in denouncing the Black Sea clauses. For the Ottoman Empire the chief significance of the discussions was the obvious fact that Britain too

6. This section is based on the excellent chapter "Epilogue: The Faith of Treaties," in W. E. Mosse, *The Rise and Fall of the Crimean System,* pp. 185-201.
7. *Ibid.,* p. 192.
8. *Ibid.,* pp. 194, 195.

would observe only the treaty obligations which suited her interests – a condition which was to be most clearly shown in relation to the Straits.

Britain Forces the Straits During the Russo-Turkish War the entire question of the Straits and the city of Constantinople occupied a major place in the discussions between the powers, in particular between Russia and Britain. After the outbreak of the war in May 1877, the British formally notified the Russian government of their interest in Suez, the Straits, and the Persian Gulf. On June 8 the Russian government accepted the position that the fate of the Straits was a matter of European importance. In July in another message Britain warned against even a temporary occupation of Constantinople. For the Ottoman Empire, who, of course, was not a party to these negotiations, the major crisis in relation to the Straits occurred in January and February 1878. At that time with a Russian army camped at the gates of Constantinople, the Porte was faced with the British determination to send a naval force through the Dardanelles, even if the Ottoman government should resist.

From the opening of the war in April 1877 until the fall of Plevna on December 11, the Ottoman armies had given a very good account of themselves on the battlefields. Thereafter it became apparent that unless foreign assistance could be obtained, Russia would have little difficulty reaching Constantinople. Although the Porte in December appealed to the mediation of the powers, it was soon clear that such intervention could only come from London. During the winter of 1877-78 the Conservative cabinet of Disraeli was in sharp conflict on the issue. The foreign secretary, Lord Derby, stood opposed to the more active and belligerent stand of Disraeli backed enthusiastically by Queen Victoria. A policy of intervention was supported by the Turkophile British ambassador at Constantinople, Sir Austen Henry Layard.[9] Musurus, still the Ottoman ambassador in London, continued

9. Layard's strong feelings are shown in his correspondence. During this period of crisis he wrote: "We are essentially a great Mohammedan Power and I cannot conceive anything more likely to strike a blow at our dominion and prestige in India than if we were to allow Russia to conquer Constantinople, and to drive out the Sultan." Gordon Waterfield, *Layard of Nineveh* (London, 1963), p. 382. In January 1878 he commented: "It is the most monstrous piece of folly that we should be ready to sacrifice the most vital interests of our country, India, our

to work for cooperation between Britain and the Porte. British policy, like the Russian, remained unclear and contradictory because of this division among the leadership of the country.

During this period, as in the preceding months, the touchstone for Russo-British relations remained the question of the Straits. Since obviously the Crimean coalition could not be reformed, Britain in this crisis did not have a continental land army at her disposal. She could thus make her influence felt only through naval action at the Straits, combined possibly with the landing of a limited expeditionary force. Under no condition could she allow full Russian control of the Straits from the land, particularly by means of the seizure of the Gallipoli peninsula. On December 13 Derby sent St. Petersburg a warning that even a temporary occupation of the Straits or Constantinople would force the British government to take action. Throughout this time Gorchakov, Peter Shuvalov, the Russian ambassador in London, and most of the responsible members of the Russian Foreign Ministry showed complete understanding of the significance of the issue. Repeated assurances were sent to Britain that Russia regarded the Straits question as one which could only be solved by agreement among the powers; Russia would not act unilaterally. Unfortunately, a division on policy on this question existed between the majority in the Foreign Ministry and some military and diplomatic representatives who held ambitious plans for the control of the Balkan area. Thus in both Britain and Russia leading statesmen were in disagreement on the policy which their governments should adopt toward the Porte and in the handling of the Straits question.[10]

In the winter of 1877-78 the Porte found itself caught between the ambitions and aims of these two contending great powers, neither of

---

position as a first-class Power, the influence that we have hitherto exercised in the cause of human liberty and civilisation, rather than stand shoulder to shoulder with the Turks, *because some Bashibazuks have murdered some worthless and unfortunate Bulgarians!*" Seton-Watson, *Disraeli, Gladstone and the Eastern Question,* p. 244.

10. For Russo-British negotiations in this period see in particular B. H. Sumner, *Russia and the Balkans, 1870-1880* (Oxford, 1937), pp. 340-398, and Goriainow, *Le Bosphore et les Dardanelles,* 341 ff. Full discussions of the attitude of the major powers toward the question of the Straits and Constantinople and of their negotiations can be found in these books and others listed in the "Bibliographical Note."

whom regarded the empire as much more than a pawn in their own diplomatic game. The Ottoman government in this crisis not only faced the danger of complete conquest by Russia, but Britain now embarked upon a policy of potentially grave consequence. Throughout the war the Porte had continued to hope for British intervention – either military or diplomatic. When none ensued, and the military situation became impossible, the Ottoman government in December commenced negotiations for an armistice and peace terms.

Despite the domestic disagreements and the ambiguous stand which had been adopted toward the Ottoman Empire, the British government was intensely worried about the situation, in particular the obvious Russian danger to Constantinople, the Straits, and the Gallipoli peninsula. At the beginning of the new year it was felt that some move to counter the threat that Russia would take over the area would have to be made. On January 12 Britain requested the Russian government that its troops not occupy Gallipoli; the peninsula had not been covered in previous assurances. At the same time Derby instructed Layard to obtain permission from the Porte for the British fleet to anchor inside the Dardanelles, "it being clearly understood that this step is no departure from the attitude of neutrality hitherto maintained. . .but is simply a precaution to guard against the channel being closed."[11] The Ottoman foreign minister, Server Pasha, discussed the question with Abdülhamid and gave a negative reply two days later. The dangerous nature of the British demand was obvious. Britain had hitherto refused to aid the Porte in its time of peril; this attitude was maintained. The British government still intended to remain neutral; it would not protect the empire from the consequences of the action. The Porte was now in the process of negotiating with Russia. This power would

11. Derby to Layard, F.O. 78/4271, tel. no. 54 secret, January 12, 1878. For an account of the entrance of the British squadron into the Straits from the point of view of its commander see Mrs. Fred. Egerton, *Admiral of the Fleet, Sir Geoffrey Phipps Hornby* (London, 1906), pp. 224-256. This episode is also covered in Arthur J. Marder, "British Naval Policy in 1878," *Journal of Modern History,* XII, September, 1940, no. 3, pp. 367-373. Summaries of despatches from the Austrian representative in Constantinople at this time are to be found in Alexander Novotny, *Quellen und Studien zur Geschichte des Berliner Kongresses 1878* (Graz-Köln, 1957), pp. 205-212. The Habsburg government also considered sending warships into the Straits.

obviously see the British move as an act of war and a menace to its army; harsher terms might be imposed in the negotiations. The Russian government might also decide to occupy Constantinople, which lay defenseless before its army. Abdülhamid thus replied that under normal circumstances he would have no objection to opening the Straits to the fleet of "so old and friendly an ally," but not at a time when such an action might endanger Ottoman interests. Server also told Sandison, dragoman in the British embassy, that if the Porte allowed the British fleet to enter the Straits, it would also have to permit a similar action by other powers.[12] Ahmed Vefik Pasha, an Ottoman statesman who was soon to become prime minister, gave the same answer. If the negotiations failed, only then would the presence of the British fleet be an advantage. Layard also saw no need for the action.[13] The fleet was not sent at this time because of disagreements within the cabinet on the advisability of the move.[14]

Meanwhile, the discussions between Russian and Turkish delegates for an armistice proceeded; the British cabinet remained tense. When rumors reached it that the terms of the peace being negotiated contained an agreement that the Straits question would be settled on a bilateral basis, contrary to Russian assurances, the British government on January 23 ordered the fleet to enter the Dardanelles. Layard was instructed to inform the sultan and to request him to direct the forts not to fire on the ships. The admiral had orders to proceed whether an agreement was reached on this matter or not.[15] In compliance with these directions Layard sent Sandison to speak with the Turkish government. Again the ministers reacted strongly. They insisted that the British government inform the Russians that the action was not being taken at the request of the Porte but only to protect British interests.[16] They feared still the grave effects which the action could

12. Layard to Derby, F.O. 78/4271, no. 61 Constantinople, January 14, 1878.

13. Layard to Derby, F.O. 78/4271, no. 67 confidential, Constantinople, January 15, 1878.

14. See Seton-Watson, *Disraeli, Gladstone and the Eastern Question,* pp. 266-269.

15. Derby to Layard, F.O. 78/4271, tel. no. 95 A secret, January 24, 1878.

16. Layard to Derby, F.O. 78/4271, tel. no. 108, Constantinople, January 25, 1878; Layard to Derby, F.O. 78/4271, no. 122, Constantinople, January 25, 1878.

have on the peace negotiations, and they were apprehensive lest it should lead to a Russian occupation of Constantinople. However, at this time and with extreme reluctance, before the threat that Britain would proceed even if the Ottoman forts fired on the fleet, the Ottoman ministers and the sultan agreed to the issuance of a firman of passage.

The British cabinet now changed its mind. On January 24 the order to the fleet was countermanded after a defective telegram from Layard led the cabinet to believe that they had been in error on the question of the Straits in the negotiations.[17] On January 25 Admiral Hornby received the rescinding order; his ships entered briefly the Dardanelles and then departed. On the same day the British government learned from Layard that the proposed peace terms did contain the suspected clause, but it was too late to change again the instructions to the fleet.[18] At this time the Porte requested the British government to allow it more time to make the necessary arrangements should it again intend to send a fleet through the Straits.[19]

The real crisis came two weeks later. As mentioned, despite repeated Russian insistence to the contrary, the armistice signed at Adrianople on January 31 did contain the type of arrangement feared by the British government. Article V provided for the bilateral negotiations which Britain so strongly opposed: "His Imperial Majesty the Sultan will come to an agreement with His Majesty the Emperor of Russia in order to safeguard the rights and interests of Russia in the Straits of the Bosphorus and the Dardanelles."[20]

This apparent violation of previous Russian promises, together with the concern caused by rumors that reached London on continued Russian troop movement in the Straits area, led the British government on February 8 to order a squadron, including the warships Alexandra, Temeraire, Swiftsure, Achilles, Ruby, and Salamis, to Constan-

17. Derby to Layard, F.O. 78/4271, tel., January 24, 1878.

18. Layard to Derby, F.O. 78/4271, no. 125, Constantinople, January 25, 1878. See also W. F. Monypenny and G. E. Buckle, *The Life of Benjamin Disraeli, Earl of Beaconsfield* (London, 1929), II, pp. 1102-1103 and Lang, *Northcote,* pp. 292-293.

19. Layard to Derby, F.O. 78/4271, tel. no. 124, Constantinople, January 27, 1878.

20. Sumner, *Russia and the Balkans,* p. 625.

tinople.[21] The reason given for the action was its necessity for "the protection of British life and property." Layard was instructed to obtain another firman if he thought it was needed.[22] This new move met even stronger opposition in Constantinople and led to a period of real tension in British-Ottoman relations. Layard himself made clear his disagreement with the action in his despatches. Musurus in London argued along the same lines. Among the Ottoman ministers there was apparently no division in their dismay over this new disaster.[23]

When Layard presented the British request for a second firman, he was met with a clear refusal. The Porte had just signed an armistice agreement with Russia; the government intended to abide by it. Server now argued that the situation had changed from the previous month; he did not see "by what right or with what object" the British fleet was coming to Constantinople. Ahmed Vefik also wrote to Layard expressing his strong disapproval:

> On my return to the council I saw the demand of M. Sandison. The Russian army is at our gates, and in addition our decision to keep our engagements is unchangeable. Is it then necessary that this immense capital and a million innocents should perish in a conflict of foreign interests and because of the state of weakness to which our heroic defense has reduced us? We will protest to England leaving to her the responsiblity for this terrible catastrophe. . . .We cannot commit suicide, we seriously want peace.[24]

21. A member of the German consulate commented on the impression made by the arrival of the British squadron: "Die Entschlossenheit, mit der sich jetzt endlich der britische Löwe erhob, überraschte die Welt. . .Die Panzer, die sich in den nächsten Tagen (15 Februar) in Mudania, dem Hafen von Brussa, bald darauf aber zwischen die Inseln Prinkipo und Chalki vor Anker legten, machten durch ihre Grösse und ihre ungewöhnlichen Formen – der eine war ein mächtiges Turmschiff – einen gewaltigen Eindruck auf die einheimische Bevölkerung. Die Sicherheit und Schnelligkeit, mit der die Schiffe. . .im Marmara-Meer ihre Manöver ausführten, imponierte den Zuschauern." Ludwig Raschdau, *Ein sinkendes Reich* (Berlin, 1934), p. 142.

22. Derby to Loftus, F.O. 78/4271, no. 119, F.O., February 8, 1878; Layard to Derby, F.O. 78/4271, no. 212, Constantinople, February 10, 1878.

23. Of the Ottoman ministers Ahmed Vefik and Said Pasha cooperated with Layard. Server was considered unfriendly to British interests. He now felt that Britain had deserted her former ally and that the Porte should make the best possible bargain with Russia. He was removed from office on February 19.

24. Ahmed Vefik to Layard enclosed in Layard to Derby, F.O. 78/4271, no. 212, Constantinople, February 10, 1878.

The Porte was particularly bitter that the British government, even when taking the step of entering the Straits, still refused to undertake any obligations toward the Ottoman Empire, even if the Russian army entered Constantinople in reprisal. As Server told Layard: "As Turkey cannot hope for help from Europe, she would only be more than ever at the mercy of Russia." Layard remained sympathetic; he was opposed to the act and the justification. He informed the foreign office: "There is no reason to apprehend at present any danger to English subjects or property here."[25] He also believed that despite the denial of the firman, the Porte would allow the fleet to pass and would content itself with a protest based on the violation of treaties.[26]

Since the Ottoman government had not sent instructions yet to the forts at the entrance of the Dardanelles, Admiral Hornby had delayed carrying out his orders.[27] When the refusal of the Porte to grant the firman was received, the British government ordered the fleet to proceed. Derby informed Layard that the ships would enter the Straits; if they were fired upon, they would return fire only if they were hit. The intention was not to silence the forts unless this action were necessary to ensure the passage of the fleet to the Sea of Marmora. It would then anchor at Princes Island.[28]

The British decision to proceed, communicated to the Porte on February 12, caused deep concern and consternation. Ahmed Vefik told Sandison that he was surprised at the determination of Britain to enter the Straits with or without the consent of the Porte. He declared that he would stand by his engagement to Russia; he would order the forts to fire on the British ships. Server reacted similarly; it was the duty of his government to resist this breach of treaties. Sandison warned him of the danger of firing on the fleet; the act would not keep Russia out of Constantinople and the empire would be faced with two enemies instead of one.[29] The two ministers still had to consult with the sultan.

25. Layard to Derby, F.O. 78/4271, tel. no. 187, Constantinople, February 10, 1878.

26. Layard to Derby, F.O. 78/4271, no. 193 most confidential, Constantinople, February 10, 1878.

27. Derby to Layard, F.O. 78/4271, tel. no. 192, February 10, 1878.

28. Derby to Layard, F.O. 78/4271, tel. nos. 195 and 196, F.O., February 11, 1878.

29. Sandison to Layard, confidential, Pera, February 12, 1878 in Layard to

In order to make absolutely clear the attitude of the Porte, Layard next instructed Sandison to request a firman of passage from the sultan in a formal manner. On the evening of February 12 Server and Said Pasha, the minister of interior, spoke with Layard and conveyed the great apprehension of the sultan on the consequences of a British entrance into the Straits. The Ottoman leaders now desperately feared a Russian occupation of Constantinople, which would be attended by acts of violence by Christians against Moslems. At this time the minister did not repeat the previous warning that a British passage might be resisted by force; Layard instead was told that protests would be made, but that the forts would remain quiet.[30]

Throughout the day of January 13 the Porte continued to try to dissuade the British government; at the same time, the fleet entered and moved up the Dardanelles. At 3 A.M. Layard received a message from the sultan that he had cabled to Queen Victoria his protests against the British action. Until an answer was received, he wished the fleet stopped. Although Layard did not have the authority to halt the naval operation, he did send a message to Hornby concerning the communication to the queen and added the advice that the fleet remain "as far from land as possible."[31] It finally anchored off Princes Island.

During the same day Ahmed Vefik dispatched two letters of protest to Layard. In the first, dated February 12, the Turkish minister reflected the Ottoman bitterness at the British attitude.

> The government that pushed us to the wall, in persuading us that even the entry of Russian troops could not force it to accept our demand for intervention, intervenes today against our will, after we are committed to peace at any price. His Majesty insists on demanding that your government absolutely desist from its plan of entrance and demands absolutely that you stop the progress of the fleet until a solution [is reached].[32]

Derby, F.O. 78/4271, no. 228, Constantinople, February 14, 1878. This long despatch covers the events through February 14.

30. Layard to Derby, F.O. 78/4271, tel. no. 206, Constantinople, February 12, 1878.

31. Layard to Hornby, Constantinople, February 13, 1878 in Layard to Derby, F.O. 78/4271, no. 228, Constantinople, February 14, 1878.

32. Ahmed Vefik to Layard, Yildiz, February 12, 1878 in Layard to Derby, F.O. 78/4271, no. 228, Constantinople, February 14, 1878.

During the day Layard held a similarly excited conversation with Server, who brought the letter quoted above. By this time the sultan had received a telegram from Alexander II stating that if the British fleet entered the Bosphorus, he would be forced to place troops temporarily in Constantinople. Server argued most forcefully that even a temporary occupation would have an "incalculable" effect on the Moslem world and on the interest of Britain. He wondered what the Moslems of India would think when they found out that Russian troops had entered the capital of Islam in the presence of a British fleet which "was unable or unwilling to interfere to prevent this great humiliation inflicted upon all Mohammedans, one which they would never forget or forgive?" At present British lives and property were not in danger, but if the Russians entered the city, the situation would change. The Ottoman government "in its absolute penury" would not be able to supply twenty to thirty thousand Russian soldiers: "They would probably help themselves, pull down the Mussulman houses for firewood, and rob to obtain provisions." These actions would lead to conflicts with the Moslems, quarrels which would spread to the Christians and end in a massacre. Britain was now proving to be "Turkey's greatest enemy" and was provoking Russia to "take a step which might bring about the final ruin of the Turkish Empire."

During this conversation Said arrived with a new proposal from Abdülhamid. The sultan now suggested that if one of the reasons why the British wished to send warships to Constantinople was the fear that the Porte might surrender its fleet to Russia and thus block the Bosphorus and Dardanelles against Britain, he would send his ships wherever the British government suggested. If it had no confidence in the Turkish officers, he would place his fleet under a British admiral and accept British officers. He emphasized that should he have "reason to believe that the Russians were about to violate the armistice or place the empire in danger," he would ask for British intervention. Because of his fears for Constantinople, he did not wish to take such a step at this time.[33]

In the next days the Porte continued to argue without success for

33. Layard to Derby, F.O. 78/4271, no. 228, Constantinople, February 14, 1878; Layard to Derby, tel. no. 208 secret, Constantinople, February 13, 1878.

the removal of the fleet. On February 14 Ahmed Vefik wrote Layard again:

> His Majesty has charged his ambassador to press your government to withdraw the fleet from the Dardanelles and the Russian government promises to await the results of this negotiation. Would you therefore have the fleet stopped where it is at this time. We are under a terrible responsibility to the nation. Wherever the Russians go, they are followed by a host of Bulgars who massacre and dishonor the Moslems.
>
> Around fifteen telegrams from last night give a heart-breaking picture of the neighborhood of Prichtina and Drama. The entrance of the Russians into Constantinople would herald [the outbreak of] violence, but against the Moslems. The foreigners would remain spectators. The Russians would enter the houses without their officers stopping them; they would express regrets but entire quarters would be burned and pillaged.[34]

In London in his conversations with Derby, Musurus also protested strongly against the British violation of the treaties and he repeated the arguments previously given.[35] On February 14 he asked Derby on what basis the British fleet had entered the Straits: as "friends and allies" or as neutrals? The British foreign secretary did not want to give a definition at this critical point, but he indicated he preferred the designation neutral. Musurus also discussed the dangers of the consequences of a Russian occupation of Constantinople. He spoke of the possibility that the sultan might be forced to leave his capital and ask for asylum with the British fleet. Derby agreed that he could do this, but the British statesman would not comment on the expediency of such a move.[36]

At the same time, of course, the Porte had to deal with Russia. The

34. Ahmed Vefik to Layard, February 14, 1878 in Layard to Derby, F.O. 78/4271, no. 228, Constantinople, February 14, 1878.

35. Derby to Layard, F.O. 78/4271, no. 204, F.O., February 12, 1878.

36. Derby to Layard, F.O. 78/4271, no. 244 most confidential, F.O., February 16, 1878. The British cabinet at this time did agree that the sultan and his family should be given asylum aboard a British warship if necessary and that the four best Ottoman warships should be purchased. There was fear at this time that Russia might seize the Ottoman fleet. Abdülhamid had already approached Layard secretly in January on the question of asylum. Waterfield, *Layard,* p. 394. See also Sumner, *Russia and the Balkans,* p. 385 and Seton-Watson, *Disraeli, Gladstone and the Eastern Question,* pp. 321-322.

British action had indeed placed the Ottoman government in a most difficult position. The British ships had entered the Straits against the wishes of the sultan and thus in violation of Ottoman territorial rights. The extremely dangerous argument of the protection of British citizens resident in Constantinople had been used – a position which appeared openly to invite a similar Russian intervention. At the same time Britain refused to take any step which would aid the Porte. The presence of the British ships in the Sea of Marmora did not certainly menace the government in Constantinople, but the obvious Russian countermove, the occupation of the city, could threaten the entire future of the empire.

With the British fleet anchored off Princes Island, the initiative for the next move lay obviously in Russian hands. Alexander II, now adopting an attitude oddly reminiscent of that of Queen Victoria, wished immediate action – an occupation of Constantinople and also of the peninsula of Gallipoli. Influenced by the moderating council of Gorchakov and of the minister of war, D. A. Miliutin, he, however, issued instructions which were unclear and contradictory. As a result the actual decision on an occupation of Constantinople came to lie in the hands of Grand Duke Nicholas, the commander in the field, who, as will be seen, was not anxious to involve his troops in further potentially dangerous battles.[37]

Meanwhile Russian diplomacy prepared the stage for a possible entrance into the city. A series of messages were exchanged between the sultan and the tsar.[38] Abdülhamid naturally argued against a Russian action; Alexander II stated the Russian position. The most important negotiations were, of course, those between St. Petersburg and London. Here, as in his explanation with other courts, Gorchakov took full advantage of the British justification for the violation of the Straits. In fact, the Russian government went one step further; it now announced it would protect "Christians" and not just its own citizens.

37. On the confusion on the Russian side see in particular Sumner, *Russia and the Balkans.* For the Russian reaction to the British entrance into the Straits see also Goriainow, *Le Bosphore et les Dardanelles,* pp. 359-367; D. A. Miliutin, *Dnevnik* (Moscow, 1950), III, pp. 15-24; and S. S. Tatishchev, *Imperator Aleksandr II* (St. Petersburg, 1911), pp. 409-422.

38. Extracts from these can be found in *Ibid.,* pp. 414-418.

In a despatch to Shuvalov of the middle of February Gorchakov declared:

> We have in view the temporary entry of a part of our troops into Constantinople with exactly the same object, with the exception that our protection, if required, will be extended to all Christians. The two Governments would thus be fulfilling a common duty of humanity. It follows that this task, being of a pacific nature, could not assume in any way the character of mutual hostility.[39]

This statement not only provided a clever justification, but it was not provocative. It also had the advantage that it was based on the concept of "humanitarian intervention," which had been recognized as valid since the involvement of the powers in the Greek revolution of the 1820s.

Like Gorchakov, Shuvalov wished this crisis to have a peaceful solution.[40] He did not oppose a Russian occupation of Constantinople, but he did not want a war with England. In his negotiations he thus preserved a firm but accommodating attitude, and again, as in the past, the similar inclinations of Derby were of great assistance. When Shuvalov first heard of the British intentions, he declared that Russia was released from her previous undertakings concerning both the Straits and Gallipoli.[41] Interestingly enough, it was this later area which proved of chief British concern. In sending its ships into the Sea of Marmora, the British government had placed itself in a bad strategic position.[42] Previously, on January 15, the Russian government had

39. Gorchakov to Shuvalov, St. Petersburg, January 31/February 12, 1878. *Accounts and Papers,* LXXXI (1878), p. 721. Layard later criticized the British action which allowed a Russian countermove. "Our ships were sent up here to protect the lives and property of British subjects which required no protection. But we gave the Russians a pretext for entering the capital and causing the very danger apprehended." Layard to Lytton, February 20. Seton-Watson, *Disraeli, Gladstone and the Eastern Question,* p. 317. Gorchakov sent similar messages to other capitals. See Gorchakov circular telegram, January 31, in *Ozvobozhdenie Bolgarii ot Turetskogo Iga* (Moscow, 1964), II, p. 470.

40. Shuvalov's explanations of his actions and certain documents pertaining to this episode can be found in V. Khvostov, "P. A. Shuvalov o Berlinskom Kongresse 1878g," *Krasny Arkhiv,* LIX (1933), pp. 86-91.

41. Shuvalov to Gorchakov, London, January 27/February 8, 1878. *Ibid.,* p. 88.

42. Layard had previously recognized the danger of the action. He wrote to

given assurances that it would not occupy the peninsula if regular Turkish troops stayed away and if the British did not attempt a landing. Now, on February 13, Derby warned Shuvalov that Russia should not move into Gallipoli or take any action to "threaten the communications of the British fleet."[43] In a telegram of February 15 Gorchakov agreed that Russian troops would not take the peninsula as long as British forces were not placed on the European or Asiatic sides of the Straits.[44] By February 17 the British fleet had moved from Princes Island to the Gulf of Mudania.

The question of the Russian occupation of Constantinople was at least temporarily settled when the tsar on February 19 telegraphed the sultan that he would not enter the city. In this decision it appears that the doubts and hesitations of Grand Duke Nicholas played the decisive role. Acutely aware of the dangerous position of his army, he did not want to contribute to the outbreak of war with Britain or Austria-Hungary. Moreover, the Ottoman troops had been able to regroup; he feared that an entry into the city would not be easy to accomplish. Although the attempt to enter the city was now relinquished, the Russians were able to improve their military position immensely. With Turkish acquiescence the Russian lines were extended beyond those in the armistice agreement and the Russian headquarters was moved to San Stefano, situated on the Sea of Marmora, very near Constantinople.

This entire episode caused great alarm in Constantinople. Since the empire was at war, the sultan in theory had full control of the Straits. The British move had been made to block Russia, but not necessarily to aid the Ottoman government. No offers of assistance or assurances of support in the peace negotiations were given. Obviously, with the Russian army at the gates of the capital, the Porte would not fire on the British squadron. A bad precedent had also been created; the incident was to be recalled in the future. Moreover, until the final peace terms

---

Admiral Hornby: "Under present circumstances how can we bring the fleet up to Constantinople, with the chance of being cut off by the Russians? We should be putting ourselves still more at their mercy." Layard to Hornby, February 6. Seton-Watson, *Disraeli, Gladstone,* p. 317.

43. Derby to Loftus, F.O., February 13, 1878. *Accounts and Papers,* LXXXI (1878), p. 722.

44. Gorchakov to Shuvalov, St. Petersburg, February 3/15, 1878. Khvostov, "P. A. Shuvalov," p. 91.

had been settled, the danger of further Russian action remained. On February 27, in a conversation with Safvet Pasha, who had replaced Server as foreign minister, Ignatiev noted that the Porte had "accepted pacifically this flagrant violation of its rights," and argued:

> Great Britain, contrary to the express stipulations of the treaties of 1840, 1856, and 1871, instigated by the London Cabinet itself, which introduced into European public law the traditional principle of the closure of the Straits to foreign fleets, today violates this principle by sending her fleet through the Dardanelles, under the pretext that it was necessary to "approach Constantinople pacifically without any hostile intent in regard to the Porte or any other power whatsoever." This decision was taken and executed without any account taken either of the repeated protestations of the Ottoman government or of the direct appeal of the sultan to the queen, and when the commandant of the fort of the Dardanelles indicated to the fleet that he would be obliged to fire on it, if it forced the strait, he was told that the first shot of the canon would be the equivalent of a declaration of war made by Turkey on England. . . .We have incontestably the right to use the arguments advanced by Great Britain and accepted by the Porte, in declaring that we also wish to approach Constantinople pacifically, without breaking the armistice and the negotiations in progress. . . .[45]

With the British fleet in the Straits area, where it remained until September, 1878, and the Russian army encamped near Constantinople, the Russian-Turkish negotiations for peace terms continued. British fears concerning Russian intentions towards both Constantinople and the Straits remained acute. On March 3 the Treaty of San Stefano was signed. Although the Straits question was omitted from this agreement, its other provisions upset the diplomatic balance in the Near East and violated previous treaties. In the next month the very real possibility existed that war might break out over the Russian conditions for peace. Under these circumstances the entire question of the presence of the British fleet in the Straits and the possible passage of British warships into the Black Sea became acute for both the Russian and Ottoman governments.

45. Ignatiev to Gorchakov, San Stefano, February 15/27, 1878. *Osvobozhdenie Bolgarii ot Turetskogo Iga,* II, p. 531.

Should Russia find itself at war with Britain, obviously the attitude taken by the Porte to the closure of the Straits would be crucial. With the conclusion of the treaty the Ottoman Empire was again technically at peace. The sultan's role as guardian of the Straits was introduced in particular by the Russian statesmen. In the period after the signature of the Treaty of San Stefano, Alexander II remained under the predominant influence of advisers from military and Panslav circles. He thus supported the preparation for strong measures such as the seizure of the shores of the Bosphorus and Constantinople in anticipation of war with Britain. Although his instructions to the increasingly reluctant Grand Duke Nicholas were in the direction of advising decisive action, the tsar never gave a definite order for the acquisition of these places. The grand duke thus concentrated on attempting to win Ottoman cooperation and to learn what that government would do should a conflict with Britain come. He also tried unsuccessfully to gain the right to use Büyükdere, situated on the Bosphorus, as a point of embarcation for Russian soldiers.

At the end of March, Abdülhamid and Grand Duke Nicholas held a series of conversations on these questions and on the possible conclusion of a treaty of alliance.[46] Under great pressure from both Britain and Russia, the sultan sought both to avoid direct answers and to win something for himself. On the question of his attitude if war broke out, he assured the grand duke that no matter what happened the Ottoman position would be that of "benevolent neutrality" toward Russia. Nicholas then inquired what the sultan meant by the word "neutrality" since:

46. The contents of these talks are reported in two resumés, marked very secret, of March 27 and March 30, 1878. *Osoboe pribavlenie k opisaniiu Russko-Turetskoi voiny 1877-78 gg. na Balkanskom poluostrovie* (St. Petersburg, 1900), II, pp. 99-103. Loftus, the British ambassador in St. Petersburg, after having heard rumors on the Russian intentions, had reported earlier his fears that Russia was trying to "obtain from the Porte a secret arrangement by which certain territory at the mouth of the Bosphorus will be ceded to Russia with a view to its acquisition as a permanent fortified position. . . ." This action would obviously strongly affect British interests which required that the Bosphorus remain open. "Should Russia obtain the entire command of those straits she becomes mistress of the Black Sea and consequently could prevent any effective naval aid on the part of England to Austria should that Power be obliged to have recourse to military operations against a Russian occupation of Bulgaria." Loftus to Derby, F.O. 78/4271, no. 244 secret, St. Petersburg, February 19, 1878.

> The neutrality of the Straits had already been violated once by the entry of the British fleet into the Sea of Marmora; it could happen a second time and – for a blow of a far more serious consequence – by the entrance of that same fleet into the Bosphorus and perhaps into the Black Sea. In allowing the latter act, the Porte would not only cease to be neutral, but even more it would commit, so to speak, an act of hostility against the shores of Russia, the access to which would thus be opened by the Turks themselves.

In the same conversation the grand duke asked directly: "should the occasion arise would Turkey open to the British the gates of the Black Sea, which she had the duty to keep closed?"

In answer Abdülhamid avoided a real reply. Instead he argued that the Russian government in exchange for a favorable Ottoman attitude should change the terms of San Stefano to restore the sultan's prestige and to "show thereby that you do not wish the total destruction of Turkey." Should this course be followed, then Ottoman policy could take a new direction and perhaps an offensive and defensive alliance could be concluded. Without concessions on the Russian side, the sultan would give no assurances on the Straits. "I repeat," Abdülhamid told Nicholas in one of several conversations, "we are too crushed to aspire to anything else than neutrality, but it depends on his Majesty the Emperor to give me a little prestige and to raise me in the eyes of my populations in softening the conditions of the peace. I would then be in a condition to render you some little services."

Meanwhile, the increasing dangers to Russia in the European diplomatic scene were becoming more apparent to Alexander II. In May, General E. I. Totleben, who had replaced Grand Duke Nicholas at the end of April, sent the tsar a frank and pessimistic report on the military situation. Thereafter the question of a Russian seizure of Constantinople or land bordering on the Straits was no longer considered. The attention of Europe had also by this time shifted from the tense situation at the Straits to the more pressing issue of the changes to be made in the San Stefano settlement.

Salisbury Reinterprets the Straits Settlement: the Congress of Berlin

With the total military defeat of the Ottoman armies on the Balkan front in December, the question of the terms of the future peace had become of immediate concern to all of the powers. In the negotiations it soon became clear that the Porte had as much, if not more, to fear from the neutral states, Britain and Austria-Hungary, as from the belligerent Russia. Not only had these powers no intention of supporting the interests of the Porte, but by 1878 it was clear to Constantinople that they too had wide designs on the empire. In fact, the eastern crisis of 1875-1878, which on the surface involved the question of the relations of the Ottoman Empire with the subject people and the Balkan governments, served to cover an equally significant action of Britain, Austria-Hungary, and Russia to carve out territories and spheres of influence from Ottoman dominated lands. Of the three powers concerned, less attention will henceforth be paid to Habsburg policy because of the secondary interest which that state had at this time in the Straits question, the problem with which this study primarily deals. What Austria-Hungary wanted had been made clear in previous agreements with Russia and in negotiations with the other powers – control of Bosnia-Hercegovina, a predominant position on the Danube, and a sphere of influence in the western Balkans, extending over Serbia and Montenegro. The attainment of these goals would, of course, all be at the expense of the Ottoman Empire.

The Russian program for the peace was developed during the war in conferences in the field between the tsar and his advisers. The division which developed among the Russian leaders concerned not only the gains which should be made, but also the extent to which the wishes of the other European powers could be ignored. Those who sought to achieve a maximum program also wanted to negotiate the peace terms unilaterally with the Porte, despite the fact that they would inevitably conflict with other European treaties. In the winter of 1877-78 a program for the peace was drawn up which would have ended Ottoman rule in Europe and which also would have given Russia a strong strategic position in Asia Minor from which she could have made further moves toward Mesopotamia and the Persian Gulf. Specifically the plan called for the Russian reacquisition of southern Bessarabia, which removed a further humiliation inflicted by the Treaty of Paris, and the annexation of Kars, Batum, and Ardahan on the Asiatic frontier.[47] In the Balkans Serbia, Rumania, and Montenegro were to be made independent. Most significant, a large Bulgaria, including all of Macedonia, was to be established, which, it was assumed, would remain in close political association with St. Petersburg. Russian dominance in this state would assure that its armies or those of its satellite would be only a short march from Constantinople and the Straits.

These controversial territorial provisions were incorporated in the Armistice Agreement of January 31, 1878 and the Treaty of San Stefano of March 3.[48] These terms, which gave Russia apparent predominance in the Balkans and a strong position in Asia, were in flagrant contradiction with other European treaties, notably the Treaty of Paris and the Reichstadt and Budapest agreements. Faced with the strong opposition of both Austria-Hungary and Britain, Russia felt compelled to submit this settlement to a congress of European powers. In 1878 she could not face the danger of the formation of another Crimean coalition. Again, as in 1870, the Russian government found it difficult to break international treaties unilaterally. It was now therefore forced to admit other powers into the sharing of the spoils of a war which it had won with difficulty and at high cost. The Habsburg price has already been mentioned. The British aims were in the process of formulation in the spring of 1878.

The British program as now developed was chiefly a countermove to the expansion of Russian influence in Asia. During the course of the war there had been much discussion and debate on policy between those who wished to continue the Crimean system of the defense of the Ottoman Empire and those whose sympathies lay more with the Christian subject nationalities. When the terms of the Armistice Agreement and the Treaty of San Stefano became known, there was a strong public reaction against Russia. It was this belligerent spirit, rather than Gladstonian sympathy for the Balkan Slavs, which was now to exercise the most influence over British leaders. The direction of this

47. See B. Jelavich, "Russia and the Reacquisition of Southern Bessarabia, 1875-1878," *Südost-Forschungen,* XXVIII, 1969, pp. 199-237, and "Great Britain and the Russian Acquisition of Batum, 1878-1886," *Slavonic and East European Review,* XLVIII, January, 1970, pp. 44-66.

48. The texts are given in Sumner, *Russia and the Balkans,* pp. 627-636.

sentiment was not, however, toward upholding Ottoman prestige and integrity, but rather toward reasserting the power and position of the British Empire. Throughout the preceding years the British government and public had been greatly disturbed by the steady advance of Russia through Asia toward India. A major Afghan crisis was soon to break out. In the Treaty of San Stefano, Russia had taken territories which placed her in a favorable position in regard to the Ottoman Asian provinces and had established a satellite Bulgaria, which gave St. Petersburg for all practical purposes predominance over the Balkan peninsula, including Constantinople and the Straits. With Russian control of the three great ports of Odessa, Varna, and Batum, the Black Sea would have become a Russian lake as much as was the Caspian.

Faced with this enormous extension of Russian influence, the British government, particularly after Salisbury became foreign secretary in March 1878, mounted a vigorous counter-offensive. It was decided that in the Balkan peninsula support would be given to the Habsburg claims on Bosnia-Hercegovina and the monarchy's desire for the partition of the large Bulgarian state. The line of the Balkan mountains was to mark the limit of the Russian satellite Bulgaria; the rest of the territory was to be returned to some sort of subject relationship with Constantinople. The national claims of the Greeks were also to be supported so that this state would form a balance against the Slavic Balkan nations. The real British gains were to be made not in Europe, but in the Ottoman Asian lands. Russia was to be compelled to yield some of her claims here. The rest of the empire was to be protected and defended through a defensive alliance with Britain and the adoption of yet another program of internal reform.

These aims were pursued through negotiations with both Russia and the Ottoman Empire. In an agreement signed in May 1878, negotiated between Salisbury and Shuvalov, Russia agreed to surrender her claim to Ardahan and the Alashkert valley, but not to Kars and Batum.[49] The settlement in the Balkans followed in general the lines desired by Austria-Hungary and Britain. Salisbury's policy toward the Ottoman Empire was more complicated. During 1877 there had been much discussion within the British government on the need to acquire a port

49. *Ibid.*, pp. 637-651.

either in the Black Sea or in the eastern Mediterranean which would provide Britain with a naval base closer to Suez and the Straits than Malta. In March 1878 the decision was made to choose the island of Cyprus.[50] Taking advantage of the desperate position of the empire, Britain now pressed on the Porte an agreement which was in many respects similar to Unkiar Skelessi. The terms stated that should Russia take Batum, Kars, or Ardahan, Britain would support the Porte in the defense of the rest of its possessions. In return the Ottoman Empire was to surrender Cyprus to Britain and to introduce reforms in her Asiatic provinces. Since the British government had already agreed to allow Russia Batum and Kars, the agreement was bound to take effect. This treaty, when taken together with the other plans for the economic exploitation of the empire, would assure Britain a predominant position in Constantinople. The British lines of imperial communication would be assured; Russian power in the Balkans and Central Asia would be balanced on a world scale by British domination in the empire.

The Treaty of San Stefano was considered and revised by the powers at the Congress of Berlin, which opened on June 13, 1878. Prior to this date Austria-Hungary and Britain had also made a separate understanding on the coming peace. With the great powers in agreement, the Porte could not hope to win from the conflicts of others over the spoils. The Ottoman position at the conference was in fact tragic. The Porte faced not only the claims of the subject peoples, but also the attempts of the great powers to gain control over its territories. In a condition of military collapse – with a Russian army and a British navy before Constantinople – it could only accept what was in fact a dictated peace.

At the Black Sea Conference in 1871 Musurus had played a major, dignified, and decisive role. He had negotiated from a position of strength and he had felt convinced that the Porte could not be forced to accede to measures which were against its own interest. A greater contrast to the part played by the Ottoman representatives at Berlin is difficult to imagine. Here the three Turkish delegates were destined to occupy a humiliating and subordinate place in the proceedings. Unfortunately, the Ottoman delegation was also basically weak. At the

50. For the negotiation of the Cyprus Convention see Dwight E. Lee, *Great Britain and the Cyprus Convention Policy of 1878* (Cambridge, Mass., 1934).

head was Caratheodory Pasha, a Phanariote Greek of apparent ability. However, the second delegate, Mehmed Ali, was a Prussian deserter and a Moslem convert, who was treated by Bismarck with exceptional rudeness and brutality. His colleague, Sadullah Pasha, the Ottoman ambassador in Berlin, was generally regarded as incompetent. To enhance their already difficult position, the representatives received entirely inadequate instructions.

In the sessions of the conference the Straits question was to occupy but little time. The actions taken, however, were to have an enormous influence on the course of international relations in subsequent years. Before the opening of the conference the issue had been discussed, of course, in detail within both British and Russian governing circles. Having naval superiority in the area, the British statesmen now considered pressing for the acceptance of the policy which they had favored in the past – the full opening of the Straits. British warships would then have free access to the ports of southern Russia and the strategic Caucasian shoreline. In a report to Disraeli (now Lord Beaconsfield), written on March 21, 1878, Salisbury listed among the desirable results of a future peace: "Effective securities for the free passage of the Straits at all times, as if they were open sea."[51] A cabinet report of March 27 on San Stefano stated a similar view:

> What would best suit the interests of Great Britain, in the altered state of circumstances, would be that the Straits should be free to ships of war, as well as of commerce, and that all forts and batteries should be removed.
>
> This would be unacceptable to the Porte; but it might possibly be made acceptable by an engagement to maintain the defense and guarantee the safety of Constantinople from the sea with an adequate naval squadron.[52]

The policy of opening the Straits, one way or another, and the conclusion of a defensive pact with the sultan was part of the general policy which found its expression eventually in the Cyprus Convention and in the British declarations on the Straits at the Congress of Berlin.

The Russian program for the Straits was, as could be expected, quite

51. H. W. V. Temperley and L. M. Penson, *Foundations of British Foreign Policy* (London, 1966), p. 366.

52. *Ibid.*, p. 369.

different. Having little naval power of consequence in the Black Sea and fearing a British attack on its shores, the Russian government wanted to assure that no unfriendly fleets passed the Straits. Throughout the war this question had remained of major concern to the Russian leaders. The military and Panslav circles, of whom Ignatiev remained a good representative, continued to desire the conclusion of a direct political agreement between Russia and the Ottoman Empire on these matters. They wished an arrangement made which would effectively close the Straits to the western powers, but open them to the passage of Russian warships. At the beginning of the war, when the Russians expected a quick and decisive victory, the plans for the Straits and Constantinople were ambitious. After the delivery of the British warnings, at least the more responsible members of the Russian foreign ministry, such as Shuvalov and Gorchakov, were well aware that Russia could not hope to solve this problem on a bilateral basis. Gorchakov too would have liked an arrangement by which Russia, or the "riverain" states, would alone have received the right of passage, but since he admitted that this could not be obtained, he preferred to maintain the existing agreements.[53]

Despite the opposition of the Foreign Ministry, the Armistice Agreement did contain a clause indicating that Russia would seek to regulate the passage of the Straits on a bilateral basis. The strong resistance to what appeared to foreshadow another Unkiar Skelessi by the powers resulted in the exclusion from the Treaty of San Stefano of any mention of the question. Article XXIV of that treaty dealt only with merchant ships and the question of a possible blockade.[54]

Because of the divergence of British and Russian views, the Anglo-Russian agreement concluded at the end of May had left the Straits question open:

> The English government reserves the right to discuss in the congress any question touching the Straits. But the ambassador of Russia at London makes note of the verbal communication which he made to the Principal Secretary of State, to let it be

53. Gorchakov to London, Berlin, and Vienna, February 8, 1878. *Osvobozhdenie Bolgarii ot Turetskogo Iga,* II, p. 413; Gorchakov to Ignatiev, January 20/February 1, 1878. *Ibid.,* pp. 439-40.

54. Sumner, *Russia and the Balkans,* p. 635.

> known that the Imperial Cabinet adheres to the declaration of Lord Derby of May 6, 1877, and notably: –
>
> "The existing arrangements made under European sanction, which regulate the navigation of the Bosphorus and the Dardanelles, appear to them (the British Government) wise and salutary, and there would be, in their judgment, serious objections to their alteration in any material particular."
>
> And the Russian Plenipotentiary at the Congress will insist on the *status quo.*[55]

Since a change in the Straits settlement was thus not part of the Treaty of San Stefano or of any other agreement preceding the peace, the subject need not have arisen as a major problem at the congress. However, the entire question had become closely associated in Salisbury's mind with that of the balance of naval power in the Black Sea and in particular with the Russian desire to acquire Batum.[56] Although the Russian Asiatic frontier appeared to have been settled in the May agreement, matters did not proceed smoothly in the congress. On June 14, a day after the conference opened, the British newspaper *Globe* published the terms of the Shuvalov-Salisbury agreement, which was, of course, secret. Because of the public outcry over what seemed to be a British surrender, particularly in the case of Batum, Salisbury and Beaconsfield felt compelled to try to gain better terms. After a sharp controversy the Russian government finally accepted a vague formulation which appeared to limit its rights on the port: "His Majesty the Emperor of Russia declares it is his intention to make Batum a free port, essentially commercial."[57] Although this wording represented a compromise, Salisbury was not satisfied with it. He apparently felt that something more must be done to satisfy British public opinion.

Salisbury had in fact already moved in this direction. On June 15 he had instructed Layard to try to gain the acceptance of the sultan to an agreement that if Russia gained control of Batum, the Porte would "not offer forcible opposition to the passage at any time of the English fleet

55. *Ibid.,* p. 649.

56. For the question of Batum and the Straits at the Congress of Berlin see Sumner, *Russia and the Balkans,* pp. 539-547, and W. N. Medlicott, *The Congress of Berlin and After* (London, 1963), pp. 101-122.

57. The text of the Treaty of Berlin is in Sumner, *Russia and the Balkans,* pp. 658-669.

through the Straits of the Dardanelles and the Bosphorus."[58] The intention of this proposal, it was argued, was to allow the Porte to obtain British assistance without the dangers which might arise by invoking the Treaty of 1871. Angered by the May convention, whose terms the sultan now also learned, and troubled by the British attitude in general, Abdülhamid refused to agree to this further extension of British influence. Although the British cabinet did not fully support Salisbury's stand at this time, it did approve on June 29 a statement which could be made if Russia took Batum.

Meanwhile, the Russian-British negotiations on the port continued; agreement was finally reached on the formula quoted above. On July 6 the questions of both Batum and the Straits were discussed in the congress.[59] At this time Salisbury declared that since Batum was to be a free port, Britain would accept the *status quo ante,* which Russia also wished, concerning the Straits. This decision was recorded in Article LXIII of the final treaty, which stated: "The Treaty of Paris of March 30, 1856 as well as the Treaty of London of March 13, 1871 are maintained in all such of their provisions as are not abrogated or modified by the preceding stipulations." On July 8 the terms of the Cyprus Convention became known. The negotiations on the exact boundaries of Batum were proceeding. On July 11, after the Batum question had been finally disposed of, Salisbury returned to the Straits issue. He now made a statement which was recorded in the protocols of the congress:

> Considering that the Treaty of Berlin will change an important part of the arrangements sanctioned by the Treaty of Paris of 1856, and that the interpretation of Article II of the Treaty of London, which is dependent on the Treaty of Paris, may thus become a matter of dispute, I declare on behalf of England that the obligations of Her Britannic Majesty relating to the closing of the Straits do not go further than an engagement with the Sultan to respect in this matter His Majesty's independent determinations in conformity with the spirit of existing treaties.[60]

58. Medlicott, *Congress of Berlin,* pp. 102-103.
59. Protocols of the Congress of Berlin in *British and Foreign State Papers* (London, 1885), LXIX, pp. 1027-1028.
60. *Ibid.,* p. 1070.

Deeply disturbed, Shuvalov at the next meeting gave the reply:

> The plenipotentiaries of Russia, without being able exactly to appreciate the meaning of the proposition of the second plenipotentiary of Great Britain respecting the closing of the Straits, restrict themselves to demanding, on their part, the insertion in the protocol of the observation: that in their opinion the principle of the closing of the Straits is a European principle, and that the stipulations concluded in this respect in 1841, 1856, and 1871, confirmed at present by the Treaty of Berlin, are binding on the part of all the Powers, in accordance with the spirit and letter of existing treaties, not only as regards the Sultan, but also as regards all the Powers signatory to these transactions.[61]

The matter was not discussed further in the congress, but the implications of the British pronouncement were to have a profound effect in St. Petersburg.

The question which Salisbury's statement now raised was what exactly had been decided in the London Conference of 1871. Since this issue was to be of major importance in future negotiations concerning the Straits, it would be well to examine this question in greater detail to determine the interpretation which could be given to past agreements on the Straits. In regard to the first, the Straits Convention of 1841, there was little controversy. In it the sultan had clearly surrendered his right to deliver firmans of passage to warships in time of peace. He had thus accepted restrictions on his sovereignty over the Straits. Moreover, this was a collective agreement and it was recognized as such. As one writer defined it, the treaty gave

> . . .rights and obligations to each contracting party as against every other contracting party. Each was empowered to protest, and was responsible for not protesting, against the contemplated passage of a foreign warship; each was entitled to reparation, in the event of a foreign warship's passage, from the parties infringing the rule, namely, the Porte, the Government to which the said warship belonged, and also any other State that aided or abetted the commission of the prohibited act or even acquiesced in its commission.[62]

61. *Ibid.*, pp. 1075-1076.

62. Coleman Phillipson, *The Question of the Bosphorus and Dardanelles* (London, 1917), pp. 153, 154.

This Straits settlement was reconfirmed in 1856. In the years after 1841 the sultan had allowed a small number of ships to pass the Straits, either in contravention of this rule or under dubious interpretations. Warships carrying heads of state were regularly granted firmans. In general, nevertheless, all of the powers had supported the observance of the closure. The alteration in the agreement in 1871, however, brought up certain difficulties in interpretation. At the London Conference, it will be remembered, the sultan was given the right to admit ships of war in time of peace to protect the stipulations of the Treaty of Paris. We have seen in the negotiations surrounding this agreement the emphasis which was placed on the idea that the sultan would resume his sovereign rights in the Straits to compensate for the action of the tsar, who now acted in the same manner in regard to his lands. This question was not directly met either in the protocols or in the text of the treaty. The final article had been a compromise; there had been little discussion of its actual meaning. Granville had not liked the wording.

Although Salisbury's statements at the Congress of Berlin were also not clear and in fact were in apparent contradiction on some points, they certainly involved two points of interpretation: first, that the Straits agreement, being between the sultan and the individual signatories separately, was not collective in nature; and, second, that the sultan had to be acting "independently" when he made a decision concerning the closure. In May 1885, during the Penjdeh crisis, Salisbury explained his statement in the House of Lords:

> The object of the declaration which I had to make on behalf of Her Majesty's Government I understood to be to establish the principle that our engagements in respect to the Dardanelles were not engagements of a general European or International character, but were engagements toward the Sultan only; the practical bearing of that reservation being that if, in any circumstances, the Sultan should not be acting independently, but under pressure from some other Power, there would be no International obligation on our part to abstain from passing through the Dardanelles.[63]

The practical application of these statements was, of course, the opening of the Straits for the British fleet. Should on any occasion the

63. Hansard, *Parliamentary Debates,* 3rd series, vol. 297, p. 1826.

sultan refuse firmans of passage, the British government could simply declare that he was not acting independently. Since the treaty was not collective in character, the approval of the other powers would not be necessary. This interpretation was completely to the British advantage given the conditions of the time. Although after 1871 the Russian government could fortify its southern coast and build a Black Sea fleet, little had been accomplished in this direction. In a time of crisis Russia could neither send ships through the Straits to threaten the British nor prevent a British entrance into the Black Sea. Britain, with a strong Mediterranean fleet and bases in Malta and Cyprus, could in contrast operate in the Black Sea and menace the Russian installations there.

The Russian government, of course, under the circumstances of the time, was bound to assume an opposing stand. During the war and the discussions on the peace terms, the Russian leaders had come to the conclusion that Russia could not attempt to gain physical control of the Straits area without running the serious risk of provoking a general war. Since it was clear that it was impossible to obtain European recognition of any Russian special privileges in the area, the Russian statesmen wished to return to the basis of the treaties. They now wanted to enjoy the benefits of a European guarantee that Britain could not sail through the Straits and attack Russia.[64]

Because of the importance of this question, it is interesting to examine the interpretation given by Musurus of the 1871 agreement. In May 1885 he reported to his government Salisbury's statement, quoted above.[65] On May 12 Asim Pasha, the Ottoman foreign minister,

64. The best statement of the Russian position is to be found in Goriainow, *Le Bosphore et les Dardanelles.* In commenting on the Treaty of London, Goriainow wrote: "En adhérant à la version italienne, la Turquie renonça à la libre disposition des clefs des détroits et se soumit à l'engagement collectif de toutes les puissances contractantes de considérer les détroits fermés, à l'exception des cas spécialement déterminés par le traité. La Russie ayant aussi adhéré, de même que les autres puissances, à la version italienne, contracta avec elles un engagement solidaire et collectif de respecter le principe de la clôture des détroits; en cas d'infraction, chacune des puissances contractantes répondait pour les autres, et toutes répondaient pour chacune d'elles. Il se trouve de la sorte établie, par tout ce qui précède, que l'engagement, contenu dans l'article 2 du traité de Londres de 1871 et la convention du 30 mars 1856 restée en vigueur, doit être considéré comme un engagement collectif et indivis. (*Ibid.*, pp. 297-298).

65. Musurus to Asim, R9/87, no. 195, London, May 8, 1885.

acknowledged his telegram, but requested Musurus to give his view of the issue.[66] On May 14 he replied:

> By the Convention of London of 1841 and the separate Convention of Paris of 1856 the powers are engaged to respect as long as the Porte is at peace the determination of His Imperial Majesty the Sultan not to admit any foreign warship into the Straits of the Dardanelles and the Bosphorus. But at the time of the abolition of the neutrality of the Black Sea the articles 11, 13, and 14 relative to that neutrality have been abrogated and replaced by Article II of the Treaty of London of 1871, which while maintaining the principle established by the separate convention of 1856 stipulates the right of H.I.M. the sultan to open the said Straits in time of peace to ships of war of friendly and allied powers in the case where the S. Porte judged it necessary to safeguard the execution of the stipulations of the treaty of [18]56, that is to say the independence and territorial integrity of the Ottoman Empire. Thus Article II of the treaty of [18]71 constitutes the status quo which was maintained by the Congress of Berlin and by article 63 of the treaty of [18]78 and which is today in force. It follows that under this status quo the S. Porte while maintaining the principle established by the separate convention of 1841 has the right to open the Straits of the Dardanelles and the Bosphorus when she judges that her independence and the integrity of the empire as it is determined by the existing treaties is menaced by Russia or by some other power. The exercise of the faculty stipulated in Article II of the treaty of 1871 could not be subordinated to the consent of the other powers because it depends only on the judgment of the S. Porte. In this regard the declaration of Lord Salisbury contained in protocol no. 18 of the Congress of Berlin conforms to the stipulations of the said article while the declaration of the Russian plenipotentiairies contained in protocol no. 19 of the same congress implies the consent of all of the signatory powers. However, Lord Salisbury put himself in contradiction when at the meeting of the 7th of this month of the House of Lords, he said that if the case occurs when H.I.M. the sultan does not act in an independent manner, but under the pressure of another power, there would be no obligation on the part of Britain to abstain from passage of the Dardanelles, for, under such an arbitrary pretext, Britain would violate her engagement to respect the independent judgment of the Porte.[67]

66. Asim to Musurus, R9/87, no. 78797/110, Porte, May 12, 1885.
67. Musurus to Asim, R9/87, no. 203, London, May 14, 1885.

This question of interpretation was to remain a major problem in the next years for the European diplomats.[68]

Although no attempt will be made here to discuss the Berlin settlement in general, it might be interesting to review briefly the arrangements made for the Danube River, since at this time the Habsburg Empire was able to gain concessions which were denied her by the Porte in 1871.[69] During the Russo-Turkish War, despite the regulations concerning the neutrality of the works and personnel, the delta had been the scene of military action; mines had been laid and ships sunk. During the negotiations for the peace, it became apparent that the political balance on the river would be drastically altered. With the reacquisition of the three provinces of southern Bessarabia, Russia again became a riverain power and held control of the Kilia channel in the delta. Since it was assumed that the new Bulgarian state would be under Russian influence, the Russian position on the river was further strengthened. Rumania, now an independent state, acquired the delta and Dobrudja; Serbia also became independent. At the congress it was again the Habsburg Empire which insisted upon a consideration of Danubian problems. Russia opposed a discussion; Bismarck did not wish the conference delayed, but he agreed to at least the examination of some of the Austrian proposals.

The chief Habsburg desire was, of course, to block Russian influence. Before the opening of the conference the monarchy had obtained from the Porte the cession of the important island of Ada Kale near the Iron Gates. Attempts were made to improve relations with Rumania, who was now in conflict with Russia over the question of southern Bessarabia. On July 2 Heinrich von Haymerle, who with Andrassy represented Vienna, introduced four proposals: the river was

68. See for example, in addition to Goriainow, Phillipson, *Bosphorus and Dardanelles,* pp. 150-162; Heinrich Mertz, *Die Schwarze Meer-Konferenz von 1871* (Tübingen dissertation), pp. 61-66, and Grigore Dendrino, *Bosporus und Dardanellen* (Berlin dissertation, 1914), pp. 209-229. Goriainow commented on Salisbury's interpretation: "L'histoire nous apprend que la Grande-Bretagne est une des puissances, qui ne tient à observer les traités, qu'elle a signés, qu'autant qu'ils s'accordent avec ses intérêts du moment." Goriainow, *Le Bosphore et les Dardanelles,* p. 298.

69. For the Danube question at the congress see Sumner, *Russia and the Balkans,* pp. 538-539, Medlicott, *Congress of Berlin,* pp. 91-93, and the books on the Danube cited in the "Bibliographic Note."

to be neutralized below the Iron Gates and fortifications were to be forbidden along the river; the European Commission was to be made permanent and given authority to Galatz; Rumania was to become a member of this body; and the Habsburg Empire was to undertake the works at the Iron Gates. Because of German and Russian objections to the wide scope of these suggestions, the Habsburg government to a degree shortened and simplified their demands. In the final treaty, articles LII through LVII dealt with the Danube. In these the river was indeed neutralized below the Iron Gates, Rumania joined the European Commission, whose jurisdiction was extended as desired, and the Habsburg Empire was named as the power to undertake the works at the Iron Gates, with the authority to collect a toll under the conditions which had been discussed in 1871. In 1883 at another conference the European Commission was made for all practical purposes permanent. The settlement was thus a Habsburg victory throughout.

The Congress of Berlin was a disaster for the Ottoman Empire, although its terms were not as severe as those of the Treaty of San Stefano. In 1871 the Porte had been able at least to discuss with the other powers the question of obtaining compensation by gaining more rights in relation to its vassal principalities. In 1878 not only was there no chance that the Porte might increase its authority in the peninsula, but the danger existed that most of its European territories would be taken away. Although Habsburg and British opposition did prevent the creation of a large Bulgaria, the Ottoman Empire lost control over the most valuable and prosperous parts of its Balkan possessions. Rumania, Serbia, and Montenegro were declared independent; each gained an accession of territory from Ottoman lands. An autonomous Bulgaria was established, which was assumed to be under Russian control. A second Bulgarian state, Eastern Rumelia, under close great power supervision, was formed also from Ottoman territory. In subsequent settlements Greece received Thessaly and part of Epirus. Russia had retaken southern Bessarabia; Austria-Hungary was in control of Bosnia-Hercegovina. The Ottoman Empire in Europe was now reduced to Albania, Macedonia, and a part of Thrace, with the city of Constantinople.

The decade of the 1870s thus ended for the Ottoman Empire quite differently than it had commenced. In 1871 the Porte had played an important and dignified role in a major conference; the state was in the process of internal reform. By 1878 the empire had been defeated in a major war and had suffered great territorial losses in the subsequent peace. In 1871 the direction of Ottoman affairs lay in the able hands of Âli; after 1876 the chief role in international affairs was taken by Abdülhamid, who was to become increasingly autocratic in internal affairs and to prove often quite inept in foreign relations. Not only had the Porte at this time been deprived of lands, but the entire empire was in grave danger of falling under the influence of one power or of suffering the fate of partition among several states. It is most significant that from this time on, Britain, who had previously not shared with Russia, Austria, and France in the large scale partition of Turkish lands, was to join those with direct designs on important areas of Ottoman possessions.

The Russo-Turkish War and the Treaty of Berlin in fact inaugurated what was to become a period of swift decline of Ottoman power in both Europe and Asia. The war and the congress had demonstrated clearly the defenselessness of the empire against the aggressive stand of the Balkan nationalities and the great powers. Throughout this period the Porte was without effective allies. Although the powers, in particular Britain and Russia, displayed much public concern about the fate of the Ottoman subject peoples and about Turkish maladministration, at the conference they had shown no hesitancy about making concrete gains for the power and supremacy of their own lands. The Habsburg Monarchy acquired Bosnia-Hercegovina; Britain took Cyprus and was soon to have Egypt. France in 1880-81 annexed Tunis. Italy, although it gained nothing at Berlin, now sought to expand in Tripoli, near the Red Sea, and to share in influence over Albania. Even the Balkans, in a peace which ostensibly benefitted the national minorities, was in fact divided into spheres of Russian and Austrian influence.

The Porte had also seen in this crisis the uselessness of the treaties which had been designed to protect its integrity. The Crimean alliance was obviously dead. The British government, as we have seen, had compelled the Porte to accept a British squadron in the Straits in the war, and at the peace conference had apparently declared itself free from the obligations of the Straits agreements. The entire relationship of the Ottoman Empire with its former protector became even worse when in 1880 the Liberal party under Gladstone returned to power. Although the new prime minister dropped the Cyprus Convention, which had involved British obligations to defend Turkish Asiatic possessions, he did not return the island. Moreover, in the fall of 1880, in connection with the crisis in Montenegro over Dulcigno, the Liberal government considered not only the forcing of the Straits, but also the landing of a military expedition.[70]

In the decade of the 1880s the Ottoman position became even weaker. Although the rivalry of the powers continued to offer a measure of protection, these states were still intent on making power gains at Ottoman expense. Most dangerous were the consequences for the Porte of the British-Russian rivalry in Central Asia and Persia and the British-French tension in the Mediterranean. When the Austrian-Russian conflict in the Balkans is considered, it can be seen that the empire was caught in the middle of a world-wide struggle for land and prestige among the great powers. Since Germany was the only state with no direct claims on Ottoman territory, it can be understood why the Porte in the next years turned more toward Berlin.

In this great imperial struggle the Straits retained its position of the prime strategic position on the map. The Black Sea remained the only area where Britain could use its supreme naval power against Russia. Access to that body of water was deemed essential for imperial interests. As we have seen, the British government had already opened the Straits in the 1870s by deed and by declaration. The Russian government was thus thrown on the defensive. Without an adequate Black Sea fleet or coastal defenses, Russia was now compelled to act to try to maintain the closure of the Straits, which was still the legal

70. The reports of the British military attaché, Capt. Leopold Swaine, are annexed to three despatches of Goschen to Granville from Therapia: they are F.O. 78/4271, no. 386 very confidential, September 24, 1880; no. 407 confidential of September 28; and no. 433 confidential of October 8. Of greater interest is the long report of C. W. Wilson, no. 1 military, secret, Therapia, October 12 enclosed in Goschen to Granville, F.O. 78/4271, no. 462 very confidential, Therapia, October 12, 1880. This is a complete description of the defenses of the Dardanelles area. Wilson suggests in a cover letter that: "In any attempt to seize the Dardanelles the greatest secrecy should be maintained until the moment comes for action, so as to allow the Turkish Government as little time as possible to assemble troops for the defense."

condition despite the British challenge, by diplomatic means. The Ottoman government was thus in the most uncomfortable position of finding the status of its own territorial waters again a pawn in international politics.

Russian Counter-Action: The Three Emperors' Alliance and the Russian Volunteer Fleet The Salisbury declaration had an effect in St. Petersburg entirely disproportionate to its real intention. From the evidence available it appears that the statement was hastily conceived and executed by a statesman who felt that some action had to be taken in the interest of the Conservative party in face of an electorate angered by what seemed to be a British surrender on some points. Moreover, the declaration had no direct practical application. In the question of the Volunteer Fleet, which will be discussed in this section, the Liberal government specifically emphasized the multilateral nature of the Straits engagements. On the question of the sultan acting independently, this issue was already clear. Quite obviously, if a Russian army was encamped in Constantinople, the Straits agreements were not in force; the sultan had to be in a position to exercise his own free judgment to fulfill the conditions of the treaty of 1871.

Nevertheless, the declaration played a great part in the formulation of Russian foreign policy after the Congress of Berlin and was the occasion of many discussions concerning the Russian aims and intentions in regard to both the Straits and the city of Constantinople.[71] Undoubtedly throughout the nineteenth century most Russian statesmen wanted the Straits to be under Russian control – directly or indirectly. This policy was certainly strongly supported by Alexander III, who came to the throne in 1881. In a letter dated September 1885 he made one of the strongest declarations in this regard ever recorded: "In my opinion we should have a single and unique aim: it is the occupation of Constantinople in order to establish ourselves once and for all in the Straits and to know that it will always

71. The Russian apprehension over British intentions is reflected in all of the standard accounts of Russian diplomacy after the Congress of Berlin. See in particular, S. Skazkin, *Konets Avstro-Russko-Germanskogo Soiuza* (Moscow, 1928), pp. 103-132; Boris Nolde, *L'Alliance franco-russe* (Paris, 1936), pp. 237-248 and J. Y. Simpson, *The Saburov Memoirs* (New York, 1929).

be in our hands."[72] The problem for the tsar and his ministers, however, remained what it had been in the past – how to accomplish this aim without provoking a major war. At this time, as before, Russia was not in a condition to take this risk. In the 1880s the Russian diplomats concentrated not on the wider goal of securing domination, but on the smaller defensive objective of gaining diplomatic support for the protection of the status quo and the treaties. They attempted to accomplish this by two methods – first, by the renewal of the alliance with Germany and Austria-Hungary and, second, by pressing when possible the idea of a special agreement with the Porte. It should be noted again that the program of Unkiar Skelessi remained a constant Russian objective in its dealings with Constantinople.

Russian dissatisfaction with the results of the Congress of Berlin had resulted in the temporary disarray of the alignment of Russia, Germany, and Austria-Hungary. In June 1881 this diplomatic combination was reestablished, this time based on a formal document. Two of its terms were detrimental to Ottoman interests: Austria-Hungary was to be allowed to annex Bosnia-Hercegovina, and Russia secured the assent of her partners to the eventual union of Bulgaria and Eastern Rumelia. For Russia the essential clause concerned the Straits. Article III obligated the Russian allies to support her interpretation of the Straits agreements:

> The three courts recognize the European and mutually obligatory character of the principle of the closure of the Straits of the Bosphorus and the Dardanelles, based on International Law, confirmed by the Treaties, and summarized by the declaration of the second plenipotentiary of Russia at the meeting of July 12 of the Congress of Berlin (protocol 19).
>
> They will together assure that Turkey does not make any exception to that rule in favor of the interests of any government whatsoever, in handing over to the warlike operations of a belligerent power the part of its empire which forms the Straits.
>
> In case of infraction, or to warn her in case such an infraction is foreseen, the three courts will warn Turkey that they consider her, in this case, as putting herself in a state of war in regard to

72. See V. Khvostov, "Zapiska A. I. Nelidova v 1882g. o zaniatii prolivov," *Krasny Arkhiv,* XLVI (1931), pp. 180-181. A strong policy was also favored by Nelidov, who was ambassador in Constantinople from 1882 to 1897. See Appendix VI.

> the party injured, and as being deprived therefore of the benefits of security assured by the Treaty of Berlin to her territorial status quo.[73]

The terms of this treaty were secret. The alignment assured that the German, Russian, and Habsburg governments would work together at Constantinople. In alliance they exerted the strongest influence at the Ottoman capital. Britain, in conflict with France over imperial issues, was again diplomatically isolated.

With the unity of the three great continental powers, often supported by France, the Porte was constrained to listen with care to any advice that came from this direction. Relations with Britain were also bound to cool with the advent to power of a Liberal government. In the first years of the 1880s no major issues arose in international relations which brought this division of influence in Constantinople into play. The single important question which involved the Straits concerned the rights of passage of ships of the Russian Volunteer Fleet.

Although in theory the Straits had been closed by international agreement to ships of war in time of peace since 1841, various vessels of this category had in fact passed the Straits with the sultan's permission since that date. Some of these had caused minor diplomatic incidents. The issue of the Volunteer Fleet, however, involved a whole category of ships and brought into question the definition of a "warship" under the Straits agreements. The ships belonging to the Volunteer Fleet had been assembled in 1877-78 under the direction of a patriotic society when it appeared that war with Britain was a possibility. In the succeeding years the Russian government wished to use these ships for the transport of convicts and recruits to the Far East. They carried the merchant flag, but the crews were under navy discipline and commissioned officers were in charge. With the opening of the Suez Canal, and before the construction of the Trans-Siberian railroad, the sea route from Odessa to the Amur Region and Sakhalin was far quicker and more convenient than the overland way. Although the Russian government at this time strongly supported the regime of the closure of the Straits, it wished the Porte to grant passage to these ships under the heading of merchant vessels, which under the prevailing regulations were under virtually no restrictions.

73. Simpson, *The Saburov Memoirs,* p. 297.

The issue was difficult to decide. Certainly the Russian government had arguments in its favor. No attempt had been made to define what a merchant ship was. But the dangers were obvious. If Russia could send ships full of soldiers through the Straits, they could also stop in these waters and land at Constantinople. In addition, vessels ostensibly destined for the Far East could in fact be disembarked at a European port. The question of whether transports in fact constituted ships of war had now to be decided.[74]

The issue became acute in March 1882, when two ships of the Volunteer Fleet passed into the Straits. The first, the Moskva, with seven hundred soldiers destined for Vladivostok, anchored in the Bosphorus; no previous communication had been made. When the Porte protested, the Russian embassy replied that the soldiers were unarmed and therefore were passengers; the ship was a commercial vessel.[75] Another ship, the *Nizhni Novgorod*, followed close behind. It had been chartered by the Russian government and carried prisoners, accompanied by a guard of one hundred soldiers. It flew the official ensign and was thus under a "flag of war." The sultan also granted this ship a firman, but with great hesitation. In this case the Russian embassy argued that the vessel was not a warship, no matter what flag it carried.[76]

In the next years, because of these controversies, the Russian government tried to make an agreement with the Porte which would allow this category of ships to pass in an almost automatic manner. The British government, as could be expected, opposed the granting of any such permanent authorization. It agreed that such vessels might indeed sail through the Straits, but insisted that they should each time be required to obtain special permission through formal application by the Russian embassy. The Porte would thus maintain control over the procedure. In 1884 the Russian attempts to gain a special arrangement failed. Thereafter ships from the Volunteer Fleet did continue to pass through the Straits, but with individual authorization and under the

74. For a historical review of the question see a memorandum by Hertslet, F.O., February 7, 1881. F.O. 78/4271.

75. Dufferin to Granville, F.O. 78/4272, no. 183, Constantinople, March 11, 1882.

76. Dufferin to Granville, F.O. 78/4272, no. 276, Constantinople, April 11, 1882.

strict scrutiny of both the Porte and the British government.[77] The entire question of the Volunteer Fleet did not become really acute until the Russo-Japanese War.

The British government was obviously not happy about the negotiations. On December 11, 1884, Granville, again the British foreign secretary, instructed the chargé in Constantinople, Wyndham, to speak with the Turkish foreign minister, Asim Pasha, and warn him that the British government considered "that no arrangement bearing upon the Treaties of 1841, 1856, 1871, and 1878 which refer to the navigation of the Straits, should be concluded with one Power, without a previous communication being made to all the Powers which were parties to these Treaties."[78]

The Penjdeh Incident Although the status of the Straits remained a constant issue in the 1880s, perhaps the most interesting episode involving this area arose in 1885 when an acute crisis developed between Britain and Russia over the question of the fate of the Afghan village of Penjdeh.[79] At this time both the ability of the Three Emperors' Alliance to keep the Straits closed and the significance of the Salisbury declaration came into question. The incident also well illustrated the immense strategic and military significance of the Straits and the difficult position of the Porte, caught between the rival

77. Dufferin to Granville, F.O. 78/4272, no. 259 A confidential, Therapia, August 4, 1884; Granville to Dufferin, *ibid.*, no. 277, F.O., September 16, 1884; Wyndham to Granville, *ibid.*, no. 343, Therapia, October 8, 1884; Wyndham to Granville, *ibid.*, no. 393, Constantinople, November 14, 1884; Wyndham to Granville, *ibid.*, no. 424 confidential, Constantinople, November 26, 1884; Wyndham to Granville, *ibid.*, no. 504, Constantinople, December 31, 1884.

78. Granville to Wyndham, F.O. 78/4272, no. 369, F.O., December 11, 1884. Also Wyndham to Granville, *ibid.*, no. 398 confidential, Constantinople, November 15, 1884. Even more interesting is Salisbury's reaction during the 1891 episode concerning the Volunteer Fleet when the Russian and Turkish governments were again in negotiation concerning the regulations to govern these ships. In contradiction to his previous stand, Salisbury instructed White: "In the opinion of Her Majesty's Government, it is of the essence that the rule thus sanctioned by the European Powers that it is applicable to all countries alike; and that any right in respect to the passage of the Straits which is a departure from the provisions of the existing Treaties will, if granted by the Sultan to one Power, be as a matter of course, and *ipso facto*, equally granted to all." Salisbury to White, F.O. 421/133, no. 214, F.O., October 2, 1891.

79. See the "Bibliographic Note" for books on the Penjdeh crisis.

pressures of the imperial powers. The great effect of the British occupation of Egypt on the entire Near East was also shown. It was, in fact, this latter event which was to determine Turkish-British relations for the rest of the decade.[80]

Although the Egyptian rulers were vassals of the sultan, they had won virtually an independent position. Because of the financial incompetence of the Khedive Ismail, the country fell in 1876 under the joint control of Britain and France. In 1879, under pressure from his own people, Ismail attempted to throw off foreign rule. As a result he was forced out of office in that same year by French and British pressure. This blatant foreign intervention gave further strength to the national movement led by Arabi Pasha. The new khedive, Tevfik, was also dominated by anti-foreign forces. Meanwhile, the Liberal government in Britain had come to power. Although Gladstone had undoubtedly no desire to intervene unilaterally in Egypt, the British government through a series of events was drawn into a military occupation, an action which was carried on without the participation of France. Alexandria was shelled and an expedition landed. In September 1882 General Wolseley defeated Arabi Pasha at Tel-el-Kebir.

This victory left Britain with a *de facto* protectorate after 1883. To the problems of the administration of this country were soon added those of the Sudan.[81] Here a religious leader, the Mahdi, defeated Egyptian and Sudanese forces under the command of General Hicks in 1883. In January 1884 the British government sent General Charles Gordon to report on the situation. His position soon became so dangerous that a relief force was dispatched to his rescue in the summer. Since the Sudan was not regarded as part of Egypt, the Liberal government, in its eagerness to rid itself of the problem, was perfectly willing to let another power take the responsibility. Italy in particular was considered. The encouragement of the Italian occupation of Massawa in February 1885 was part of a policy aimed at gaining Italian support for the British interests. After the massacre of Gordon at Khartoum in January 1885 it was more difficult for the British to

80. See John Marlowe, *A History of Modern Egypt* (Hamden, Conn., 1965), pp. 112-164.

81. On the Sudan see L. A. Fabunmi, *The Sudan in Anglo-Egyptian Relations* (London, 1960), especially pp. 33-46.

disengage from the Sudan. As the occupying power in Egypt, the British government not only had the Sudanese problem on its hands, but also that of the Egyptian debt, which involved other powers. Negotiations on this were held in 1883 and 1884, with the Ottoman government participating in a secondary role. By March 1885 the European powers, but not the Porte, had found a basis of agreement.

In 1885, in addition to the very real dangers to its interests involved in British activities in Egypt and the Sudan and those of Italy in the Red Sea area, the Ottoman government was disturbed by the events in Central Asia. Although the Russian advance did not involve Ottoman territories, it was clear to all powers that if Britain and Russia went to war over their conflicting interests in Asia, the Black Sea would be a major, if not the most important, field of battle. In the question of Egypt, Ottoman interests obviously required that Britain leave the country; in Central Asia the Porte had more desire to see Britain maintain a firm position. A clear Russian victory there would affect the Ottoman neighbor Persia and would also increase Russian pressure on the Turkish eastern borders. The position of the Porte, was, however, to be finally influenced by the superior strength of the Three Emperors' Alliance, supported by France, and by the uncompromising British stand on the Egyptian question.

In 1884, with the acquisition of the city of Merv, the Russian boundaries closely approximated the territories of the amir of Afghanistan, a state which was under British protection. The Russian advance greatly alarmed many in Britain who feared that the Russian government aimed at the acquisition of Herat and thereafter India. Although at this time both governments agreed upon the establishment of an arbitration commission to settle the boundary, it did not meet because of a disagreement over its duties. On March 16, 1885 the Russian foreign minister, N. K. Giers, gave the British government assurances that Russian troops would not move forward. Nevertheless, on March 30 a Russian force defeated an Afghan detachment at Penjdeh. Since the accounts of the British commissioner on the spot, Colonel Lumsden, and the Russian general responsible for the skirmish differed on the question of who had initiated the fighting, both the British and Russian governments felt that justice was on their side. Gladstone, in another emotional speech, denounced the action as a

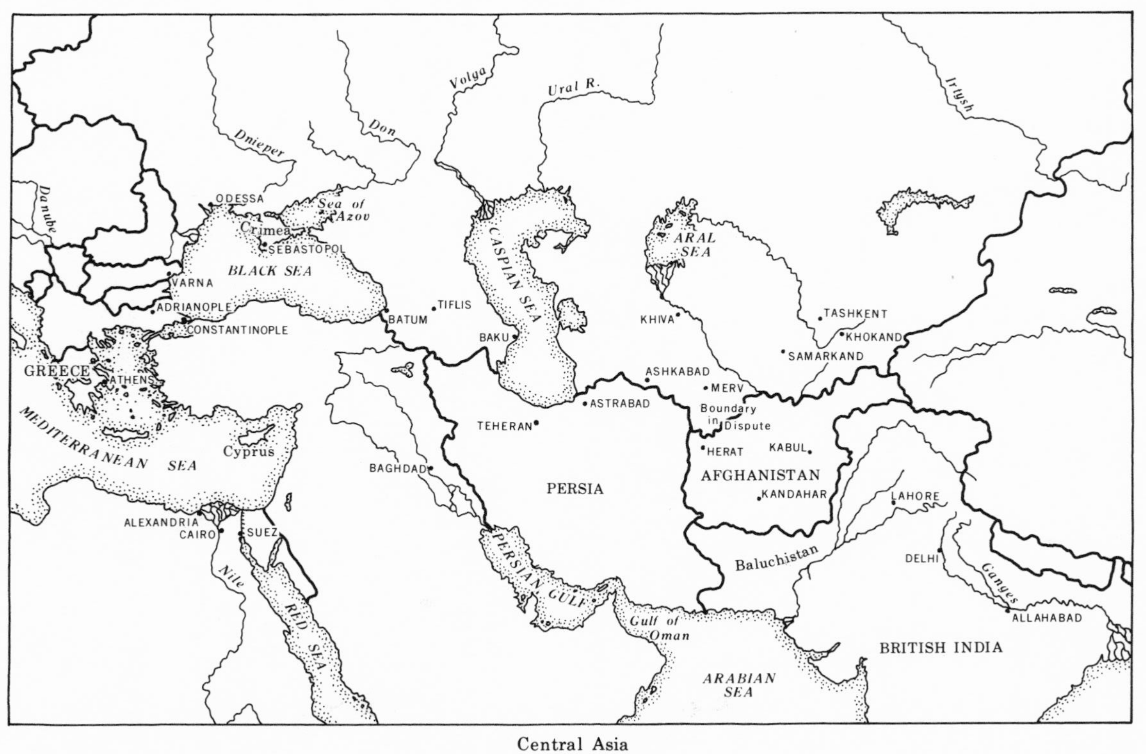

Central Asia

breaking of a "very solemn covenant"; the British press took a similarly strong stand. During the period of the crisis which now occurred, two issues were involved: first, the question of responsiblity for the incident, and, second, the fate of Penjdeh. For a period of about three weeks, because of the firm position taken by both governments, it appeared that war could break out.

Should such a conflict occur over Central Asian issues, the power at a grave disadvantage was obviously Britain. Her tremendous weight in seapower could not be brought to bear on the Afghan frontier. It was recognized that she did not have sufficient land troops to wage a major war here and also keep up her commitments in other areas. It was obvious that the only logical way that Britain could fight Russia would be through an attack on the Russian lands bordering the Black Sea. Here British naval strength could be exploited. An attack on Batum would be particularly advantageous, since this action would cut Russian communications with the Central Asian sector and could be used as a point from which to promote uprisings against Russia in the Caucasus.[82]

In order to conduct such a campaign British warships would have, of course, to pass the Straits in contravention of the international agreements. Not only did these treaties close the Straits to ships of war, but in 1871 the sultan's right to open the Straits was limited to the defense of the Treaty of Paris. By no stretch of the imagination could the conflict on the Afghan border be linked to this pact. Nevertheless, despite this prohibition, the powers expected Britain to attempt to come to some sort of an agreement with the Porte to prepare for the passage of the Straits and to offer large compensations in return for this right. Such a move was entirely logical. In fact, it is hard to believe that a responsible government could have committed itself in the manner which the Liberal government now did without making the minimum necessary moves to wage war. Yet that is apparently what happened. As will be explained in the next pages, the British government did not ask for concessions on the Straits, and in the Egyptian question a hard and uncompromising line was maintained. The pressure in Constantinople

82. See Appendix V for the British military report, "England's means of Offence against Russia."

came almost completely from the side of Russia and her allies who wished to guard against a move which never materialized.

In the winter of 1884-85 the first concern of the Ottoman Empire in its relations with Britain was to secure an agreement for the evacuation of the British forces from Egypt. The Porte also desired to improve relations in general in London. Therefore a special mission, that of Hasan Fehmi Pasha, was sent to Britain to try to obtain a statement on exactly when British troops would leave Egypt. The announcement of the mission caused immediate apprehension in St. Petersburg, where it was feared that the real goal was the negotiation of a political agreement which would affect the situation in Central Asia.[83] On January 19, 1885, Hasan Fehmi held his first interview with Granville.[84] In this and in subsequent meetings, when he was usually accompanied by Musurus, Hasan Fehmi presented the Ottoman viewpoint, but with a notable lack of success. Granville repeatedly assured the Ottoman representatives that the British government had no intention of annexing Egypt or of establishing a protectorate; the British action, he maintained, consisted of removing "from that province harmful people like Arabi and the Mahdi," and that would be "a service rendered to the rights of sovereignty and the caliphate of H.I.M. the Sultan."[85] Other matters concerning the British occupation and Egyptian administration were discussed, but on the essential point, the evacuation, no agreement could be reached. Granville found the problem difficult to solve. He argued against setting a time limit, both because he was against the fixing of a date in principle and also because of the difficulties in choosing one – a given period might be too long or too short.[86] He was willing to give assurances that, as long as Egypt retained its exceptional position, it would remain a part of the Ottoman Empire and that the rights of the sultan would be respected. He also

83. Shakir to Asim, E263/46A, no. 4298/4, St. Petersburg, January 8, 1885. Giers complained that when Onou, the Russian chargé in Constantinople, asked Asim the aim of the mission, the Turkish minister had been evasive and reserved. Shakir commented: "Il m'a semblé voir que la démarche projetée du Gouvt. Imp. auprès du Cabinet de St. James préoccupait beaucoup Mr Giers et que celui-ci désirait qu'elle fut ajournée."

84. Hasan Fehmi to Asim, E263/46A, no. 3, London, January 19, 1885.

85. Hasan Fehmi to Asim, E263/46A, no. 7, London, January 23, 1885.

86. Hasan Fehmi to Asim, E263/46A, no. 11, London, January 28, 1885.

told Hasan Fehmi that the British government did not want to continue the occupation longer than necessary, but he remained adamant on the date. When Hasan Fehmi asked "what result he should in effect be able to take back to Constantinople as having been accomplished by his visit to England," Granville replied that the Ottoman representative had been able to discuss the wishes of the sultan fully and frankly and he had been able to form his own opinion of the sincerity of the British intentions and the friendly character of its policy[87] – a small consolation indeed.

Relations between Britain and the Ottoman Empire were also not improved by the Italian occupation of Massawa with obvious British approval.[88] The death of Gordon also affected the general situation.[89] With these events in mind the Ottoman government pressed Hasan Fehmi to even greater efforts to reach an agreement with Britain. What the Porte really feared was that Britain and France would settle their differences over Egypt and make an arrangement which would permanently alienate that land from Ottoman control. Italy, it was obvious, would stand by Britain.[90] However, despite its worsening

87. Granville to Wyndham, F.O. 195/1492, no. 50A, F.O., February 3, 1885.

88. When Hasan Fehmi spoke to Granville in protest against the Italian action, the British statesman was not sympathetic. Hasan Fehmi to Asim, E. 263/46A, no. 16, London, February 4, 1885; Hasan Fehmi to Asim, *ibid.*, no no., London, February 11, 1885. Giers was more sympathetic; he said to Shakir: "La conduite de cette Puissance est étrange. . .au début elle était d'accord avec nous puis elle s'est rapproché de l'Angleterre, Massouah sert-elle de base à ce rapprochement? L'Angleterre désire-t-elle faire occuper cette place par les troupes italiennes pour retirer les (soldats) et pouvoir les envoyer ensuite à Khartoum en cas de besoin? Tout cela reste encore en état de mystère." Shakir to Asim, no. 4319/14, St. Petersburg, January 25, 1885 in Asim to Hasan Fehmi, E263/464, no. 77397/4, January 27, 1885.

89. The Ottoman reaction to Khartoum was mixed. Wyndham first reported: "The feeling at the Palace and amongst all Mussulman classes here at the fall of Khartoum is one of undisguised satisfaction. But I believe some anxiety prevails at the Palace at the possible increase of prestige and power which may accrue to the Mahdi and so affect the position of the Sultan as Caliph." Wyndham to Granville, F.O. 195/1505, no. 15, Constantinople, February 10, 1885. On the next day he wrote: "Although the Sultan is said to have been pleased at hearing of the fall of Khartoum, I am now told that H. M. deeply regrets it, as he sees that it will entail further military operations and a consequent prolongation of the occupation of Egypt." Wyndham to Granville, F.O. 195/1505, no. 18, Constantinople, February 11, 1885.

90. Asim to Hasan Fehmi, E263/46A, no. 77512/14, February 7, 1885; Asim to Hasan Fehmi, E263/46A, no. 77843/37, Constantinople, March 6, 1885.

general situation in both the Sudan and Central Asia, and its isolated position in diplomacy, the British government made no attempt to assuage Turkish feelings. Agreement was reached on certain minor questions, but not on the major issues.[91] Relations, in fact, reached a low point at the end of March when, after the Porte hesitated to sign a financial convention which had been under negotiation for over a year, Granville threatened to give the Ottoman representatives their passports if they did not agree at once.[92] The Russian fear that the mission would lead to a wider political accord was thus without foundation.

The Penjdeh crisis found the British ill-prepared. Deeply involved in the Sudan, alienated from most of the continental powers, Britain yet appeared willing to enter a costly war in Central Asia. In the past years it had been recognized that if war broke out with Russia, the most favorable, in fact about the only, area for direct combat was the Black Sea, but no attempt had been made to approach the Turkish government on the question of the Straits. Should the Porte in case of war not only refuse to allow passage but be prepared to defend its decision, it would be difficult for Britain to go to war over Penjdeh, despite all of the strong words spoken by the British leaders during the crisis. The Russian government was fully aware of this situation.

Therefore, as could be expected, at the height of the Penjdeh crisis the Porte found itself the center of diplomatic attention, particularly from the powers of the Three Emperors' Alliance. The Ottoman

91. Asim spoke repeatedly with Wyndham on the necessity of an agreement. The goal remained an understanding on the evacuation of British troops within a certain period even with the reservation that the time could be prolonged if necessary. Wyndham to Granville, F.O. 195/1505, no. 22, Constantinople, February 22, 1885; Wyndham to Granville, F.O. 78/3749, no. 106, Constantinople, February 25, 1885. The negotiations for the Turkish representatives were complicated by the arrival in London of Hobart Pasha, an Englishman in Ottoman service who was a confident of the sultan. Asim warned Hasan Fehmi to handle him carefully. He also confused Granville. Arriving with "quasi-credentials" from the sultan to call on the British leaders, Hobart reported that the sultan feared that the British government wished to "deprive him of his authority as Caliph over Egypt." He wanted assurances as to a future evacuation, but he did not insist on a date. This latter statement was, of course, in strong contradiction to the position of the Hasan Fehmi mission. Asim to Hasan Fehmi, E263/46A, no. 77789/32, March 1, 1885; Granville to Wyndham, F.O. 195/1492, no. 61 confidential, F.O., February 9, 1885.

92. Hasan Fehmi to Asim, E263/46A, no. 71, March 24, 1885.

government was now under strong pressure not only to keep the Straits closed, but to defend them against any British attempts at passage. On April 8 Giers spoke with Schweinitz, now the German ambassador in St. Petersburg, on the question of calling into effect the relevant clause of the Three Emperors' Alliance.[93] Bismarck had in fact already instructed Radowitz, the German ambassador in Constantinople, to warn the Porte that the opening of the Straits would be a break in Ottoman neutrality and would put the Porte in a state of war with Russia.[94] The German chancellor used the entire crisis to gain favor in St. Petersburg in the interest of his other diplomatic goals in Europe. He turned next to Vienna, where he urged that the Habsburg ambassador in Constantinople, Calice, cooperate with Radowitz in putting pressure on the Porte. He feared that if the alliance did not withstand this test, other issues would be gravely affected.[95] As a consequence the Porte was strongly warned by the Habsburg government through both the Austrian ambassador and the foreign minister, Gustav Kalnoky. Kalnoky told Sadullah, the Ottoman ambassador in Vienna, that if the Ottoman Empire let the British fleet into the Black Sea, Russia would consider this a *casus belli* and war would break out. Should Britain force the Straits, the Ottoman Empire could still remain neutral. If war came under these circumstances, the Habsburg Empire would advise the Balkan states to keep calm.[96]

Bismarck also turned to France. In a conversation with the French ambassador in Berlin, Courcel, he repeated the widely held opinion that Britain and the Ottoman Empire were arranging a deal in which Turkish troops would enter Egypt and in return the Porte would open the Straits.[97] The French foreign minister, Charles de Freycinet, subse-

93. Schweinitz to Bismarck, no. 58 secret, St. Petersburg, April 8, 1885. *G.P.*, IV, p. 112.

94. Bismarck to Schweinitz, no. 64 secret, Berlin, April 9, 1885, *G.P.*, IV, p. 113. The German pressure was maintained the entire month. In Berlin Hatzfeldt told Said: "Si vous vous engagez dans une guerre. . .Dieu sait qu'elle en serait la conséquence." Said to Asim, R9/87, no. 136 confidential, Berlin, April 14, 1885.

95. Bismarck to Reuss, no. 60 secret, Berlin, April 9, 1885. *G.P.*, IV, pp. 113-114.

96. Sadullah to Asim, R9/87, no. 15013/131, Vienna, April 15, 1885; Sadullah to Asim, *ibid.*, no. 15037/146, Vienna, April 29, 1885.

97. Courcel to Freycinet, Berlin, April 11, 1885. Ministère des Affairs Etrangères, *Documents diplomatiques français*, first series, (Paris, 1929-1959), VI, p. 6. Cited hereafter as *D.D.F.*

quently instructed the French representative in Constantinople, Imbert, to warn Asim that an opening of the Straits would be a direct violation of the treaties and a very dangerous path to follow.[98] Similar advice was given the Ottoman representative in Paris.[99] By the end of April the Italian government had let it be known that its attitude coincided with that of the other continental powers.[100]

As could be expected, Russian warnings were even stronger. On April 15 Shakir Pasha, the Ottoman representative in St. Petersburg, spoke with Giers, who expressed his satisfaction with the reports of the Russian ambassador, A. I. Nelidov, on the Turkish attitude in case of a British-Russian war. At this time the Russian foreign minister "renewed his recommendation concerning the Straits adding that a permission of passage accorded the English would be a breach of the neutrality promised and would completely destroy the Treaty of Paris, in a word it would be the declaration of war on Russia."[101] Shakir also reported in this period that in Russia the partisans of war had the upper hand. The "lordly manner" with which Britain had treated the matter had so excited the spirits of the country that each class was prepared for war.[102] The British government through its representatives in the capitals received accurate information of this and the other warnings which had been delivered to the Porte.[103]

The Ottoman government was thus under strong pressure from the powers of the Three Emperors' Alliance and from France. During this period, the foreign minister, Asim Pasha, was in continual close touch with both Hasan Fehmi and Musurus. Both diplomats regarded the situation as critical. They reported that British public opinion was for war, but they felt that the government desired a settlement.[104] On April 15 Asim telegraphed Hasan Fehmi to request his opinion on what actions

98. Freycinet to Imbert, Paris, April 12, 1885, *D.D.F.*, VI, pp. 8, 9; Courcel to Hatzfeldt, private letter, Berlin, April 14, 1885. *G.P.*, IV, pp. 12, 13.

99. Esad to Asim, R9/87, no. 2470/112, Paris, April 13, 1885.

100. Radowitz to F.O., no. 56, Pera, April 24, 1885. *G.P.* IV, pp. 118-119.

101. Shakir to Asim, R9/87, no. 4429/75, St. Petersburg, April 15, 1885.

102. Shakir to Asim, R9/87, no. 4442/83, St. Petersburg, April 23, 1885.

103. Wyndham to Granville, F.O. 195/1505, no. 65, Constantinople, April 15, 1885; Paget to Granville, tel. no. 8, Vienna, April 15, 1885; Wyndham to Granville, F.O. 195/1505, tel. no. 67, Constantinople, April 17, 1885.

104. Musurus to Asim, R9/87, tel. 156, London, April 12, 1885; Hasan Fehmi to Asim, E263/46A, no. 81, London, April 13, 1885.

the Porte should take. On the next day Hasan Fehmi replied that the situation was uncertain; war seemed probable but the hopes for peace were not lost. Because of this he believed that the Ottoman government should observe an attitude of great reserve and study the possibilities of using the situation for its own advantage. It should therefore maintain its freedom of action and only make a choice of a policy when it became clear whether there would be war or not.[105]

At this time the Ottoman representatives also received an indication of the course which the British government wished them to follow. On April 17 Musurus spoke with Granville and requested information on the course of the negotiations over the Penjdeh incident. The British minister replied that he had nothing to communicate. Musurus then informed him that heavy pressure was being put on the Ottoman government to induce it to preserve an attitude of strict neutrality if war should come. Granville commented that "it seemed to me advisable in the interests of Turkey that the Porte should not fetter its liberty of action by any hasty engagements."[106] On the next day Granville spoke in a similar manner to Hasan Fehmi, who reported to his government that the British minister had:

> . . .told me confidentially. . .that the Sublime Porte would assume engagements of a nature to fetter its liberty of action in case of a war between Britain and Russia. His Lordship observed to me at the same time that although the British government had not requested anything until now from the Imperial Government to this effect, it thinks that such a bond would not be in accordance with the interests of Turkey and that as a consequence it would rather believe that there is nothing in it.

Hasan Fehmi reported that he had replied to Granville that he did not know what the Porte had decided, but that it would undoubtedly follow its own best interests.[107]

On April 20, clearly unsatisfied with the reply of April 16, Asim again telegraphed Hasan Fehmi asking advice on what course the Porte should pursue and requesting that the Ottoman representative express

105. Hasan Fehmi to Asim, E263/46A, no. 84, London, April 16, 1885.

106. Granville to Wyndham, F.O. 195/1493, no. 138A confidential, F.O., April 17, 1885; Musurus to Asim, R9/87, tel. no. 165, London, April 17, 1885.

107. Hasan Fehmi to Asim, E263/46A, no. 92 confidential, London, April 18, 1885.

his opinion in a precise and detailed fashion and "in a manner to leave room for no ambiguity and no doubt."[108] On the next day Hasan Fehmi replied much as he had before, that the situation was not clear. Therefore the Porte should maintain a strict neutrality, preserve its freedom of action, and not declare its future policy.[109] This advice was, of course, in line with that expressed by Granville.

On April 21 Asim spoke of the problems of the Porte in a conversation with Wyndham, who subsequently telegraphed to Granville: "I am earnestly requested by M. [Minister] for F.A. [Foreign Affairs] to explain to Y.L. [Your Lordship] difficult position of the Porte with regard to the Straits in case of war and to express the hope that Turkey being anxious to remain neutral will not be called upon under present circumstances to commit itself to any declaration on the subject."[110] On April 28 Granville replied: "With regard to the attitude of Turkey in the event of a war between England and Russia I have abstained from putting any pressure on the Sultan and have confined myself to urging upon Fehmi Pasha and Musurus the importance in the interests of Turkey of his not fettering his liberty of action by any hasty engagements."[111]

Thus in April the Porte was under strong pressure from two opposing sides. The British government wished the empire to make no engagements and to keep its full freedom of action. In practice this policy would mean that the Porte would neither declare its neutrality nor state its intention to abide by the Straits agreements. In contrast, the five continental powers warned the Ottoman government against an understanding with Britain and pressed for a statement on neutrality and the Straits. Neither side was confident of the Turkish position. The Russian representatives, for instance, expressed fears not only of the Ottoman willingness, but also of its ability to fulfill its role of "guardian of the Straits" and to supply the force necessary to stop a British

108. Asim to Hasan Fehmi, E263/46A, no. 78466/69, April 20, 1885.

109. Hasan Fehmi to Asim, E263/46A, no. 96, London, April 21, 1885.

110. Wyndham to Granville, F.O. 195/1505, no. 74 confidential, April 21, 1885.

111. Granville to White, F.O. 195/1504, tel. no. 46 secret, F.O., April 28, 1885. White, now ambassador in Constantinople, had already on April 23 advised Asim that the Porte should "keep itself free from any hasty engagements." White to Granville, F.O. 78/3751, no. 245, Constantinople, April 29, 1885.

passage. Nelidov repeatedly stated his opinion that should a British fleet actually appear in the Straits, the Porte would not have the courage to act. Instead the ships would be allowed to remain and, once stationed before Constantinople, this force would command the Ottoman government. The sultan, Nelidov believed, would be afraid to flee Constantinople and he would thus fall in the power of the English.[112] The governments of the Three Emperors' Alliance also continued to fear that the Porte would use the situation to bargain for concessions in Egypt in return for the opening of the Straits. The apprehension over the goals of the Hasan Fehmi mission remained acute.

While the British government was advising the Porte to refrain from all action, the representatives of the three allied courts, in particular Radowitz, urged the Ottoman government not only to declare its policy openly, but also to prepare to defend the Straits against a possible British attempt to force a passage. They now wished the sultan to take three actions. First, he was to make an open statement on his intention to remain neutral and to close the Straits. This declaration was to be given at once before the outbreak of hostilities. Second, military measures were to be taken to make certain that the Straits could be defended. Third, the Hasan Fehmi mission was to be recalled.

The greatest efforts by the allied powers were devoted to the attempt to obtain a clear declaration of Turkish policy. Although the sultan was willing to state privately that he would pursue a policy of neutrality,[113] he and his ministers naturally hesitated to go further before war actually broke out. From the Ottoman point of view it would be very disadvantageous to anger needlessly the British, who could then put further pressure on Egypt. If war did not come, the Porte's attitude could cause further friction with Britain. The Ottoman government thus preferred to take openly no decided stand. If war came, then neutrality and the closure of the Straits could be proclaimed; assistance could then be sought to maintain this policy.[114]

112. Calice to Kalnoky, H.H.S. XII/146, tel. no. 78, Constantinople, April 24, 1885; Calice to Kalnoky, *ibid.,* no. 25D, Constantinople, May 2, 1885.

113. Calice to Kalnoky, H.H.S. XII/146, tel. no. 68, Constantinople, April 12, 1885.

114. Calice to Kalnoky, H.H.S. XII/146, no. 22D, Constantinople, April 18, 1885; Calice to Kalnoky, *ibid.,* no. 22C, Constantinople, April 18, 1885.

One of the chief concerns of the Porte at this time was just this question of its capability of resisting a British attack in case the Straits were kept closed. It was felt that the Straits could be defended, but fears were expressed over possible British action against Turkish shores and islands. Egypt might also be declared independent of the Porte. On April 22 Reshid Bey, the secretary of the sultan, approached both Calice and Radowitz about what their governments would do against the British threat and "if Turkey could count, should the occasion arise, on the support of the friendly powers, to what degree and in what form. His Majesty thinks among other things of the sending of the friendly fleets before the Straits and he believes that their presence, by itself, will hold back the English."[115]

Under continual pressure, particularly from Berlin, the Porte finally issued to the powers concerned the statement which they wished. On April 29 Calice reported that although the Ottoman government would make no public declaration, the position of the Porte would be communicated through the ambassadors of the friendly powers.[116] In early May the Ottoman government thus informed in identical notes the Russian, German, French, and Austrian governments that it intended to keep the Straits closed, and that it counted on their aid to maintain this policy.[117]

The powers of the Three Emperors' Alliance were if anything more concerned than the Porte itself over Turkish defenses against Britain. They thus pressed for definite action, in particular in regard to the Dardanelles. Despite the assurances of the sultan that the Straits would be closed if war came, Asim admitted to Radowitz that it might be difficult to put such an action into force. Nelidov, as has been mentioned, felt that the Turkish government would not show the necessary courage at the decisive moment.[118] As a result of pressure

115. Calice to Kalnoky, H.H.S. XII/146, tel. no. 76, Constantinople, April 22, 1885; Radowitz to F.O., no. 53 secret, Pera, April 23, 1885, *G.P.,* IV, pp. 117, 118.

116. Calice to Kalnoky, H.H.S. XII/146, tel. no. 82, Constantinople, April 29, 1885.

117. Asim to Sadullah, R9/87, no. 78660/69, May 3, 1885; Asim to Esad, *ibid.,* no. 78659/106, May 3, 1885; Asim to Said, *ibid.,* no. 78658, May 3, 1885; Calice to Kalnoky, H.H.S. XII/146, tel. no. 84, Constantinople, May 5, 1885.

118. Radowitz to Bismarck, no. 84 very confidential, Pera, April 13, 1885, *G.P.,* IV, pp. 114, 115.

from the representatives of the Three Emperors' Alliance, the Turkish government did send a commission composed of the director of the artillery of the War Ministry and three German officers in the Ottoman service to superintend and inspect the defenses of the Straits. Although their report was positive, fears still existed that at the last moment the Porte would not take the necessary actions to keep the Straits closed.[119]

The allied powers had thus been able to obtain a declaration from the sultan and they had seen that the Porte took steps in regard to the defenses of the Straits. They now were able to secure the recall of the Hasan Fehmi mission. Throughout the period of the Penjdeh crisis rumors circulated freely on the actions and attitude of the special envoy. He had certainly been sent with the intention not only of gaining an agreement in Egypt, but also of improving if possible the relations between the two governments. When his advice had been requested on what attitude the Porte should take, he had indeed supported the policy desired by Granville – that is, that the Porte should maintain its freedom of action. Although he was completely unsuccessful in the main objects of his mission, the Russian and German governments had, of course, no way of knowing this. Russia in particular remained greatly concerned over exactly what was being discussed. Both Russia and Germany now pressed for his recall. On April 23 in a discussion with Shakir, Giers expressed his satisfaction with the action taken by the Porte, but he regretted "the double policy of its ambassador at London."[120] On the same day, in Berlin, Hatzfeldt complained to Said that Hasan Fehmi was following a "personal policy" at London, and that this had given rise to interpretations of Ottoman conduct that were not in the interest of the Porte.[121] Nelidov and Radowitz spoke in a similar manner in Constantinople.[122] As a result of this united pressure, Hasan Fehmi was recalled at the end of the month. The action was justified by the obvious failure of his mission.[123]

119. Calice to Kalnoky, H.H.S. XII/146, no. 22E, April 18, 1885.

120. Shakir to Asim, E263/469, no. 4443/84, St. Petersburg, April 23, 1885.

121. Said to Asim, E263/46A, private letter, Berlin, April 23, 1885.

122. Calice to Kalnoky, H.H.S. XII/146, no. 24E, Constantinople, April 28, 1885; Radowitz to F.O., no. 57, Pera, April 28, 1885, *G.P.*, IV, p. 119.

123. Asim to Hasan Fehmi, E263/46A, no. 78594/77, April 28, 1885. The

The Penjdeh crisis ended during the first week of May. At this time the British governments agreed to submit the question of responsibility to arbitration. The major issue over the Afghan boundary was subsequently settled by awarding Penjdeh to Russia and another disputed point, the Zulficar Pass, to Afghanistan. A commission then undertook the task of delimiting the rest of the boundary between Russia and Afghanistan; a final agreement was signed in September 1887. In this crisis certainly the Russian government had showed itself in a stronger position than its opponent. In the end Penjdeh, the cause of the crisis, remained in Russian hands. The Russian allies gave firm support in Constantinople. The Ottoman government would obviously be responsive to the influence of the stronger combination.

Salisbury Replies: The Mediterranean Agreements

Although Penjdeh had been a Russian victory and had shown the strength of the Russian diplomatic position in Constantinople, the British government under the leadership of Lord Salisbury was able in the next three years to reverse the situation completely and in fact to break again the Russian alignment with the central European courts. The weapon he used was the crisis in Russian-Bulgarian relations which existed by 1885.[124]

At the Congress of Berlin and in the Three Emperors' Alliance, the autonomous Bulgaria had been assigned to the Russian sphere of influence. However, contrary to the expectation of the powers, that state had refused to be a Russian client. By 1885 St. Petersburg and Sofia were in fact in sharp conflict. Therefore when a revolt broke out in Eastern Rumelia in that year, Russia, despite her previous support of a large Bulgarian state, did not favor the union of the two provinces. Instead it was Britain, now under a Conservative government, who stood behind the Bulgarian national aims. In a compromise settlement in March 1886, Alexander of Battenberg, the ruler of Bulgaria, was

---

recall notification stated: "V.E. nous ayant successivement signalé l'impossibilité de fixer un terme pour l'evacuation qui était la base et le but essentiel de sa mission à Londres. . . ." White believed that Hasan Fehmi was recalled to please Russia. White to Granville, F.O. 78/3751, no. 246 confidential, Constantinople, April 30, 1885.

124. This section on Bulgaria is based on Charles Jelavich, *Tsarist Russia and Balkan Nationalism* (Berkeley, 1958).

named also governor of Eastern Rumelia. This action further weakened the sultan's hold on the Bulgarian lands, but in a sense it added to the security of his empire against Russia. The balance in the Black Sea had improved; Varna could no longer be considered a Russian port. Russian-dominated military forces no longer stood within striking distance of the Straits.

The Bulgarian episode was undoubtedly a blow to Russian prestige. In order to balance the account the tsar in the summer of 1886 proceeded to abrogate Article LIX of the Treaty of Berlin concerning Batum.[125] The powers were notified of the Russian intention in the first part of July. Once again a Liberal cabinet in Britain had to deal with a unilateral action against a treaty. In the notification to the signatories of the Treaty of Berlin, the Russian government denied that it was in fact violating the agreement, since unlike other stipulations, it was not "a product of a general agreement, but it simply records a free and spontaneous declaration of His Majesty the Emperor Alexander II of imperishable memory."[126]

In reply Gladstone, again in power, attacked the principle rather than the fact. In a despatch of July 13 the Earl of Rosebery, the foreign secretary, denied the validity of the Russian argument and maintained that the declaration was on the same footing as the other articles: "This being so, the terms of the Protocol of London of the 17th January 1871 are applicable in all their force." The sanctity of treaties was once again proclaimed.

> One direct, supreme and perpetual interest, however, is no doubt at stake in this transaction – that of the binding force and sanctity of international engagements. Great Britain is ready at all times and in all seasons to uphold that principle, and she cannot palter with it in the present instance.[127]

With these noble words the British government in fact let the matter drop. There was no demand for a conference as in 1870 and no

125. See B. Jelavich, "Great Britain and the Russian Acquisition of Batum," pp. 57-66.

126. Enclosure in Rosebery to Morier, Foreign Office, July 3, 1886. *Accounts and Papers,* LXIII, no. 1 (1886), p. 4.

127. Rosebery to Morier, no. 157, July 13, 1886. Temperley and Penson, *Foundations of British Foreign Policy,* pp. 437-441.

question of compensation. The other powers accepted the change at once. Although the ending of the free port status of Batum would, of course, have some commercial effects, the real significance of the Russian action was that the city could now be openly fortified. The importance of the port for British strategy in case of a war with Russia has already been mentioned; it formed a most important link at this time in the direct communications between St. Petersburg and Central Asia. At the Congress of Berlin this question had been joined with the closure of the Straits. This connection was mentioned in the British reports, but only as a point of interest. In 1886, in contrast to 1878, Batum was not a matter to fight about.

Although the interests of the Porte in the Black Sea were affected by the change in the status of Batum, they were far more involved in the Bulgarian lands. In July 1886 the Conservative party, with Salisbury as prime minister and Lord Iddesleigh as foreign secretary, came again to office. During the next eighteen months Bulgarian issues, centering on the kidnapping of Alexander of Battenberg, his abdication, and the subsequent election of Ferdinand of Coburg dominated the diplomatic scene. Apprehension was felt in Britain that Russia would march into the country, overthrow the anti-Russian regime in power, and establish a puppet government. Britain would then be faced with what she had avoided at the Congress of Berlin – a big Bulgaria under Russian domination, far too close to Constantinople and the Straits. Although there was division within the Conservative ministry on the policy of blocking Russia in the Balkans, Salisbury personally emphasized the defense of the Turkish capital. In October 1886, after the forced abdication of Alexander of Battenberg, Salisbury wrote to Randolph Churchill, now chancellor of the exchequer, who opposed his policy:

> I consider the loss of Constantinople would be the ruin of our party and a heavy blow to the country: and therefore I am anxious to delay by all means Russia's advance to that goal. A pacific and economical policy is up to a certain point very wise: but it is evident that there is a point beyond which it is not wise either in a patriotic or party sense – and the question is where we shall draw the line. I draw it at Constantinople.[128]

128. Winston Churchill, *Lord Randolph Churchill* (London, 1951), p. 520.

In his opposition to Russia, Salisbury could count on little support in Constantinople. The question of Egypt still deeply strained the relations of the two countries. The pressure which could be exerted by Russia, France, and Germany outweighed any that could be brought by Britain, even in combination with Italy and Austria-Hungary. In the Bulgarian crisis the issues in regard to the Porte were similar to the situation at the time of Penjdeh. The British navy was the best weapon which England had to use against Russia, but it had to pass the Straits. In October 1886 Iddesleigh wrote to Sir William White, the British ambassador in Constantinople, that the question then at issue was if the Porte in the Bulgarian crisis would "not act herself, will she give us the power of acting by admitting our fleet into the Black Sea." White was further instructed to warn Abdülhamid:

> I think you may very well take some opportunity of hinting to the sultan that if he allows Russia to gain such an ascendency in Bulgaria as to appear to threaten the independence of Constantinople England will probably change her tactics, and try to safeguard her Eastern Empire by measures of her own, which would not be framed on the old model. Our position in Egypt for instance might have to be reconsidered.[129]

More important than the pressure on the Porte, however, was to be Salisbury's very successful diplomacy in relation to the great powers. During the Penjdeh incident, the Three Emperors' Alliance had been effective in the Straits question; this combination had also held together during the first stages of the discussions on the unification of Bulgaria and Eastern Rumelia. Salisbury was now to use the greater crisis arising from the kidnapping of Alexander of Battenberg and the establishment of Ferdinand of Coburg as prince of Bulgaria to break the Three Emperors' Alliance. Like Disraeli in 1878, he was able to exploit the natural antagonism of Austria-Hungary to Russian expansion in the Balkans to draw that power from alliance with St. Petersburg. He also had the tacit support of Bismarck, who feared the outbreak of a European war, to the establishment of a new diplomatic combination. Thus in March and December 1887 Britain signed with Italy, Austria-Hungary, and Spain the Mediterranean Agreements. These

129. Iddesleigh to White, F.O. 364/1, confidential, October 12, 1886.

understandings were designed to prevent a Russian occupation of Bulgaria and in general to preserve the status quo in the Mediterranean and the Black Sea against both French and Russian action. Although the treaties directly concerned the Ottoman Empire, that state was expressly not informed of the terms.

In the Three Emperors' Alliance of 1881 we have seen how Russia won support for her interpretation of the Straits agreements, i.e. that they were European and multilateral in character. In the Mediterranean Agreements of 1887 Britain changed the emphasis in the entire question and gained the approval of the signatories of the treaty to one portion of Salisbury's declaration in 1878: that Britain was bound by the decisions of the sultan only if he were acting "independently." The Mediterranean Agreement of December stated:

> 4. The independence of Turkey, as guardian of important European interests; the Caliphate, the freedom of the Straits, &c., to be independent of all foreign preponderating influence.
> 5. Consequently, Turkey can neither cede nor delegate her rights over Bulgaria to any other Power. . . .Neither will Turkey, who has by the Treaties been constituted guardian of the Straits, be able to cede any portion of her sovereign rights, nor delegate her authority to any other Power in Asia Minor. . . .
> 8. Should the conduct of the Porte, however, in the opinion of the three Powers, assume the character of complicity with or connivance at any such illegal enterprise, the three Powers will consider themselves justified by existing Treaties in proceeding either jointly or separately to the provisional occupation by their forces, military or naval, of such points of Ottoman territory as they may agree to consider it necessary to occupy in order to secure the objects determined by the previous Treaties.[130]

In addition to these agreements, with their decidedly anti-Turkish edge, Salisbury made an attempt to settle the Egyptian question. In 1885 Sir Henry Drummond Wolff had been sent to Constantinople to negotiate on the same questions which had concerned the Hasan Fehmi mission. This time, however, it appears to have been the British government which had the intention of using the negotiations for laying a basis for wider political arrangements. The discussions did not proceed smoothly, but in May 1887 an agreement was reached. The

130. C. J. Lowe, *The Reluctant Imperialists* (London, 1967), II, pp. 61, 62.

terms provided for a definite period of three years for the withdrawal of British troops, as the Porte wished, but the action was not to be carried through if either internal or external dangers arose in the meantime. Moreover, provision was made that British troops could return under some circumstances. Upon the strong recommendation of Russia and France, the Porte did not ratify this engagement. Like the Hasan Fehmi mission the bilateral negotiations went down to defeat largely because the British did not want to leave Egypt. If they did, they wished to provide for their return or to assure themselves large concessions. The Russian and French representatives in Constantinople also constantly influenced the Porte not to come to the type of understanding which Britain wished.

Another agreement, dealing with the Straits and concluded without the knowledge or participation of the Porte, was also signed in 1887. With the growth of Austro-Russian antagonism over Bulgaria, it was obvious that the Three Emperors' Alliance, which came up for renewal at this time, would have to be dropped. Austria-Hungary, as we have seen, joined the Mediterranean alignment. Unwilling to abandon all diplomatic connections with St. Petersburg, Bismarck now concluded with Russia the Reinsurance Treaty. In this Germany gave support to the Russian desire to see the establishment of a "regular and legal government in Bulgaria" and agreed to give "moral and diplomatic support" should the tsar "find himself under the necessity of defending the entrance to the Black Sea in order to safeguard the interests of Russia"[131]

Although the Ottoman government was not informed of the contents of these secret agreements, the change in alignments in Europe was obvious in Constantinople. The continental nations no longer stood united against Britain, as they had in the Penjdeh incident. Instead the powers of the Mediterranean Agreements were now joined against Russia and France, who, although not yet formally allied, had similar interests and opponents in some matters. As long as Bismarck remained in office, the German position straddled the two camps. After 1890, when Bismarck left office and the Reinsurance Treaty was dropped,

131. The text is in *Grosse Politik,* V, pp. 253-255. See Appendix VI for a letter from Nelidov to Giers on the question of using the German friendship for Russian interests at the Straits.

Germany joined the Mediterranean powers. She had, of course, been since 1882 a partner in the Triple Alliance with Italy and Austria-Hungary. This shift in alliance systems was neither a benefit nor an injury to the Ottoman Empire. In individual questions the lines of the alignments often blurred. Both camps held policies that in some issues were a danger and in others a benefit to the Porte. Certainly, no trace of a "Crimean" alliance remained.

IV

CONCLUSION

In the previous pages the question of the Straits and certain other related issues have been discussed for the years 1870 through 1887. During this period we have seen a shift in the Ottoman position in international relations and in the attitude of the powers toward the Ottoman possessions. In 1870 the Porte was probably in a relatively stronger relationship with the states of Europe than at any other period in the century. The attention of continental Europe was concentrated on the national unification of Germany and Italy and on the reorganization of the Habsburg Monarchy. Russia was in a period of internal reform and in foreign policy was primarily concerned with rectifying the losses of the Crimean War. The "Crimean alliance" of Britain, Austria-Hungary, and France to support the Ottoman Empire still held even though these powers were willing to impose some losses on the Porte. The national movements among the subject nationalities made progress between 1856 and 1870, but they as yet did not pose the danger to the Ottoman state that they did in later periods.

With a favorable international situation and a stable internal regime, the Ottoman leaders were thus during the Black Sea crisis of 1870-71 able to play an important and honorable role. They could not prevent the Russian alteration of the Treaty of Paris, but they did hinder the Habsburg Empire from making gains on the Danube. The change made in the Straits settlement was intended to strengthen the Ottoman position. Most important, at the conference the Porte was able to act independently and to take a stand against the united wishes of the representatives of the great powers.

The succeeding years were to prove quite different. Most significant for the fate of the Ottoman Empire was the change in the atmosphere of European politics following the unifications on the continent. After the consolidation of the national states of central Europe, all of the great powers entered on a period of imperial expansion, one of whose prime targets was the possessions of the Ottoman Empire. The powers concentrated on those lands most open to their military and naval pressure. Russia and Autria-Hungary, as has been shown, in the pre-war agreements and at the Congress of Berlin in effect partitioned the Balkan peninsula, with Habsburg control in the western half balanced by Russian predominance in Bulgaria. With the loss of the greater part of its Christian Balkan possessions, the Ottoman Empire after 1878 shifted its prime attention to the Moslem Asiatic and African lands. Here Britain was the principal threat. In the Cyprus Convention the British government aimed at the establishment of a general protectorate over the Turkish Asiatic provinces; in 1882 Egypt was occupied, to be abandoned entirely only in 1956.

Although Britain and Russia remained the states with a major interest in Constantinople, Austria-Hungary, France, Germany, and Italy were also in contention for influence in the empire. The powers not only directly attacked Ottoman domains through military and economic means, but they continued when convenient to exploit the national movements within the empire, particularly in the Balkans. They thus used both the weapon of the national, or the liberal-national, ideology, which they claimed to represent, and the power gained in money and guns from their own more successful internal organizations to bring down a weaker opponent. Europe moved into the Ottoman lands, buttressed by material power and a triumphant western ideology.

The heightening imperial conflicts were reflected in the attitude of the powers to the status of the Straits. The Ottoman Empire in this question was caught between the two great rival powers – Britain and Russia. Since the Black Sea was the most effective point where British naval supremacy could be brought into play against Russia, the British government needed an assurance that it could pass through these

Turkish territorial waters if needed. In the 1880s it was Britain who remained on the offensive, Russia on the defensive. The Salisbury statement in 1878 was designed to open the Straits for the British navy. There is certainly no doubt but that Britain would have forced the Straits in 1885, as was done in 1878, if war had broken out in Central Asia. Although certainly the Russian government would have welcomed any opportunity to acquire control over the area, in the 1880s it was primarily concerned with assuring the closure of the Straits and in organizing the continental powers in support of the treaties. It is interesting to note that both Britain and Russia sought essentially the same goal – that expressed in the Treaty of Unkiar Skelessi. Each would have liked a treaty of alliance with the Ottoman Empire which would have put that state in a subject relationship and would have assured free passage for its ships and closure for those of its opponents.

The pressure of Europe on Constantinople was almost impossible for the Porte to resist. The best means of defense lay, as we have seen, in the competition of the states and their rivalry over the same lands. The Habsburg Monarchy and Russia contended over influence in the Balkans; Britain and Russia over Asia; France and Britain and later Italy over African territories. The general field of economic exploitation showed a similar division and competition. In the final analysis, however, as far as the Ottoman Empire was concerned, this system of balance failed. The powers found that they could settle their mutual rivalries also by a policy of partition. Ottoman territories and dependencies thus often became prizes handed out to calm the international tensions or to compensate or divert the attention of other powers. Thus Germany was to encourage France to turn to Tunisia rather than Alsace-Lorraine, and Italy to Africa rather than the Tyrol.

The relationship of the great powers to the national movements of the subject people was even more subtle and difficult to meet. Throughout the nineteenth century certain groups, particularly in Britain and Russia, developed a fantastic ability to see what they wanted to see and to close their eyes to any facts which disturbed their theories. Many English liberals and Russian Panslavs were sincerely indignant about what they considered atrocious political conditions in the Balkans in particular. They did not view their own subject populations or the condition of their own people in the factories and on the farms with the same critical standards. Moreover, a similar blindness afflicted them in regard to the Moslem population of the empire and the sultan's obligations toward them. Very little indignation was expressed concerning the repeated Christian atrocities committed against Moslem civilians in times of crisis.

The attack of liberal elements certainly proved effective. It gave the moral justification for territorial dismemberment and economic exploitation. It also allowed the governments concerned to envisage the partition of the empire and to alter treaties without regard for Ottoman interests with little fear of political repercussions at home. The Russian government used national and religious arguments – the British liberal and national themes. These considerations were of particular importance in influencing public opinion in Britain, where not only Gladstonian Liberals but also Conservatives came to attack the continuation of the Crimean policy. If a government is considered evil, backward, sick, or decadent, it is easy to imagine that one is doing a good deed by undermining it, no matter what methods are used. Yet certainly these same groups would have been highly indignant had international attention been focused in a similar manner on their own Irish, Welsh, and Scotch populations and on the conditions of life in many parts of the British Empire. Russia too would have rejected any attempt to apply to her Polish, Baltic, Jewish, and Central Asian people the same political principles which she often demanded for the Balkan Orthodox Christians. It is to the credit of the Italian, German, Habsburg, and French governments that they were less inclined to cover practical policies with noble motives.

In the following years the question of the passage of the Straits and the interpretation of treaties remained a major factor in international relations. The provisions of the Treaty of London were only finally superceded by those of the Treaty of Lausanne of July 24, 1923, but numerous attempts were made to change them before that date, particularly by Russia, who by the end of the century began again to press for special rights for the warships of the riverain states of the Black Sea. As long as the center of the Ottoman Empire remained Constantinople, the question of passage was closely bound with that of the control of the Ottoman government. For the Porte the best solution remained that established in the Treaty of London: the closure of the

Straits to ships of war, with the exception that in a period of emergency the sultan could summon the assistance of "friendly and allied powers." It was this settlement that the Ottoman government sought to maintain in the future.

V

POSTSCRIPT: THE BOSNIAN CRISIS

Although this narrative is designed to concentrate on the period from 1870 to 1887, a brief discussion will be included of another episode, the Bosnian crisis of 1908-1909, because of certain similarities between this event and the questions which have already been covered. The Austrian annexation of Bosnia-Hercegovina, which broke the Treaty of Berlin, is the last of the three most notable unilateral denunciations of international treaties in the last half century before the First World War. The other two, the Russian denunciation of the Black Sea clauses of the Treaty of Paris and of Article LIX of the Treaty of Berlin concerning Batum, have already been discussed. Like the Russian action in 1870, the Habsburg move harmed Ottoman interests; as in previous episodes, however, it was again the great powers who decided the matter according to their own desires. All three incidents were also closely bound to the Straits question. It will be noted too that in 1870-71 the Ottoman Empire had been under the reform government of the Tanzimat ministers, in the succeeding period under the autocratic rule of Abdülhamid, and in the Bosnian crisis under the constitutional government of the Young Turks. The great powers, despite their frequent urging that the Ottoman government reform itself, treated these three regimes in almost precisely the same way.

Although the Bosnian crisis thus offers certain comparisons with previous events, it also demonstrates the effects on the Ottoman Empire and the status of the Straits of the radical changes in international alignments which took place between 1887 and 1908. In this period Britain and Russia were still the two powers with a decisive influence over the fate of the Ottoman Empire and the Straits. Austria-Hungary, Germany, France, and Italy usually regarded the question as a diplomatic weapon or a bargaining point in their relations with other powers. However, a notable change in attitude occurred in London. Two practical considerations influenced British opinion . First, Britain did not have the predominant political position at Constantinople which she had enjoyed in previous periods when she had been the chief protector of the Porte. Particularly after the fall of Bismarck and the advent to the German throne of William II, Germany came to play an increasingly important role in Ottoman affairs. Second, the British military and naval leaders in effect abandoned the Black Sea as a field of action against Russia. Of particular influence in this decision was the fact that in 1891 and 1894 Russia and France concluded a military alliance which could be directed against England as well as against Germany. Thereafter the British Mediterranean fleet had to assume that if it became involved in a naval war with Russia it would also have to deal with the French fleet. Under these circumstances British Naval and Military Intelligence came to the decision, as expressed ironically by Salisbury, that it was "not only not possible. . .to protect Constantinople, but that any effort to do so is not permissible."[1] In 1903 similar discussions within the British government led to the even more significant conclusion that the balance of power in the Mediterranean would not be decisively changed if Russia succeeded in opening the Straits for riverain powers only: ". . .while Russia would no doubt obtain certain naval advantages from the change, it would not fundamentally alter the present strategic position in the Mediterranean."[2]

1. Memorandum by Salisbury of June 4, 1892 on the Joint Report of the Director of Military Intelligence and the Director of Naval Intelligence. Lowe, *Reluctant Imperialists,* II, p. 86.

2. Hardinge Memorandum on the passage of Russian warships through the Straits, November 16, 1906. G. P. Gooch and Harold Temperley, eds., *British Documents on the Origins of the War, 1898-1914* (London, 1929), IV, p. 59. This series will be cited hereafter as *B.D.O.W.*

Despite these military and naval judgments, the British Foreign Office was certainly not prepared to concede to Russia easily in this question. It was the major bargaining point which could be used in negotiations, particularly over Asiatic questions. Most political leaders also believed that British public opinion would not accept the surrender of the Straits. Nevertheless, British policy did begin to shift, as was shown in the Armenian crisis of 1895. The Mediterranean agreements were also dropped at this time, because the British government would not accept the obligation to defend Constantinople.

Although British policy was now to change, Russia in contrast kept its main goals in view, but with an added emphasis. Until the end of the century the Russian posture remained largely defensive; Russia feared chiefly a British penetration into the Black Sea in a time of crisis. During the years when Nelidov was ambassador in Constantinople, he continued to support an aggressive and active policy toward the Straits, but his main emphasis was on the necessity of countering a British move. Alexander III remained favorable to such an attitude, but general international conditions prevented practical steps from being taken. In fact, in its negotiations with the other powers, the Russian government continued to place more weight on the defensive and European aspects of the Straits problem. Moreover, at this time the attractions of an active Far Eastern policy outweighed all Balkan and Near Eastern issues.[3] In order to pursue its interests in this area, Russia in 1897 came to an agreement with Austria-Hungary which was designed to keep peace in the Balkans so that an advance could be made in Manchuria and Korea. The section referring to the Straits stated:

> It was equally recognized that the question of Constantinople and of the adjacent territory as well as that of the Straits (Dardanelles and Bosphorus), having an eminently European character, is not of a nature to be made the object of a separate understanding between Austria-Hungary and Russia.
>
> Count Muravieff [the Russian foreign minister] did not hesitate to declare in this connection that, far from striving for any modification of the present state of things, sanctioned by the

3. On Russian policy toward the Straits question see in particular A. N. Mandelstam, "La Politique russe d'accès à la Mediterranée au XXe siècle," *Recueil des cours* (1934), XLVII, pp. 597-802. On this period see also Y. Hekmet Bayur, "Boğazlar Sorumunun Bir Evresi, 1906-1914," *Belleten,* VII, 1943, pp. 89-215.

> Treaty of Paris and the Convention of London, the Imperial Government held, on the contrary, to the complete maintenance of the provisions relative thereto, which gave full and entire satisfaction to Russia in prohibiting, by the closing of the Straits, access to the Black Sea to foreign war vessels.[4]

During this period and at the time of the Russo-Japanese War, controversies arose over the sultan's granting of passage through the Straits to certain ships under dubious circumstances. The war demonstrated again to the Russian government the danger and inconvenience of the closure to their warships. Nevertheless, despite the disadvantages of the regime in force, the Russian statesmen preferred to continue the status quo rather than to accept a full opening. Their goal remained, as before, the granting of passage to riverain states only. They could obtain this aim through the two methods employed repeatedly previously. They could press for a bilateral agreement with the Porte, or they could seek to obtain their objective through negotiations with the powers signatory to the treaties. Both paths were once again pursued.

In the negotiations preceding the Russo-British entente of 1907 the question of the Straits occupied a major position. The Russian government pressed hard for an opening for the riverain states exclusively; under no condition did it want the privilege extended to all the powers. The Liberal party, under Lloyd George with Sir Edward Grey as foreign secretary, was now in power. Grey handled the question in a very clever manner, recognizing fully the value of the problem as a bargaining point. Because he could not antagonize the power with whom he wished to make an agreement, he conceded the principle that the Straits agreements should be altered, but he used the excuse of the hostility of British public opinion to argue that the time had not yet come for the change. He also now indulged in a form of polite diplomatic blackmail to influence the Russian government to come to terms on other issues. Russia was informed:

> . . .if the negotiations now in progress between the two Governments with regard to Asiatic questions had a satisfactory result,

4. The agreement is in the form of an exchange of notes. This quotation is from the Austrian statement written by the foreign minister A. von Goluchowski. A. F. Pribram, *The Secret Treaties of Austria-Hungary* (Cambridge, 1920), I, pp. 187, 188.

> the effect upon British public opinion would be such as very much to facilitate a discussion of the Straits question if it came up later on. I have no doubt whatever that, if as a result of the present negotiations, the British and Russian governments remained on good terms in Asia, the effect on British public opinion and on any British Government with regard to other questions, including this, would be very great.[5]

It can thus be seen that the powers were continuing their previous policies of using Ottoman rights and properties as a source of compensation to each other. Meanwhile, within the empire the same problems of national revolt and internal reform remained. After 1890 the chief centers of tension were Macedonia, Armenia, and Crete. In 1897 the Porte waged a victorious war against Greece, but it was largely deprived of the benefits because of great power intervention. It will be noted that in these years the Ottoman government was able to retain control of its remaining Balkan and Asiatic domains. Discontent with the government of Abdülhamid, however, led to the organization of a military conspiracy, which in the summer of 1908 carried through a successful revolt. Although Abdülhamid remained as sultan, it appeared that a new era of reform would be initiated. The Young Turk revolution was particularly welcomed by Britain. It was hoped that the change in the government would open a better era in Turkish affairs and that German influence would be neutralized.

Unfortunately for Britain and for the prestige of the new regime, the Habsburg Monarchy and Russia chose precisely this moment to inaugurate a more active policy in eastern affairs. Both states now had foreign ministers who wished to make positive gains for their governments to aid their own careers. Neglecting to consult their respective allies, A. von Aehrenthal and A. P. Izvolsky met at Buchlau in Moravia in September 1908 and came to an understanding in line with previous Austrian-Russian agreements on the Balkans. Although the two ministers later hotly disputed exactly what had been decided at the meeting, it is clear that Izvolsky accepted an Austrian annexation of Bosnia-Hercegovina in return for a promise of Habsburg support on the Straits issue. After this meeting Izvolsky made other visits and then

5. Memorandum by Sir Edward Grey, F.O., April 27, 1907. *B.D.O.W.*, IV, p. 291.

proceeded to France; there in the first week in October he learned not only that the monarchy had proceeded to announce the annexation, but that Bulgaria had declared its independence. Two governments had thus simultaneously broken the Treaty of Berlin by unilateral denunciations.

With the Austrian action, much the same situation had arisen as in 1870. Once again a great power had freed itself from treaty obligations by a simple declaration. Moreover, as in the case of Russia previously, the Habsburg move was difficult to meet. Austria was in occupation of the two provinces. Without launching an offensive war it would be impossible for the powers to impose upon her a settlement which she would not willingly accept, particularly in view of her strong alliance with Germany. Since the act could not well be undone, again, as in 1870, the powers concentrated on the question of compensation and on the issue of principle – that is, how the changes could be made "legally" and how the consent of the powers signatory to the Treaty of Berlin could best be registered. Once again the Ottoman Empire was the power most damaged by the action. Not only did the Porte lose complete control of the areas in question, but other states now demanded compensation at Ottoman expense. Immediately after the announcement, Serbia, Greece, and Montenegro presented their demands for gains to balance the rival Austrian and Bulgarian advances in power and prestige. Most dangerous for the Ottoman Empire, however, was Izvolsky's attempt to achieve his part of the Buchlau bargain. As in 1870, the Porte found itself again on the defensive on the question of the Straits. The situation was in a sense now reversed; Russia, not Britain, sought a policy inimical to the interests of the empire. In 1870-71 Britain had preferred a settlement which would open the Black Sea to her ships while closing the Mediterranean to those of Russia. Now the Russian government sought access to the Mediterranean, but still declined to allow western fleets to enter the Black Sea.

Immediately after hearing of the annexation, Izvolsky acted to protect his own interests and those of his country. He at once pressed the Russian desire for compensation on the other powers, and he suggested a European conference of the signatories of the Treaty of Berlin to consider the changes which had been made. However, by this time Izvolsky in fact no longer represented the policy favored by the

Russian government. When the foreign minister left for the meeting with Aehrenthal he undoubtedly had the sanction of the tsar, Nicholas II, to pursue a policy of agreement with Austria-Hungary and to exchange recognition of the annexation for support at the Straits. Both these actions were at the expense of the Ottoman Empire. Under the Russian system at the time, the tsar had full control of foreign policy, a right which Nicholas II exercised. Neither P. A. Stolypin, the premier, nor V. N. Kokovtsov, the minister of finance, knew in advance of Izvolsky's intentions. When they learned of the negotiations with Aehrenthal, they strongly disapproved. In opposition to cooperation with the Habsburg Empire, they and others in the government preferred a policy of the formation of a coalition of Balkan states, including Turkey, against the monarchy and a disavowal of the annexation. At this time Nicholas II shifted his position to conform more to this view. This change in policy was communicated to Izvolsky in London.[6]

Although these two lines of policy were in contradiction in regard to the Habsburg Empire, both involved an agreement with the Ottoman Empire and a change in the status of the Straits. Thus as far as Constantinople was concerned the conflict within the Russian government had little significance. Both Izvolsky and N. V. Charykov, who was in charge of the Russian foreign ministry temporarily, spoke in the same terms to the Turkish representatives. It will be noted that at this time the Russian government continued to pursue the same double policy seen before. In the negotiations with the powers it emphasized a European solution – an opening of the Straits under certain limitations, but on the basis of an international understanding. In secret and private conversations with Turkish representatives the Russian diplomats spoke in favor of a return to the relationship of Unkiar Skelessi, which, of course, was quite another matter. Charykov held discussions along this line with Turhan Pasha, the Turkish ambassador in St. Petersburg. On October 6, immediately after the annexation, Izvolsky in a conversation

6. On the Russian position see in particular N. V. Charykov, "Reminiscences of Nicholas II," *Contemporary Review,* CXXXIV (October, 1928), pp. 445-453; N. V. Charykov, *Glimpses of High Politics* (New York, 1931), pp. 268-272; I. V. Bestushev, *Borba v Rossii po voprosam vneshnei politiki, 1906-1910,* (Moscow, 1961), pp. 199-294.

with Naum Pasha, the Ottoman representative in Paris, clearly indicated the Russian position.[7]

In this meeting the Russian minister first told Naum that Russia would insist on a conference to deal with the double infraction of the Treaty of Berlin and to decide on compensation for Russia, the Balkan states, and the Ottoman Empire. Izvolsky emphasized that the Ottoman territories would not be further endangered: "it is understood that neither Serbia nor Montenegro will be allowed to advance their claims on any part whatsoever of Turkish territory." Montenegro would as compensation be released from the restrictions placed on her in favor of Austria-Hungary in Article XXIX of the Treaty of Berlin. Izvolsky then proceeded to present the Russian desires:

> . . .Russia has no territorial appetites and does not covet anything on the Balkan peninsula. She is the sincere friend of Turkey and desires her maintenance and strengthening. Her single interest consists in modifying in an open, purely juridical manner the stipulations concerning the Straits and that in common accord with Turkey and in a manner so as not in any way to endanger the interests of the Ottoman Empire or to put in peril the security of that state.
>
> The present situation as it is confirmed by the Treaty of Berlin constitutes a crying injustice with regard to Russia, who can neither move out of the Black Sea nor enter it.
>
> This situation was recently stressed for us at the time of the war in the Far East, and if it continues, it will make necessary for us excessive expenditures in order to construct and maintain three fleets.
>
> It appears just to us that the riverain states of the Black Sea, Turkey among them, should have a particularly privileged position and the possibility of passing freely through the Straits, while maintaining the principle of closure for non-riverain states. In a word we wish to return to the principles which regulated the relations between Russia and Turkey at the time of the Treaty of Unkiar Skelessi.
>
> It is clear that if the question of the Straits were regulated in this fashion Russia would have the highest interest in the continuation of Turkish domination at Constantinople and at the Straits and she would have no desire either to establish herself

7. Naum Pasha to Tevfik, C535/D77, no. 262, Paris, October 6, 1908. See also Ismail Kemal Bey, *Memoirs,* pp. 327-328.

> there or to see any other power whatsoever come there. This is what you should understand correctly at Constantinople and the best course would be for Turkey to come to a frank understanding with Russia, France, and Britain on the further road to follow in the present grave circumstances.

Izvolsky further stated that among other compensations which the empire could receive would be the gradual abolition of the restrictions imposed by the capitulations and other treaties. In conclusion, he emphasized the friendship of his country for the Ottoman Empire.

Upon receiving this report from Paris, the Turkish foreign minister, Tevfik Pasha, communicated its contents to the German ambassador, Marschall.[8] At the same time the grand vezir, Kâmil Pasha, spoke with the British ambassador, Lowther. He reported on October 8 that Kâmil had told him that it had been learned from both St. Petersburg and Paris that: ". . .Russia was prepared to go to a Conference on condition that the riverain Black Sea States should have exclusive freedom of passage of Dardanelles, in return for which, if obtainable, Russia would abandon the capitulation of the war indemnity, amounting to some 25,000,000 £. . . ."[9]

On October 9 Izvolsky proceeded from Paris to London, where he met with Grey and the Ottoman ambassador, Rifat Pasha. The chief questions discussed were those of the holding of a conference and of the Russian desire for compensation in the Straits question. The British government was in a difficult position not only on the Straits issue, but even on that of a conference. Because of the Russo-British entente, Grey did not wish to antagonize the Russian government; he was also concerned to protect the personal position of Izvolsky, who had supported the British alignment.[10] However, he also did not wish to damage the new Turkish government, particularly in the first period of its rule. It was hoped that this new regime would introduce a satisfactory reform program and adopt a pro-British attitude in foreign

8. Marschall to Foreign Ministry, no. 17 very secret, Therapia, October 8, 1908, *G.P.*, XXVI/1, pp. 118, 119.

9. Lowther to Grey, tel. no. 304 confidential, Therapia, October 8, 1908. *B.D.O.W.*, V, p. 414.

10. Izvolsky told Grey that he must return home with some compensation or he would be forced to resign. Harold Nicolson, *Lord Carnock* (London, 1930), p. 282.

affairs. Moreover, certain sections of the agreement with Russia, particularly those on Persia, were not being carried out smoothly. The Liberal party had to think of its position in future elections; many voters would still react strongly against surrendering on an issue such as the Straits which had been so important in previous years. A middle course had to be found.

When notified officially of the annexation and the Bulgarian declaration of independence, Grey had reacted as could be expected; the British government could not "approve of an open violation of the Treaty of Berlin nor recognize an alteration of it when the other Powers and in this case especially Turkey have not been consulted."[11] At the same time the Ottoman Empire was advised that it should seek a monetary and not a territorial compensation and that a conference might be held.[12] The British government, however, soon showed a lack of enthusiasm for such a gathering. In 1870 Britain had insisted that a conference be held and that there were to be no prior agreements among the participants. In 1908 Grey's position was in fact similar to that of the Porte earlier. He did not want the question of the Straits to arise and he feared that if a congress met it would proceed to the further partition of the Ottoman Empire. He thus wished a strict understanding limiting the topics to be discussed and was willing to forgo such a meeting altogether.[13] This attitude was also favorable to Turkish interests.

The Ottoman government thus did find support in London for its strong position against an alteration of the Straits regulations.[14] When

11. Grey to Goschen, tel. no. 96, F.O., October 5, 1908. *B.D.O.W.*, V, p. 390. When Sir A. Nicolson, the British ambassador in St. Petersburg, saw Charykov, the acting minister of foreign affairs, he was told that Russia too "did not admit one Power could free herself from any Treaty provision without consultation with all other Signatory Powers." Nicolson to Grey, tel. no. 184 confidential, St. Petersburg, October 5, 1908. *B.D.O.W.*, V, pp. 390-391.

12. Grey to Lowther, tel. no. 284, F.O., October 5, 1908. *B.D.O.W.*, V, p. 388; Grey to Lowther, tel. no. 287, F.O., October 6, 1908. *Ibid.*, V, p. 397.

13. Grey to Bertie, tel. no. 156, F.O., October 6, 1908. *B.D.O.W.*, V, p. 396; Grey to Bertie, no. 473, F.O., October 6, *Ibid.*, V. pp. 233-400.

14. On October 12 Grey told Rifat "that while not opposing in principle the opening of the Straits for Russia, we are not satisfied yet that there is any proposal to which we can agree and that in any case we should make agreement to any proposal conditional upon its being voluntarily accepted by Turkey on terms satisfactory to her." Grey to Lowther, tel. no. 339, F.O., October 12, 1908. *B.D.O.W.*, V, p. 425.

Izvolsky spoke with Grey, he found himself blocked in his main purpose, which was to gain British acceptance of a change in the Straits settlement. He now did not ask that the question be discussed at a congress, but he did want the British government to agree not to oppose a Russian attempt to negotiate a bilateral agreement with the Ottoman Empire. He proposed an arrangement by which the Porte would allow ships of war of riverain powers to pass, but not remain in, the Straits. No more than three were to pass at one time and at an interval of twenty four hours. These stipulations were to apply in time of peace. In war the Ottoman Empire was to act as it pleased.[15]

While Izvolsky was speaking in a conciliatory manner with Grey, his words with Rifat were stronger. On October 12 the Turkish ambassador reported that Izvolsky "let me understand in courteous terms that what he asks of us today in a friendly manner Russia can demand by force the day when she feels herself strong enough to do it." Rifat replied that he was not prepared to discuss the question but that "the closure of the Straits was considered by the Ottoman people as the symbol and the security of the capital." It would be very difficult to accept a change, particularly at a time when the Porte was under attack from all sides. At this meeting the Russian minister also brought up a further question: "M. Izvolsky let me understand that his sovereign is ready to conclude an alliance with us in exchange for the opening of the Straits. He insists only that this alliance be held secret." Rifat commented that he did not believe that such an agreement would be made unless Britain were favorable.[16] In a later meeting the same themes were discussed further. Rifat reported:

> M. Izvolsky was not satisfied with my language and showed me a paragraph appearing in a Russian journal, saying that there were only two solutions for the Russians in the affair of the Straits: complete and free possession of the Bosphorus and the Dardanelles or an offensive and defensive alliance between Turkey and Russia.[17]

15. Grey to Nicolson, tel. no. 484, F.O., October 12, 1908. *B.D.O.W.*, V, p. 424; Grey to Nicolson, no. 317, F.O., October 12, 1908. *Ibid.*, V, pp. 429, 430; Grey to Nicolson, no. 318 secret, F.O., October 14, 1908. *Ibid.*, pp. 442-444; Grey to Lowther, no. 434, F.O., October 15, 1908. *Ibid.*, V, pp. 447-448.

16. Rifat to Tevfik, D535/C77, no. 538, London, October 12, 1908.

17. Rifat to Tevfik, D535/C77, no. 552 confidential, London, October 14, 1908.

In St. Petersburg Charykov spoke along the same lines with Turhan,[18] but with some obvious misrepresentations. He told the Ottoman ambassador that the British government did not oppose the Russian desires on the Straits. He said that it had been agreed in London that the matter would be handled between Russia and Turkey.[19] Moreover:

> M. Charykov added next very confidentially that which follows: "your ambassador at London has hinted at the thought expressed from Constantinople that one could add to that technical accord dispositions of a political character."
>
> If in fact, he told me, such is the thought of the government, the Russian government would in no way oppose making it the object of an exchange of views at St. Petersburg, considering that the technical accord in question does establish an important and lasting identity of interest between the two governments.[20]

These approaches were not received with sympathy by the Porte. In their conversations with the British representatives both Rifat and Kâmil were similarly strong in their rejection of a change in the Straits settlement. Rifat told Grey that he "thought the Turks would feel that an alteration in the status of the Straits would lay their country open to a *coup de main*."[21] Kâmil told Lowther that "Turkey could never consent."[22]

18. Tevfik communicated the contents of a telegram from Turhan to Marschall on October 9 stating: "Russland werde von dem Recht der freien Durchfahrt seiner Kriegschiffe durch die Meerengen nur in Spezialfällen und in einer Weise Gebrauch machen, die für die Pforte keinen Anlass zu Besorgnissen gebe. Dagegen sei Russland bereit, der Türkei noch eine weitere wichtige Konzession zu machen, nämlich die Garantie ihres europäischen Besitzstandes. Auch würden mit den Kapitulationen die fremden Postanstalten wegfallen. Endlich verpflichte sich das Petersburger Kabinett, die Pforte in allen politischen Fragen zu unterstützen und zu schützen.

Was Tscharykow heir sagt, hat Iswolsky dem Botschafter in Paris mit einem Wort ausgedrückt: 'Unkiar Iskelessi'. . . ." Marschall to the Foreign Ministry, tel. no. 346 very secret, Therapia, October 9, 1908. *G.P.*, XXVI/1, p. 120.

19. Charykov spoke with Nicolson in much the same sense on October 15. He may have been misled by Izvolsky's reports from London. Nicolson to Grey, no. 457, St. Petersburg, October 16, 1908. *B.D.O.W.*, V, pp. 453-455.

20. Turkhan to Tevfik, D535/C77, no. 471 very confidential, St. Petersburg, October 14, 1908.

21. Grey to Lowther, no. 428, F.O., October 9, 1908. *B.D.O.W.*, V, pp. 418, 419.

22. Lowther to Grey, tel. no. 327, Therapia, October 15, 1908. *B.D.O.W.*, V,

Although Grey would personally have been willing to allow some compensation in this line to Russia, his opinions were opposed by the majority of the British cabinet.[23] As Grey informed Izvolsky, the problem still remained of "the disadvantage it would be to us if in time of war, when Turkey was at peace, one or two cruisers could come out through the Straits and harry British Commerce without our being able to pursue them back into the Black Sea."[24] Izvolsky in a meeting later on the same day proposed that the problem be met by a provision that in time of war "when Turkey was neutral, she should observe her neutrality by giving equal facilities for passage through the Straits to all the belligerents."[25] Such proposals, of course, could not outweigh the fact that most of Grey's colleagues were unwilling to negotiate on the question.

Faced with the problems of accepting the cabinet's decision, saving Russian prestige, and aiding the Young Turk regime, Grey met the situation in a most intelligent manner. Although he did emphasize to Constantinople that a change would have to be made eventually, he insisted that it would depend on "Turkey's willing consent." Britain, moreover, would agree that the Straits be open only under conditions "which would be safe for Turkey, which would leave Turkey perfectly free in time of war to open or close the Straits as she pleased, and which if Turkey was neutral would not place any of the belligerents at a disadvantage."[26] The entire emphasis in the British recommendations was that the whole question be postponed.

The answer to the Russian proposal was contained in a memorandum dated October 14. The British government here agreed "that the

---

p. 447. Kâmil opposed giving Russia and the riverain states special rights: "I cannot but believe that these privileges, given in no matter how restricted a form, would be fatal to Turkey." Lowther to Grey, private letter, October 13, 1908. *B.D.O.W.*, V, pp. 439, 440.

23. Hardinge to Nicolson, private letter, F.O., October 13, 1908. *B.D.O.W.*, V, pp. 434-436.

24. Grey to Nicolson, no. 317, F.O., October 12, 1908. *B.D.O.W.*, V, pp. 429, 430.

25. Grey to Nicolson, no. 324, F.O., October 13, 1908. *B.D.O.W.*, V, pp. 433, 434.

26. Grey to Lowther, no. 434, F.O., October 15, 1908. *B.D.O.W.* V, pp. 447-448; Grey to Lowther, tel. no. 358, F.O., October 16, 1908. *B.D.O.W.*, V, pp. 452-453.

opening of the Straits is fair and reasonable, and in principle they will not oppose it." If the full opening had been proposed, Britain would have agreed, but it could not now accept an "exclusive, though limited, right" for the riverain powers. An arrangement would also have to be made, such as had been proposed by Izvolsky, to deal with questions relating to time of war. In addition, "the consent of Turkey would be a necessary preliminary to any proposal"; no pressure was to be put on Constantinople at this time.[27] Thus once again Britain accepted the principle but not the fact. Indeed if the question were to depend on the free acceptance of the Porte, it was obvious that no change would be made in the status of the Straits for many years to come. The treaty of 1871 thus remained intact.

In 1909 the Ottoman government accepted both the Austrian annexations and the Bulgarian declaration of independence in return for a monetary compensation. After a major crisis over Serbian claims, the other powers also acquiesced in these changes. They were not in a position to go to war over the questions which had been raised by the Habsburg actions; no conference was held. Although the Ottoman Empire was not compelled to accept an alteration in the treaties concerning the Straits, her authority and control in Bosnia, Hercegovina, and Bulgaria had obviously been taken away forever. The monetary compensation was, of course, entirely inadequate in face of the great loss in position and prestige. Although both Britain and Russia now sought to follow a policy of cooperation with Constantinople, neither would obviously offer any material assistance in a time of crisis.

27. Memorandum by Grey, October 14, 1908. *B.D.O.W.*, V, p. 441. Grey explained to Izvolsky that the Porte did not want the question raised at the moment, but that he had told the Ottoman government that some arrangement was necessary for continuing good relations between Turkey and Russia. Grey to Nicolson, no. 319 secret, F.O., October 19, 1908. *B.D.O.W.*, V, p. 356.

APPENDICES

APPENDIX I

Âli to Musurus, December 21, 1870.[1]

La confiance de Notre Auguste Maître Vous investit de la mission importante de représenter son Gouvernement au sein de la Conférence convoquée pour résoudre la question qui vient d'être inopinément soulevée par la Russie.

Nous n'avons pas répondu à la dépêche circulaire du 19 Octobre du Prince Gortchakoff. Nous avons pensé qu'un échange de pièces diplomatiques n'aboutirait à aucun résultat pratique et ne servirait au'à aigrir les esprits. Nous nous sommes donc bornés à faire nos réserves et c'est maintenant devant l'aréopage Européen qui va se réunir à Londres que nous croyons devoir nous expliquer.

Je crois également superflu de commencer par une longue argumentation pour combattre les assertions du Chancelier de Russie en faveur de sa thèse: d'autres plumes plus autorisées et incomparablement plus éloquentes ont déjà rempli cette tâche. D'ailleurs, il n'y a pas de raison humaine qui puisse justifier l'abolition unilatérale d'un acte signé par plusieurs Puissances.

J'entre donc tout de suite en matière:

La neutralisation de la Mer Noire et la limitation des forces navales Russes dans cette mer était une garantie beaucoup trop important à la sécurité de l'Empire pour que la S. Porte ne soit pas profondément affectée de la perdre. Aussi n'estñce pas la forme seule, mais surtout le fond de la démarche du Cabinet de St. Pétersbourg qui nous a surpris et affligés.

La meilleure solution à donner à ce regrettable incident serait à nos yeux le maintien de statu quo. Par ce moyen on aurait restauré et renforcé l'habitude déjà affaiblie du respect des traités, on aurait complètement effacé le mauvais effet produit par la brusque déclaration

1. No. 29158/252, M.N. 20/6.

dont nous nous occupons et on aurait donné au monde entier une garantie réelle de sécurité. Nous voudrions naturellement que cette politique pût prévaloir au sein de la Conférence et fût couronnée d'un succès complet. Mais pour atteindre cet heureux résultat il faudra ou que la Russie se désiste volontiers de sa prétention ou qu'il y ait une coalition prête à lui déclarer une guerre offensive. Chacune de ces deux alternatives nous semble malheureusement et également hérissée de difficultés insurmontables. La Russie ne se décidera jamais à retirer purement et simplement sa résolution: l'humiliation en sera bien autrement sensible que celle dont Elle se dit atteinte par l'existence des clauses restrictives du Traité de Paris; il sera plus que puéril de se livrer à une illusion pareille. Reste la guerre. La Russie assure qu'Elle ne la cherche pas. Il est certain que n'y étant pas encore prête, Elle n'entreprendra pas une guerre offensive. C'est chez Elle qu'il faudra aller la combattre. – Grâce à Dieu et à la nouvelle organisation de notre armée nous espérons pouvoir nous défendre assez sérieusement contre une invasion étrangère. Mais quand il s'agit d'une opération offensive contre un Empire comme la Russie il serait insensé d'y prétendre ou de la provoquer. C'est la coalition de plusieurs Puissances qui peut seule affronter avec chance de succès les immenses difficultés de tout genre dont une expédition en Russie est entourée. Cette coalition pourra-t-elle se former dans l'état où se trouve actuellement toute l'Europe? Supposons au moment qu'Elle puisse se réaliser, quel en sera le résultat pour l'Empire? Pouvons-nous être sûrs d'en sortir sans rien perdre ou moralement ou matériellement? Devons-nous, en conséquence, agir de manière à attiser le feu, c'est-à-dire diriger tous nos efforts à entraîner les Puissances à une politique extrême ou bien sera-t-il plus utile, plus prudent de suivre une ligne de conduite ferme et modérée?

Le Conseil des Ministres a examiné une à une toutes ces questions et après mûre réflexion il a émis l'opinion dont le résumé suit:

Nous ne devons pas pousser à la guerre, parce qu'il est impossible d'en prévoir les conséquences. Il y a des circonstances où un Gouvernement ne doit pas hésiter un seul instant. Mais dans le cas dont il s'agit c'est la modération qui s'impose sous tous les rapports! Nous avons la conviction que nous n'obtiendrons pas le retour à l'ancien ordre de choses. La majorité de nos co-signataires ayant déjà donné son assentiment tacite au fond de la question, ne saurait aller à présent jusqu'à en faire un casus-belli. En outre, l'expérience nous a démontré que des Alliés plus Puissants deviennent des demi protecteurs et sont obligés d'exiger de celui pour lequel ils ont versé leur sang et dépensé leur argent des sacrifices qu'on ne peut leur refuser sans se montrer ingrat. De là, une immixtion plus ou moins déguisée dans les affaires intérieures du pays, immixtion qui finit par amoindrir le prestige de l'autorité légitime et rendre la tâche du gouvernement presque impossible. C'est donc une de ces armes qu'il faut réserver pour des cas extrêmes. Ce qui nous importe le plus maintenant c'est de pouvoir gagner une dizaine d'années de paix et de tranquillité afin de completer nos réseaux de chemin de fer, d'achever l'organisation de nos finances comme celle de nos forces de terre et de mer. Nous devons faire tout notre possible pour atteindre ce but et tâcher d'arranger la question actuelle d'une manière pacifique et moyennent certaines garanties pour l'avenir. Quant aux garanties à demander, elles peuvent être de différentes espèces. Nous pourrions exiger entre autres l'abolition des clauses restrictives du Traité de Paris relativement aux Principautés de Moldo-Valachie et de Servie et la faculté de les contraindre même avec des moyens coërcitifs à rentrer dans les limites des devoirs que les traités leur ont imposés. Quinze années d'épreuve ont suffisammant prouvé que le sentiment d'une impunité assurée a rendu ces pays non seulement un sujet de préoccupation continuelle pour le Gouvt. Impl. et un foyer de toutes sortes de machinations contre la tranquillité intérieure de l'Empire, mais aussi une source inépuisable de difficultés internationales. Ce sont ces mêmes pays qui ont obligé les Puissances Signataires du Traité de 1856 à se réunir à plusieurs reprises pour consacrer les différentes violations qu'il leur a plu de porter au dit traité; ce sont eux, qui, par ces violations ont donné à la Russie une puissante arme dont Elle se sert aujourd'hui. On ne saurait taxer d'exagération ce que je viens de tracer. Il n'y a là que des faits dont il est impossible de nier l'exactitude. Eh bien! est-il juste, est-il sage, est-il équitable de perpétuer un état de choses si préjudiciable et si dangereux et tout cela pour conserver aux pauvres habitants des contrées en question l'anarchie qui est devenue leur état normal?

Nous serions parfaitement fondés à dénoncer, de notre côté, les articles qui interdisent toute action repressive; nous aurions pu proposer d'y substituer des dispositions qui accorderaient à la Turquie le droit d'occuper militairement les Principautés toutes les fois qu'Elles méconnaîtraient les stipulations existantes, qu'Elles permettraient ou qu'Elles toléraient sous quelque prétexte que ce soit la formation des bandes ou des Sociétés dans leur sein contre la sécurité des autres parties de l'Empire. Ce qui nous arrête, c'est la quasi-persuasion où nous sommes de rencontrer une opposition insurmontable de la part de la majorité de nos Alliés et dans ce cas nous aurions rendu la situation encore pire que celle dont nous nous plaignons aujourd'hui. Nous craignons en même temps de compromettre l'existence de tout le traité de Paris dont nous désirons ardemment la conservation. Vous pourriez peut-être pressentir l'opinion de Lord Granville à cet égard, *mais à la seule condition d'imprimer à vos ouvertures le cachet d'une conversation intime et toute personnelle.*

La répudiation des capitulations eût pu être mise en avant si nous n'étions pas également convaincus d'avoir à essuyer ou un refus unanime ou des conditions inadmissibles. Il est bien préférable de rester encore quelque temps sous le régime de ces traités que de subordonner la justice du pays à des restrictions internationales.

Les considérations qui précèdent ont induit le Conseil à chercher les garanties nécessaires dans un sens qui ait une certaine connexion avec l'incident soulevé par la Russie et n'en soit en apparence comme au fond que la conséquence inévitable.

La question des détroits du Bosphore et des Dardanelles s'est présentée tout naturellement. La dernière convention qui confirme la clôture aux bâtiments de guerre étrangers a été conclue en vue de donner à la Russie une garantie en retour de la neutralisation de la Mer Noire et de la limitation de ses forces navales dans cette Mer. Maintenant qu'il s'agit d'abandonner ce système et de rendre à la Russie la plénitude de sa liberté il est incontestable, il est plus que logique que, de son côté, Notre Auguste Souverain recouvre son droit absolu sur les deux portes de Sa capitale. Vous êtes, par conséquent, chargé, Mr. l'Ambr., par S.M.I. de déclarer à la Conférence que la S. Porte, tout en étant décidée à maintenir le principe de la fermeture des deux détroits, principe sanctionné par son ancienne législation, demande à être libérée de toute engagement international y relatif et se réserve le droit de les ouvrir ou de les fermer aux navires de guerre des autres Puissances selon que ses intérêts et sa sécurité l'exigeraient et sans que ce changement puisse autoriser aucun Gouvt. étranger à demander en sa faveur une exception quelconque.

Vous savez l'origine de la Convention en question. C'est le fameux traité de Hunkiar Iskelessi qui en a jeté les bases. Elle a ravi au Sultan une partie de son droit de la Souveraineté territoriale et S.M.I. le revendique aujourd'hui non seulement comme une compensation de ce que l'Empire perd du côté de la Mer Noire, mais aussi comme une garantie contre toute éventualité à venir.

Cette demande amenera peut-être de la part de quelques-unes des Puissances celle de l'ouverture complète des dits détroits à toutes les flottes étrangères. Le Gouvt. de S.M.I. n'admet à aucun prix une telle transaction; vous vous opposerez formellement et catégoriquement si une proposition de cette nature vient à surgir au sein de la Conférence.

V. E. formulera en outre la proposition de confirmer et de consolider les restes des stipulations du traité de Paris et de ses accessoires de manière à interdire à l'avenir à chacune des parties contractantes de les violer ou de les répudier selon ses convenances et sans un accord préalable entre tous les co-signataires. Les dispositions de la Convention du 15 Avril de 1856 peuvent être insérées dans le nouvel acte confirmatif comme une mesure efficace de précaution contre le renouvellement des cas analogues à celui dont nous nous occupons actuellement.

Je ne parle pas d'une autre combinaison qui consisterait à protester officiellement et à laisser les choses à leur cours. C'est le pire de tout ce qu'on peut imaginer de mauvais et de dangereux.

Voilà, Mr. l'Ambr., les vues et les voeux du Gouvt. Impl. Vos talents éprouvés et Votre dévouement aux intérêts de Notre Auguste Maître, sauront, nous en avons la conviction, les faire prévaloir auprès de qui de droit.

APPENDIX II

Musurus to Âli, confidential, London, January 27, 1871.[2]

Conformément aux instructions éventuelles de Votre Altesse sur les démarches personnelles et confidentielles que je pourrais faire auprès de Lord Granville dans le but d'obtenir, s'il est possible, par son concours, quelque chose dans le sens des garanties indiquées dans la Dépêche confidentielle de Votre Altesse du 22 Décembre dernier, No. 29158/252, j'avais fait de sérieux efforts auprès de Sa Seigneurie pour l'engager à s'intéresser à la réalisation de nos voeux à cet égard.

Lord Granville a opposé un refus formel à toutes mes sollicitations, en alléguant toujours qu'il était convenu d'avance entre toutes les Puissances que la Conférence ne s'occuperait que de la question de la Mer Noire; que toute autre question devrait être soigneusement écartée, et que Sir Henry Elliot l'avait assuré que telle était aussi la décision de la Sublime Porte. Mais, comme je revenais toujours à la charge, il a fini par me demander de lui exposer par écrit mes observations verbales sur les infractions commises dans les Principautés et le moyen d'y mettre fin à l'avenir. Aussi ai-je rédigé, et lui ai-je remis l'exposé ci-joint, où j'ai mis en tête un extrait de la Dépêche précitée de Votre Altesse du 22

2. No. 4356/15, M.N. 20/6.

Décembre, afin de prouver à Sa Seigneurie que ce n'était pas de mon chef, comme le faisaient présumer les Rapports de Sir Henry Elliot, que je l'entretenais confidentiellement de cette question, mais que j'agissais par ordre de Votre Altesse.

Ainsi que Votre Altesse l'observara par la lecture de cet exposé, c'est à titre de simple interprétation des stipulations existantes relativement aux Principautés, et non pas à titre d'une modification de ces stipulations, que j'ai demandé à insérer dans le nouveau Traité un article ayant pour objet le maintien de ces stipulations et les mesures à prendre pour en prévenir dorénavant la violation et assurer le repos ultérieur de ces provinces.

Lord Granville, après l'avoir étudié, et tout en me faisant des compliments sur ce travail, m'a déclaré que ses collègues, qu'il avait consultés, tous les Plénipotentiaires des autres Puissances et lui-même personnellement, s'opposaient à ce que la proposition que je suggérais fût portée devant la Conférence.

Me conformant aux instructions de Votre Altesse, j'ai renoncé à insister davantage; mais je n'ai pas manqué de dire à Lord Granville que mon exposé développait d'une manière raisonnée l'interprétation que la Sublime Porte donnait aux stipulations existantes relativement aux Principautés, et qu'Elle était résolue de maintenir à l'avenir.

Veuillez agréer, Altesse, les assurances de ma très haute considération.

[Enclosure:] Personnelle et Confidentielle

"Quant aux garanties à demander en compensation de la perte importante qui résulterait pour nous de l'annulation des stipulations relatives à la neutralisation de la Mer Noire elles peuvent être de différentes espèces. Nous pourrions exiger, entre autres, l'abolition des clauses restrictives du Traité de Paris relativement aux Principautés de Moldo-Valachie et de Servie, et la faculté de les contraindre même par des moyens coercitifs à rentrer dans les limites des devoirs que les traités leur ont imposés. Quinze années d'expérience ont suffisamment prouvé que le sentiment d'une impunité assurée a rendu ce pays non seulement un sujet de préoccupation continuelle pour le Gouvernement Impérial et un foyer de toutes sortes de machinations contre la tranquillité intérieure de l'Empire, mais aussi une source inépuisable de difficultés internationales. Ce sont ces mêmes pays qui ont obligé les Puissances signataires du Traité de 1856 à se réunir à plusieurs reprises pour consacrer les différentes violations qu'il leur a plu de faire au dit traité; ce sont eux qui, par ces violations, ont donné à la Russie une arme puissante dont elle se sert aujourd'hui. On ne saurait taxer d'exagération ce que je viens de tracer. Il n'y a là que des faits dont il est impossible de nier l'exactitude. Eh bien! est-il juste, est-il sage, est-il équitable de perpétuer un état de choses si préjudiciable et si dangereux, et tout cela pour conserver aux pauvres habitants des contrées en question l'anarchie qui est devenue leur état normal? "

Les observations qui précèdent sont extraites textuellement des instructions confidentielles que j'ai reçues de Son Altesse le Grand Vizir.

Cependant, ce que je demande, ce n'est ni une modification aux stipulations du Traité de Paris, ni l'introduction d'une nouvelle stipulation; c'est une simple interprétation des stipulations existantes, interprétation dont l'absence a favorisé jusqu'ici les déplorables infractions effectuées en Moldo-Valachie, tandis que la légitimation de ces infractions par les Conférences a pour effet d'en encourager de nouvelles.

Je m'explique. Le Traité de Paris a passé sous silence le cas où les Principautés violeraient les stipulations qui les concernent; il n'a pas non plus indiqué les moyens de faire cesser ces violations. Mais ce silence même prouve à l'évidence que c'est à la Puissance Suzeraine qu'il appartient de veiller à l'application fidèle de ces stipulations dans les Principautés et de faire cesser toute infraction qui y serait commise. En effet, par l'Art. XXIII de ce Traité, la Sublime Porte s'engage à conserver aux Principautés leur administration indépendante et nationale, ainsi que la pleine liberté de culte, de législation, de commerce et de navigation. Tous ces privilèges, toutes ces prérogatives de l'autonomie des Principautés ont été déterminés par la Convention de 1858 qui règle d'une manière complète et détaillée leur organisation administrative. Or, comment la Sublime Porte pourrait-elle remplir l'engagement qu'elle a pris par l'Article précité, si on lui contestait le droit et le devoir de maintenir et de faire respecter les stipulations découlant dudit Traité? Il y a plus. Aux termes de l'Art. XXV du même Traité, toutes les stipulations de la Convention de 1858 et des stipulations subséquentes résultant d'un accord entre la Puissance Suzeraine et les Puissances Garantes ont été promulguées dans les Principautés par Hatti-Chérif ou Ordonnance autographe de Sa Majesté Impériale le Sultan. Dès lors, n'est-il pas évident que la Puissance Suzeraine a le droit et le devoir de maintenir et de faire respecter les dispositions de ses Hatti-Chérifs et de ses Firmans? Autrement pourquoi les promulguerait-elle? Serait-ce pour voir son Autorité méconnue et sa dignité compromise? Le droit des Puissances garantes est de veiller à ce que la Sublime Porte n'enfreigne pas elle-même les stipulations relatives aux Principautés; mais le droit de veiller à ce que ces stipulations ne soient pas violées par les Principautés appartient à la Puissance Suzeraine, qui, d'un autre côté, ne saurait y apporter des modifications sans un accord préalable avec les Puissances garantes.

On pourrait assimiler la Puissance Suzeraine qui promulgue un Hatti-Chérif contenant des dispositions arrêtées avec le concours des Puissances garantes, au pouvoir exécutif qui promulgue des lois à la confection desquelles ont participé les grands Corps de l'Etat.

On ne saurait soutenir une interprétation contraire sans être réduit à l'absurde. En effet, supposer que les Grandes Puissances, des gouvernements sérieux ont entrepris la tâche laborieuse de régler par des stipulations internationales l'organisation définitive des Principautés sans s'attendre à voir ces stipulations maintenues et respectées, prétendre que, toutes les fois qu'il se serait produit dans les Principautés une infraction à ces stipulations, la Puissance Suzeraine serait tenue de la soumettre à l'examen d'une Conférence destinée, comme l'expérience l'a constamment démontré, a légitimer l'infraction et à sanctionner les faits accomplis, ce serait révoquer en doute leur sagesse, leur prévoyance, leur sollicitude pour les Principautés elles-mêmes qui, par un tel systême, seraient exposées à l'anarchie et à la guerre civile; ce serait leur attribuer des intentions qu'on ne saurait concilier avec la loyauté qui les caractérise.

Une conséquence naturelle de la seule interprétation qu'on puisse donner au silence du Traité de Paris à l'endroit des violations commises dans les Principautés, c'est que si la cessation d'une telle violation nécessite l'emploi de moyens coercitifs, cette tâche incombera à la Puissance Suzeraine. Tout ce que les Puissances garantes pourraient réclamer dans une pareille éventualité, serait, en cas qu'elles voulussent par précaution s'assurer que la Puissance Suzeraine ne saisirait pas cette occasion pour attenter à l'autonomie des Principautés, d'adjoindre chacune un Délégué au Commissaire Impérial qui accompagnerait le Chef Militaire chargé de la mission de remettre en vigueur la stipulation violée. D'ailleurs, les deux Puissances limitrophes les plus directement intéressées au maintien de la légalité dans les Principautés ont reconnu ce droit de coercition de la Puissance Suzeraine. Dans la séance du 13 Avril 1859 des Conférences de Paris, le Plénipotentiaire d'Autriche adhéra aux observations par lesquelles le Plénipotentiaire de Turquie avait alors proposé ce mode d'action pour faire cesser l'infraction résultant de la double élection du Colonel Couza. Il est vrai que la Russie ne se déclara pas du même avis à cette occasion-là; mais elle était tout à fait d'accord sur ce point avec la Sublime Porte lors des Conférences tenues à Paris en 1866 à la suite d'une nouvelle infraction.

Du reste, par sa Circulaire, le Prince Gortschakoff constate cette identité de vues, quand il rappelle le langage que le Représentant de Russie a tenu dans ces Conférences; et l'on ne saurait supposer que cette Puissance ait changé d'avis, aujourd'hui qu'elle reproche aux Puissances garantes des tolérances en contradiction avec les stipulations explicites du Traité, et qu'elle soutient le principe de la dignité des Gouvernements.

Comme déduction des observations qui précèdent, je propose d'insérer dans le nouveau Traité, à titre d'interprétation, un article dont le premier paragraphe serait ainsi concu:

> "Les hautes parties contractantes reconnaissent à la Puissance Suzeraine le droit et le devoir de veiller au maintien des stipulations du Traité de 1856 et des stipulations subséquentes, relatives aux Principautés de Moldavie et de Valachie, ainsi qu'à la Principauté de Serbie, et de faire cesser toute infraction qui se commettrait à l'avenir dans lesdites Principautés. Si, pour faire cesser l'infraction, la Puissance Suzeraine se trouve dans le cas d'avoir recours à l'emploi de moyens coercitifs, les Puissances garantes pourront adjoindre chacune un Délégué au Commissaire Impérial qui accompagnera le Chef Militaire chargé, sous la direction dudit Commissaire, de remettre en vigueur la stipulation violée."

L'Art. XXVIII du Traité de Paris, en prévoyant le cas où le repos intérieur des Principautés se trouverait menacé ou compromis, porte qu'une intervention armée ne pourra avoir lieu sans un accord préalable entre la Sublime Porte et les autres Puissances contractantes. La Sublime Porte veut bien continuer à se soumettre à la restriction qui subordonne à un accord préalable avec les Puissances garantes l'exercice du droit d'intervenir militairement pour rétablir l'ordre s'il venait à être troublé dans les Principautés. Mais la lettre de cet Article ne dit pas que c'est à la Puissance Suzeraine qu'appartient exclusivement le droit de l'intervention armée; et la Sublime Porte désire qu'il soit suppléé du moins à une omission qui est de nature à encourager l'audace des fauteurs de troubles. En effet, inférant à tort de cette omission que la Puissance Suzeraine ne peut pas seule intervenir militairement, et sachant qu'une intervention armée collective des Puissances est impossible, les ennemis de l'ordre se croient libres de se livrer impunément à toute tentative et à toute menée subversives. Personne ne saurait contester à la Puissance Suzeraine l'exercice exclusif de ce droit. Par l'Art. XXVI du même Traité, les Puissances ont reconnu à la Sublime Porte le droit de s'entendre directement avec les Principautés, sans entrave ni immixtion des Puissances garantes, sur les mesures extraordinaires de défense à prendre pour repousser une aggression étrangère. Or, les Puissances, en reconnaissant que la Sublime Porte a seule le droit d'envoyer une armée dans les Principautés pour la défense de leur territoire en cas d'agression extérieure, admettent implicitement qu'elle a également seule le droit d'intervenir militairement sans une entente préalable avec les Puissances garantes, pour le rétablissement de l'ordre s'il venait à être troublé. D'ailleurs, ce n'est que la Russie qui pourrait désirer se charger d'une intervention armée dans les Principautés ou y participer; et il n'y a pas de raison pour que les autres Puissances, qui, par leur position géographique, sont dans l'impossibilité de prendre part à une telle intervention, hésitent aujourd'hui à suppléer à une omission qui pourrait, le cas échéant, être mal interprétée par la Russie, et occasionner de graves complications. Quant à la Sublime Porte, pour donner une preuve de ses intentions loyales, elle admet qu'en cas d'une intervention armée faite à la suite d'une entente préalable pour le rétablissement de l'ordre s'il venait à être troublé, les Puissances garantes pussent adjoindre chacune un Délégué au Commissaire Impérial qui accompagnerait le Commandant de la force armée.

Je propose donc d'ajouter à l'article à insérer à titre d'interprétation, dans le Nouveau Traité, un second paragraphe ainsi conçu:

> "De même, si, le repos intérieur de ces Principautés venant à être menacé ou compromis, la Puissance Suzeraine, d'accord avec les Puissances garantes, reconnaît la nécessité d'une intervention armée, la Sublime Porte se chargera exclusivement de cette intervention avec l'assistance des Délégués des autres Puissances contractantes."

APPENDIX III

Beust to Prokesch-Osten, Vienna, March 24, 1871.[3]

Au moment où la Conférence de Londres vient de terminer son oeuvre, nous éprouvons le besoin de reporter nos regards sur l'ensemble des faits qui ont marqué cette page de l'histoire diplomatique, et de faire part à la Sublime Porte de quelques réflexions que ce coup d'oeil rétrospectif nous suggère.

La réunion de la Conférence a été virtuellement, sinon officiellement

3. Enclosure in no. 29952/97, M.N. 20/6.

motivée par la circulaire du Cabinet de St. Pétersbourg tendant à déclarer la Russie déliée des obligations que lui avait imposées le traité de Paris relativement à la Mer Noire. La Puissance qui se trouvait atteinte en première ligne par cette déclaration était la Turquie. La clause qui neutralisait l'Euxin avait pour objet principal de constituer à l'Empire Ottoman une situation assurée, en le prémunissant contre le retour de ces entreprises de son redoutable voisin qui avaient donné naissance à la guerre de Crimée. D'autre part, la démarche brusque du Cabinet russe et les formes impérieuses qu'elle revêtait, étaient faites pour semer tout particulièrement l'agitation parmi les sujets chrétiens du Sultan, et ce n'est que d'une manière indirecte, et pour ainsi dire par ricochet, que les effets de cet acte pouvaient s'étendre à nos populations.

Quant à l'Empire austro-hongrois, son attention, par une suite naturelle de sa position, se portait davantage à l'époque dont je parle, sur la lutte engagée dans l'Ouest de l'Europe. C'est en cela que son attitude différait de celle de la Porte, plus exposée à subir le contrecoup de l'intimation russe.

Néanmoins, les préoccupations qu'excitaient en nous les événements de la guerre ne nous empêchèrent point de prendre une attitude très ferme et très accentuée en face de la démarche du Cabinet de St. Pétersbourg. Nous sommes même allés, Votre Excellence le sait, jusqu'à provoquer l'application du traité trilatéral du 15 avril 1856, nous déclarant prêts à remplir les engagements qu'il nous imposait vis-à-vis de la Turquie. Toutes les instructions qui Vous sont parvenues depuis attestaient invariablement notre désir empressé de prêter notre appui moral et matériel au Gouvernement du Sultan pour peu qu'il eût voulu lui-même pourvoir à sa sûreté. C'est dans le même esprit amical que nous lui avons successivement proposé plusieurs combinaisons qui nous paraissaient de nature à remplacer utilement le régime de neutralisation de la Mer Noire, destiné à disparaître, régime dont, je n'en disconviens pas, nous avions nous-mêmes, quelques années auparavant suggéré l'abrogation légale, parce qu'il nous semblait contraire aux lois naturelles et d'un avantage pratique assez douteux. Que l'arrangement adopté maintenant par la Conférence, pour servir de compensation à la garantie supprimée, laisse fort à désirer, nous ne l'ignorons pas; mais ce n'est pas sur nous que peut en retomber la faute. La Porte a préféré se placer sur le terrain d'une indépendance absolue et se priver de l'assistance de l'Europe durant les dernières négociations; c'était son droit et nous n'avons pu ni voulu nous y opposer pour notre part. Seulement, nous ne saurions nous dissimuler qu'il va en résulter pour nous un double inconvénient: d'abord, la Russie pourra y puiser un sentiment d'aigreur à notre égard, provenant de ce que nous nous sommes montrés moins coulants pour elle que ne l'a fait le Gouvt. Ottoman; puis, l'issue de la Conférence entraînera nécessairement pour la position de la Sublime Porte une modification sensible et dont, à notre tour, nous ne pourrons manquer de nous ressentir dans une certaine mesure.

Dans une autre de mes dépêches de ce jour, j'ai fait ressortir comme quoi, en ce qui touche la question du Danube, la Porte, au lieu de nous venir en aide, a fait opposition à nos vues. L'harmonie qui, à ce propos, s'est révélée entre la Cour suzeraine et la Régence serbe a lieu de nous surprendre. Nous nous expliquons, jusqu'à un certain point, les répugnances que la correction du Bas Danube rencontre auprès du Gouvernement de Belgrade; elles sont dues surtout à ce que l'on assure, à la crainte de voir le pays mis à la merci des forces navales de la Turquie. Mais cette considération ne peut avoir fait agir la Sublime Porte et nous renonçons à démêler les motifs de sa résistance.

Nous sommes obligés de constater les faits que je viens de retracer, non que nous ayons l'intention d'empiéter sur l'indépendance du Gouvt. du Sultan, ni la prétention de lui faire modifier sa politique. Mais force nous est bien d'accepter les conséquences d'une situation que nous n'avons point contribué à créer. Que l'on veuille bien, à Constantinople, ne point taxer notre marche d'hésitation, lorsqu'elle ne fera que se conformer à la logique des faits. Au moment où le Gouvt. Ottoman cherche à se faire bien venir de la Russie, il ne saurait exiger que nous nous montrions nous-mêmes démesurément revêches de ce côté-là. Demander tout à la fois que les populations slaves soient animées de sentiments de confiance à l'égard de la Russie, qu'elles tournent des regards d'esperance vers Constantinople, et qu'en même temps elles n'éprouvent pour nous que de la méfiance, c'est ce qui n'est réellement pas admissible. Moins que jamais il nous sera permis désormais de tenir compte d'insinuations telles qu'on nous a fait entendre maintes fois, lorsqu'on nous dénonçait certaines complaisances attribuées aux autorités de la Dalmatie pour les aspirations slaves. Il est loin de notre pensée de favoriser des projets ou des menées dirigées contre l'Empire Ottoman, et la Porte aurait grand tort de se laisser égarer par des suggestions qui tendraient à nous en accuser; mais, d'un autre côté, nous croyons accomplir un devoir en la mettant en garde contre des illusions du genre de celles que je viens d'indiquer.

Votre Excellence voudra bien donner confidentiellement lecture de la présente dépêche à son Altesse le Grand Visir et recevoir l'assurance. . . .

APPENDIX IV

Âli to Halil, Constantinople, April 19, 1871, confidential.[4]

Mr le Baron de Prokesch vient de me faire la communication confidentielle d'une dépêche de S. E. le Chancelier d'Autriche-Hongrie contenant les appréciations du Gouvt. Impl. et Royal sur les résultats de la dernière Conférence de Londres et sur l'attitude observée par la S. Porte dans les négociations du nouveau Traité dont la signature a clôturé la dite Conférence.

Cette revue rétrospective des circonstances qui ont précédé et suivi la réunion des Conférences, nous attribue un rôle qu'il nous est impossible d'accepter sans nous assumer la tâche d'une noire ingratitude et le crime d'une insouciance complète de nos propres interêts.

Aussi, ai-je cru devoir entrer de mon côté dans quelques détails pour éclaircir certains points auxquels la dépêche de Mr le Comte de Beust fait allusion et pour expliquer franchement tout le mobile de notre politique dans l'importante question de la Mer Noire.

Au moment où la circulaire du Pce. Gortchakoff est venue notifier aux Puissances la résolution de l'Empereur Alexandre de se délier de ses engagements concernant la neutralisation du Pont Euxin, le Gouvt. du Sultan s'est posé les questions suivantes:

1° S'il fallait en faire un Casus-Belli;

2° S'il valait mieux de ne pas pousser les choses jusqu'à cette extrémité et de se borner à demander la retraite de cet acte arbitraire par des protestations énergiques ou bien s'il n'était pas plus avantageux d'agir avec modération afin de ne pas tomber à la fin dans de cruelles déceptions.

Nous nous sommes arrêtés à cette derniére alternative; en voici les causes:

La situation d'alors de l'Europe nous avait suffisamment convaincus de l'impossibilité d'une guerre offensive contre la Russie, je dis offensive, parce que le Gouvt. Russe n'aurait assurément pas manqué de nous laisser cet honneur et aurait continué à construire ses vaissaux blindés dans ses ports de la Mer Noire en nous defiant d'y aller l'en empêcher. Il eût été insensé de notre part d'entreprendre à nous seuls une guerre de cette espèce. Aurions-nous trouvé des auxiliaires résolues? Non. Deux des Puissances Contractantes du Traité de Paris étaient engagées, en ce moment-là, dans une lutte gigantesque et toute l'attention des autres était naturellement absorbée par les immenses

4. No. 29952/97, M.N. 20/6.

soucis que ce terrible duel à mort leur donnait. C'était la situation matérielle de l'Europe. Quant à la situation morale, nous savions d'avance que la plupart des Signataires du dit Traité s'étaient déjà prononcés en faveur de l'abolition des clauses contre lesquelles la Russie s'élevait. L'opposition de ces Puissances ne pouvait donc se porter que sur la forme unilatérale que le Cabinet de St. Petersbourg avait cru pouvoir donner à sa résolution. Il est évident qu'on n'aurait pas trouvé dans une question de forme des motifs suffisants pour une grande guerre au milieu des circonstances dont je viens de parler. Nous sommes, cependant, très reconnaissants à l'Autriche-Hongrie de s'être déclarée prête à l'application du Traité trilatéral du 15 Avril 1856. N'étant pas cosignataire de ce Traité la S. Porte ne pouvait qu'en souhaiter la mise à exécution par les hautes parties contractantes dont l'une complètement paralysée et l'autre nous faisait observer, toutes les fois que nous lui en parlions, que cet acte garantissait uniquement l'intégrité territoriale de l'Empire et la démarche actuelle de la Russie n'y touchait pas et n'autorisait, en conséquence, aucun recours aux stipulations qu'il contient.

Je prends la liberté de demander au Comte de Beust si ce qui précède n'est pas la reproduction exacte de la situation générale au moment où le Pce. Bismarck a proposé et fait accepter par tous les Cabinets la réunion d'une Conférence à Londres.

Mais avant d'entrer dans les détails des négociations, je désire compléter l'exposé des causes générales qui ont, comme je le dis plus haut, déterminé toute notre attitude dans cette question. La persuasion de l'impossibilité de la guerre nous à conduit à celle de l'imminence d'un arrangement dans le sens des désirs de la Russie. Nous avons cru et tout le monde partageait notre croyance que les notes diplomatiques les plus énergiques, les protestations les mieux motivées n'auraient pu décider le Gouvt. Russe à retirer sa résolution tant qu'elles n'étaient pas appuyées par la certitude d'une coalition sérieuse des Puissances Signataires du Traité de Paris. Ces' notes et ces protestations n'auraient servi, à notre avis, qu'à envenimer les choses et à rendre au Gouvt. la tâche de souscrire à la fin au même résultat, qu'on avait commencé par combattre beaucoup plus désagréable. En conséquence, nous n'avons pas répondu à la première communication Russe par une protestation violente; nous nous sommes bornés à faire des réserves. L'espérance de maintenir l'état de choses qui venait d'être dénoncé si brusquement par le Gouvt. Russe nous a donc paru chimérique et nous nous sommes vus dans la nécessité de chercher d'autres garanties pratiques. V.E. possède en copie les instructions adressées à Musurus Pacha où je passe en revue les garanties que nous serions en droit de demander si nous n'étions pas sûrs de rencontrer de la part de la majorité des Puissances une opposition invincible. La manière dont la simple énonciation confidentielle de quelques-unes d'Elles a été reçue a pleinement confirmé notre prévision. Les conversations intimes que notre Plénipotentiaire a cru devoir entamer sur ce sujet avec certains de ses Collègues a suffi pour attirer sur nous des soupçons d'arrières-pensées que nous n'avions jamais eues et pour nous démontrer une fois de plus l'impossibilité d'arriver à un accord.

C'est ainsi que nous avons dû nous contenter de la nouvelle consacration du Traité de Paris avec les additions relatives aux détroits des Dardanelles et du Bosphore. Les vraies garanties auxquelles nous avions le droit d'aspirer, nous ayant été refusées par tout le monde, il serait injuste de venir nous taxer de faiblesse là où nous sommes restés completement isolés. Il y a des cas où ni l'isolement, ni aucune autre considération ne doivent arrêter les Gouvts. de se défendre par tous les moyens avec la résolution de vaincre ou de mourir. Dans de telles occurrences la S. Porte ne manquerait pas à son devoir. Mais, entre la défense de son intégrité et de son indépendance et la provocation d'une guerre offensive avec la perspective d'aboutir à des conditions encore plus dures il y a une très grande différence; différence qu'il était également du devoir des Conseillers de S.M. le Sultan de bien peser avant de pousser leur pays vers une aventure semblable dans le but de conserver un régime que Mr. le Comte de Beust qualifia *de contraire aux lois naturelles et d'un avantage pratique assez douteux.*

Certes, nous nous sommes rendus à la Conférence rempli du désir très sincère d'y agir de concert avec les Augustes Alliés de Notre Auguste Souverain. Nous n'avons jamais cessé d'attacher une importance très grande à leurs conseils et à leur bienveillance; nous n'avons pas voulu et nous ne pouvions pas vouloir nous *priver de l'assistance de l'Europe* par un excès d'amour-propre mal placé. Mais d'un autre côté les vrais amis de l'Empire Ottoman parmi lesquels nous sommes heureux de compter l'eminent Chancelier de l'Autriche-Hongrie nous auraient reproché bien plus justement si nous n'entrions à cette réunion que comme simples auditeurs n'ayant ni opinion ni souci de l'indépendance, et des intérêts de notre pays et seulement pour apposer notre signature au bas des documents que d'autres auraient confectionnés. Non, ce rôle, nous ne pouvions pas le jouer sans manquer à nos devoirs et sans perdre à jamais l'estime des Gouvts. Si nous avons été dans le cas de décliner durant les négociations quelques-unes des propositions, ce n'est nullement pour satisfaire une absurde vanité ou par suite d'injustes sentiments de méfiance à l'endroit des Puissances proposantes, mais c'est par des motifs très sérieux et dans la conviction profonde qu'on ne prendrait pas en mauvaise part les observations que la connaissance particulière des affaires de notre pays, de ses intérêts et de ses besoins nous obligeait de soumettre à leur appréciation amicale. Quoique toutes ces observations aient été développées à mesure que les cas se sont présentés, je crois cependant utile d'y revenir encore une fois afin de dissiper tous les doutes.

Les propositions principales émanées du Cabinet Impl. et Royal auxquelles nous n'avons pas pu nous associer sont les suivantes:

1° l'érection d'un Arsenal maritime international dans un des ports Ottomans de la Mer Noire;

2° l'augmentation illimitée des stationnaires étrangers dans les bouches du Danube; et 3° la première rédaction de l'article concernant les travaux à entreprendre aux portes de fer.

Les raisons qui nous ont empêchés d'entrer dans les vues de l'Autriche-Hongrie sont tellement justes et claires qu'il suffira de les rappeler à l'esprit éclairé de l'homme d'état auquel j'essaye de répondre pour que les nuages qui ont pu couvrir un instant à ses yeux la vraie situation se dissipent.

La création d'un port militaire international pouvait-elle être envisagée comme une garantie réelle contre les empiétements probables de la Russie? Selon notre opinion, non. Ce système eût occasionné dans son application des dangers et des conflits innombrables. Peu à peu cette partie des possessions de S.M.I. eût été convertie en domaine international d'où l'autorité de Notre Souverain aurait naturellement disparue et le principe de la clôture des détroits, principe que nous considérons comme une mesure importante de sûreté n'aurait plus eu de raison d'être. Ces inconvénients et tant d'autres que nous aurions ainsi accepté étaient-ils, au moins, capables de procurer quelque avantage moral ou matériel? Ici aussi nous répondons négativement. La Russie eût trouvé dans cette mesure un acte de méfiance à son égard et aurait redoublé d'efforts pour avoir une force navale bien plus considérable que celle que les Puissances auraient assumé les dépenses d'entretenir dans la Mer Noire. Quant au plan d'une augmentation illimitée des stationnaires aux bouches du Danube V. E. doit se rappeler des motifs puissants qui nous l'ont fait décliner. Nous espérions d'en avoir amplement prouvé l'inefficacité absolue.

Venons maintenant à la question des portes de fer et de l'appui qu'on nous accuse d'avoir donné aux Serbes contrairement à nos intérêts. J'avoue franchement mon inaptitude de bien saisir la signification de ce reproche. Avons-nous jamais prononcé un mot qui ait pu faire supposer que la S. Porte avait une opinion contraire à l'accomplissement de cette oeuvre? Nos observations ne se sont portées que sur la rédaction de l'Article y relatif.

Aurions-nous mieux fait de ne pas tenir aucun compte en ce qu'il pouvait avoir de légitime dans les réclamations du Gouvt. Servien et de le laisser chercher ailleurs la protection qu'il n'aurait pas trouvée auprès de nous? Le dernier Traité n'a-t-il pas, du reste, consacré le principe que l'Autriche-Hongrie voulait faire adopter? La S. Porte a-t-elle fait la moindre opposition à l'adoption de ce principe?

Nous avons eu d'autant plus de raison de protéger les Serviens dans ceux de leurs intérêts qui ne touchaient pas au fond de l'affaire que nous savions pertinemment qu'on cherchait à persuader les trois Principautés Danubiennes que la S. Porte seule mettait des obstacles à la réunion de la Commission Riveraine pour éviter l'admission de leurs délégués. Cette question ayant été donc résolue quant au fond selon les désirs du Gouvt. Impl. et Royal Apos., je confesse encore une fois l'insuffisance de mon esprit pour saisir la nuance qui a pu décider Mr le Comte Beust à blâmer notre conduite.

Les explications qui précèdent me semblent établir très clairement que nous n'avons pas *cherché à nous faire bienvenir de la Russie.* Si le Cabinet de St. Pétersbourg montre depuis quelque temps des dispositions amicales à notre égard ce n'est nullement par suite d'une entente ou alliance secrète dont il a plu à quelques nouvellistes de parler. Je pense que ni Mr le Chancelier d'Autriche-Hongrie, ni personne ne nous conseillerait de répondre par des impolitesses aux politesses que nous recevons. Il est certainement de l'intérêt de la paix de ne pas nous mettre systématiquement et sans nécessité mal avec un puissant voisin. Mais cela ne saurait supposer des deux côtés un revirement complet de politique.

Chacun garde ses traditions, et sa liberté.

Si donc le résultat de la Conférence n'a pas été aussi satisfaisant qu'on l'aurait désiré, si la Russie est parvenue à détruire la garantie que la neutralisation de la Mer Noire offrait, il faut en accuser la situation générale et non pas la conduite de tel ou tel Gouvt.

Nous serions au désespoir si le Gouvt. d'Autriche-Hongrie concevait le moindre soupçon sur la réalité de notre désir d'être toujours en bon et intime rapport avec lui. Les intérêts des deux Empires sont identiques et l'ennemi de l'un ne peut pas être l'ami de l'autre.

Veuillez donner lecture *confidentielle* de cette dépêche à S.E. Mr. le Comte de Beust et agréer la nouvelle assurance etc. etc.

APPENDIX V

The Treaty of London[5]

Art. I. Les Articles XI, XIII, et XIV du Traité de Paris du 30 Mars, 1856, ainsi que la Convention spéciale conclue entre la Sublime Porte et la Russie, et annexée au dit Article XIV, sont abrogés et remplacés par l'Article suivant.

II. Le principe de la clôture des Détroits des Dardanelles et du Bosphore, tel qu'il a été établi par la Convention séparée du 30 Mars, 1856, est maintenu, avec la faculté pour Sa Majesté Impériale le Sultan d'ouvrir les dits Détroits en temps de paix aux bâtiments de guerre des Puissances amies et alliées, dans le cas où la Sublime Porte le jugerait nécessaire pour sauvegarder l'exécution des stipulations du Traité de Paris du 30 Mars, 1856.

III. La Mer Noire reste ouverte, comme par le passé, à la marine marchande de toute les nations.

IV. La Commission établie par l'Article XVI du Traité de Paris, dans laquelle les Puissances co-signataires du Traité sont chacune représentées par un Délégué, et qui a été chargée de désigner et de faire exécuter les travaux nécessaires depuis Isaktcha, pour dégager les embouchures du Danube, ainsi que les parties de la Mer Noire y avoisinantes des sables et autres obstacles qui les obstruent, afin de mettre cette partie du fleuve et les dites parties de la Mer dans les meilleures conditions de navigabilité, est maintenue dans sa composition actuelle. La durée de cette Commission est fixée pour une période ultérieure de 12 ans, à compter du 24 Avril, 1871, c'est à dire jusqu'au 24 Avril, 1883, terme de l'amortissement de l'emprunt contracté par cette Commission sous la garantie de la Grande Bretagne, de l'Allemagne, de l'Autriche-Hongrie, de la France, de l'Italie, et de la Turquie.

V. Les conditions de la réunion nouvelle de la Commission Riveraine, établie par l'Article XVII du Traité de Paris du 30 Mars, 1856, seront fixées par une entente préalable entre les Puissances Riveraines, sans préjudice de la clause relative aux 3 Principautés Danubiennes; et en tant qu'il s'agirait d'une modification de l'Article XVII du dit Traité, cette dernière fera l'objet d'une Convention Spéciale entre les Puissances co-signataires.

VI. Les Puissances Riveraines de la partie du Danube où les Cataractes et les Portes de Fer mettent des obstacles à la navigation, se

5. Great Britain. Foreign Office. *British and Foreign State Papers* (London, 1877), LXI, pp. 9, 10.

réservant de s'entendre entr'elles à l'effet de faire disparaître ces obstacles, les Hautes Parties Contractantes leur reconnaissent dès à présent le droit de percevoir une taxe provisoire sur les navires de commerce sous tout pavillon qui en profiteront désormais, jusqu'à l'extinction de la dette contractée pour l'exécution des travaux; et elles déclarent l'Article XV du Traité de Paris de 1856 inapplicable à cette partie du fleuve pour un laps de temps nécessaire au remboursement de la dette en question.

VII. Tous les ouvrages et établissements de toute nature créés par la Commission Européenne en exécution du Traité de Paris de 1856, ou du présent Traité, continueront à jouir de la même neutralité qui les a protégés jusqu'ici, et qui sera également respectée à l'avenir dans toutes les circonstances par les Hautes Parties Contractantes. Le bénéfice des immunités qui en dérivent s'étendra à tout le personnel administratif et technique de la Commission. Il est, cependant, bien entendu que les dispositions de cet Article n'affecteront en rien le droit de la Sublime Porte de faire entrer, comme de tout temps, ses bâtiments de guerre dans le Danube, en sa qualité de Puissance territoriale.

VIII. Les Hautes Parties Contractantes renouvellent et confirment toutes les stipulations du Traité du 30 Mars, 1856, ainsi que de ses annexes, qui ne sont pas annulées ou modifées par le présent Traité.

IX. Le présent Traité sera ratifié, et les ratifications en seront échangées à Londres dans l'espace de 6 semaines, ou plus tôt si faire se peut.

En foi de quoi les Plénipotentiaires respectifs l'ont signé et y ont apposé le sceau de leurs armes.

Fait a Londres, le 13ème jour du mois de Mars, de l'an 1871.

(L.S.) GRANVILLE.
(L.S.) BERNSTORFF.
(L.S.) APPONYI.
(L.S.) BROGLIE.
(L.S.) CADORNA.
(L.S.) BRUNNOW.
(L.S.) MUSURUS.

APPENDIX VI

Secret England's Means of Offence against Russia.[6]

It has been asserted that the only effectual method of checking

6. P.R.O., CAB. 37/13. The footnotes designated by letters are part of the original document.

Russian advances in Asia is to cause it to be distinctly understood that any further step in the direction of India will be treated by England as a declaration of war,[a] and it is proposed in this paper to discuss the mode in which, under such circumstances, the power of England might most effectively be brought to bear against Russia.

Blockade. A declaration of war by England would doubtless be followed by the immediate capture of any Russian merchant vessels which might be found on the high seas, and by the blockade of the principal Russian ports; but these measures would have no serious effect on the general prosperity of such a huge empire, and would be absolutely without result so far as a Russian invasion of Afghanistan was concerned.

Russian Trade. That this is the case will be perceived by the following statement of the Russian exports and imports for the year 1882:-

	Exports	Imports
	£	£
*Sweden and Norway	1,210,000	660,000
†Germany	17,800,000	21,420,000
Holland	2,960,000	990,000
Belgium	2,910,000	1,210,000
*Denmark	350,000	Nil.
*England	21,010,000	12,470,000
†France	5,130,000	1,990,000
*Italy	880,000	930,000
Austria	3,330,000	2,990,000
*Greece	450,000	190,000
*Turkey	1,390,000	2,050,000
Roumania	690,000	200,000
*United States	Nil.	3,450,000
Finland	1,330,000	1,560,000
†Other countries	970,000	3,260,000
	60,410,000	53,370,000

If these are divided into two portions – viz., sea-borne and land-borne, the trade with the countries marked thus * may be considered as exclusively sea-borne, that with those marked † as partially so, and that with the remainder as land-borne.

[a]*See* Sir Lopel Griffin's letter to the *Times* of 26th May 1884.

Assuming that three-quarters of the trade with Germany is land-borne and one-quarter sea-borne, and that the trade with France and "other countries" is carried in equal proportions by sea and by land, the external trade of Russia will stand, approximately, as follows: –

	Exports £	Imports £
Sea-borne	32,790,000	27,730,000
Land-borne ..	27,620,000	25,640,000

As the English trade would naturally be stopped, a blockade of the Russian ports would have no very important effect, except on the trade with the United States, as most of the remaining sea-borne trade would be carried by the railways of Germany, Austria, or Roumania, and we may conclude that the total amount of injury which an English blockade would inflict on Russian commerce would be represented by the stopping of about 3,400,000£. of Exports, and 7,200,000£. of Imports, or a total of some 10,500,000£. on a trade of 80,300,000£. Even of this much would no doubt reach its destination through other channels, and a simple blockade must accordingly be regarded as a very ineffectual means of coercing Russia.

Objective points. If we now consider where it is possible for England to undertake naval or military operations against Russia, it will be seen that the only points, other than Afghanistan where the powers can come into direct collision are to be found on the shores of the White Sea, the Baltic, the Black Sea, and the North Pacific. In the war of 1854-55, hostilities were carried on by England in portions of the Russian Empire, adjoining each of these seas, but it was only in the Black Sea that any results were obtained.

The conditions of a contest would, at the present time, be far less favourable to England than they were in 1854-55, as Russia can now, by means of her railways, assemble vast forces at any threatened point in a comparatively short time, while her position in Asia has been so much improved as fully to counterbalance the advantage, which the power of transferring Indian troops to a Western theatre of war by the Suez Canal, has conferred on us.

Supposed case. To form a just estimate of the strategical situation it will be convenient to take a supposed case. Russia is securely established in the Turkoman and Merv Oases, and has her frontier post at Sarakhs, and we assume that the frontier between her possessions and Afghanistan has been accurately delimitated. This frontier Russia, for her own purposes, chooses to violate, and an army of 50,000 men marches on Herat and besieges it. The question is how we should be able to retaliate?

Two courses would be open to the Government of India. An army might be despatched from our advanced posts at Quetta and Pishin through Afghanistan, with the object of compelling the Russians to raise the siege, or else it might be decided simply to occupy Candahar, and await the further advance of Russia in the neighbourhood of that fortress.

English forces available. Whichever of these courses were adopted, the condition of India does not encourage us to hope that any troops could be withdrawn from the garrison ordinarily maintained, and, therefore, for the blows which we would wish to strike against Russia elsewhere, we can only count on our Navy, and on such military forces as can be spared, after adequate provision has been made for the defence of our other foreign possessions.

As it is to be presumed that only a small portion of our Navy would be required to clear the seas of hostile cruizers and privateers, the great majority of our ships of war would be available for offence against Russia; but the military force which could be despatched from our shores cannot be estimated, under the most favourable circumstances, at more than about 36,000 men of all arms. It, therefore, is of great importance to consider how such forces may be employed to the best advantage.

Of the four seas on whose shores Russian possessions are to be found, only two – viz., the Baltic and the Black Sea, are situated so that operations conducted in them could have any serious influence on the Central Asian Question; and though, as in the Crimean War, minor expeditions might be sent to Archangel or Eastern Siberia, it is in those seas alone that England's power could make itself felt.

Baltic. On the Baltic Russia possesses three naval stations, Helsingfors, Wiborg and Cronstadt, and in these harbours the bulk of the Russian Baltic fleet would doubtless take refuge in the event of hostilities with England. The Baltic being more or less blocked with ice during the winter a naval expedition sent into this sea would be obliged to return in the autumn as did those of 1854 and 1855, and therefore no prolonged operations against any of these places could be undertaken. An attack on Helsingfors might be made in a manner similar to that adopted in 1855; the town might be bombarded and the forts of Sweaborg might be destroyed, but as an extensive system of torpedo defence would be employed it is by no means certain that an entrance into the harbour could be effected, or, if it were, that any adequate result would be obtained.

Wiborg. With regard to Wiborg, a similar conclusion may be arrived at with even greater confidence, as the fortified channels lead merely into a shallow bay, navigable only by vessels of light draught, while there is no dockyard, and the naval establishments are on a very small scale.

Cronstadt. Cronstadt, on the contrary, is quite worthy of the labour which has been expended on it, and operations against it, if brought to a successful termination, would place St. Petersburg at the mercy of the invader. Such a result would repay great efforts, but the prospects of success are very slight. Recent experience does not give good grounds for believing that a fleet of iron-clads could silence heavily armed cupola forts, such as those of Cronstadt, especially when the narrow channel, which these forts protect, is further defended by every appliance, in the shape of torpedoes which modern science has been able to design.

A direct naval attack on Cronstadt may thus be removed from the list of possible operations in the Baltic.

Kotlina. A combined naval and military attack, by means of a landing on the island of Kotlina, on which the town of Cronstadt stands, must also be discarded, on account of the exposed anchorage, the shelving beach, the defensive works in existence, and the large Russian force which would certainly be at hand to repel a descent on this island.

St. Petersburg. St. Petersburg, however, has no defences on the land side, and is open to attack either from the north or from the south by a military force capable of defeating the army charged with the defence of the capital. The ordinary peace garrison of St. Petersburg is about 30,000 men, and could be raised to over 100,000 in the course of a fortnight, even if Russia were at the same time engaged in hostilities on a large scale, in some distant theatre of war.

A British military expedition, destined to land on the shores of the Baltic could not be of greater strength than one Army-Corps (36,000 men), and therefore such an enterprise could only be undertaken under circumstances of extraordinary weakness on the part of Russia.

If in the event of Russia being in such a condition, it were considered desirable that a British force should make a descent on the shores of the Baltic with the object of gaining possession of St. Petersburg, a landing might be made on the coast of Finland, either at Biorko, about 90 miles from the Capital, or at Sestroretsk, which is only 20 miles off, good anchorage and suitable landing places existing at both these points. It must, however, be remembered that all transports and other vessels passing up the Gulf of Finland would be peculiarly liable to attack by torpedo boats, which, issuing from the labyrinth of islands on the southern coast of Finland, would find safety in these channels when pursued; and this risk might be considered a sufficient obstacle to extended operations in these waters.[b] Torpedo boats would, no doubt, cause less annoyance if the force were disembarked in Esthonia, to the south of the Gulf of Finland; but the only suitable landing place on this side is Baltic Port, which is more than 200 miles from St. Petersburg, and an advance on the Capital from such a distance could hardly be undertaken by so small a force as that which we are considering. For the landing place of a large force, however, Baltic Port has considerable advantages, as it is only closed by ice for a comparatively short period each year. It is, moreover, connected with Revel, both by road and railway, and on the capture of this city (which is unfortified on the land side) both harbours would become available for landing supplies for the Army.

From the foregoing brief consideration of the position of Russia in the Baltic, it may be concluded that a British expedition to this sea, beyond what is necessary for establishing a blockade and making a demonstration, could only promise good results provided Russia were in a very enfeebled condition; in which case, the necessity for attacking her in defence of British supremacy in India would, probably, have disappeared.

Black Sea. The Black Sea can only become the scene of British operations against Russia with the consent of Turkey; but it is not likely that, in the event of a war between England and Russia, access to the Black Sea would be denied to our fleet, and we may discuss the case in which Turkey takes no active part in the contest, but merely allows a secure passage through the Bosphorus to our ships.

It has been mentioned above that the operations under consideration are those which might be undertaken by us for the purpose of retaliating on Russia for an invasion of Afghanistan; and the presence of a British fleet in the Black Sea would undoubtedly have its effect on the events which might be in progress in that country.

Russian Lines of Communication. The Lines of Communication for the Russian Army, which we have assumed to be laying siege to Herat, would be by way of Sarakhs, Askhabad,[c] Kizil Arvat, and Krasnovodsk, being thence connected with Moscow, the heart of the Empire, either

[b]The channels among these islands have been the peculiar study of Russian Naval Officers in recent years.

[c]The railway between this place and Kizil Arvat is to be at once commenced.

by Astrakhan and the Volga, or by Baku, Tiflis, Batoum, and so to Odessa or Sebastopol. The entry of a British fleet into the Black Sea will at once close the latter route, and supplies for the Russian forces in Afghanistan must be sent either by the Volga, which is frozen up between November and April, or reach the western shores of the Caspian, either by crossing the Caucasus from Vladikavkaz to Tiflis and using the railway thence to Baku, or else by road transport from a point on the railway north to Vladikavkaz, to Petrovsk. As the presence of a British fleet in the Black Sea would not endanger the Russian communications, but only necessitate the adoption of a less convenient route, it is clear that naval operations alone would be ineffectual, and to produce decisive results they must be supplemented by a military expedition.

We must therefore now consider on what point such an expedition should be directed. In 1854 the destruction of the Naval Power of Russia in the Black Sea was one of the main objects of the operations undertaken by the Allies, but under the circumstances here discussed no project need be considered which would not hamper Russia in the prosecution of an Eastern campaign. We may accordingly confine our attention to the eastern part of the Black Sea, and here there is only one good harbour to be found, namely, that of Batoum.

Batoum. Batoum, from being the railway terminus, is well suited for the base of operations of an army advancing into Trans-Caucasia from the West. An invader established here would doubtless first move on the railway junction of Samtredi, and thence on the important town of Kutais, from which, under favourable circumstances, Tiflis or Vladikavkaz might be reached.[d] It cannot be denied that the formidable defile of Bielogorskaya,[e] through which the railway and road leading to Tiflis has been constructed, would form a most serious obstacle if properly defended; but the importance of the interests, which in the supposed case would be involved, and the security which would be afforded to the left flank of an invading army by the mountain barrier of the Caucasus, might bring about the adoption of such a scheme as here indicated. Its prospects of success remain to be considered.

Batoum, in accordance with the intentions of the Czar, as set forth

[d]It is unneccessary here to enter into the details of further possible operations, but if a British force did succeed in occupying Tiflis, an advance on Baku, and the construction there of vessels wherewith to dispute Russian supremacy on the Caspian, would be the natural sequel.

[e]Otherwise known as the Suram pass.

in Article 59 of the Treaty of Berlin, is unfortified; but the old gun emplacements exist, and it is known that at least four 11-inch guns of 30 tons, with their ammunition and stores, are kept ready at the Artillery depôt some three miles from the harbour. These and other guns of smaller calibre, said to be 60 in number, could be brought down to the batteries by means of the branch railway which connects the depôt with the town, and could be mounted at a few days' notice. A force attacking Batoum would thus undoubtedly find it defended both by Artillery and by torpedoes. The latter, however, would probably be comparatively harmless on account of the great depth of the water, and our estimate of the defensive value of the place may be based on the number of guns which would be found in position, and on the strength of the garrison.

According to the most recent reports, there are only three batteries in existence, and these might be supplemented by others if time were allowed for their construction; it is not probable that they could hold out against the fire of a fleet of ironclads which would be unhampered by rocks or shoals, and free to take up whatever position seemed most favourable.[f]

The ordinary garrison of Batoum is about 800 strong, and so long as trains can run on the railway, this number might be largely and rapidly increased. But though the entry of a British Fleet into the Black Sea would probably be known, its destination might remain secret, and on its arrival off Batoum, the railway which runs close to the shore for the first 10 miles after leaving the town might easily be cut, and could not be repaired under the guns of a man-of-war lying in deep water close at hand. We may thus conclude that, unless it were known beforehand that Batoum was the point selected for attack, the garrison which would be found there would not be of such exceptional strength as to prevent the capture of the town, and the surrounding heights. If these were seized by *coup de main,* the works thrown up by the Turks in 1878, which are still in existence, might be as efficacious for the defence of the harbour as they were at that period.

From these considerations, it appears, therefore, that if a descent on Batoum were carried out with promptitude, it would be successful, but to insure this, it is essential that our relations with Turkey should be such as to secure for our fleet an immediate entry into the Black Sea, in

[f]Since the above was written the works of Batoum are reported to have been restored and strengthened. As this restoration commenced in October last, the defences should now be in a forward state.

case of hostilities with Russia.[g] There would, of course, be no question as to this right of access to the Black Sea if the invasion of Afghanistan by Russia was part of a scheme in which a movement on Constantinople had a place, instead of being merely an isolated act of aggression, and under such circumstances the strategical importance of Batoum would be even greater than if England were acting independently. For from this point the communications of the Russian troops in Armenia as well as in Afghanistan would be threatened, while the military strength of Turkey would occupy a large portion of the Russian Army and thus diminish the forces with which an English Expedition would have to deal.

It is, perhaps, too much to expect that the arrival of English troops would produce revolts in the Caucasus, though in 1878 a whole Division was necessary to keep order in Daghestan, but it may be fairly anticipated that the people of Lazistan would sympathise more or less openly with the invaders, and that consequently supplies and transport animals could be obtained more easily in this district than in other parts of the Russian dominions.

If the remainder of the Black Sea Coast is examined it will be perceived that Russia is practically invulnerable.

Odessa, Nicolaiev, Sebastopol, Kertch. It would, probably, be within our power to occupy the great trading centre of Odessa; but the majority of the residents in that city, who would be the principal sufferers, are not Russians, and the Russian Government would be little influenced by any losses which they might experience. Nicolaiev, the principal naval establishment now maintained in the Black Sea, is so situated that any attack on it would be most tedious and difficult, while Sebastopol has hardly yet regained sufficient importance to make it worthy of serious operations. The fortress of Kertch, guarding the entrance to the Sea of Azov, might be selected as the object of an expedition; but the strength of the place is such that enormous difficulties would be here encountered; and even if our efforts were successful they would only have an indirect influence on the course of events in Asia.

Summary. From this review of England's means of offence against Russia, it appears that while a simple blockade would be useless, military operations could only be successful in the Baltic under exceptional conditions, and in the Black Sea if directed against a single point. This point is Batoum, and, unless its strategic importance has

[g]If no delay were experienced, Batoum might be reached in about seven days from Malta, in six from Cyprus, or in less than four from Besika Bay.

been greatly overestimated, it should be at the present time an object of our special attention. The maps and other information which we now possess do not convey all the minute particulars which should be in our hands as to a region where hostilities might have to be commenced with the utmost promptitude, and it is therefore respectfully submitted that steps should be taken to prepare for such a contingency, and that the country near Batoum should be studied with as much care as is bestowed on the military features of a district in England.

This can only be done by adopting the method successfully employed by the Germans previous to 1870, and sending one or two carefully selected, Russian speaking, officers to reside as sportsmen or artists in the neighbourhood of Batoum until the necessary data have been fully obtained.

J. S. Rothwell, Major, D.A.Q.M.G.

Intelligence Branch
7th July 1884.

Examined 27th January 1885, forwarded to the Adjutant-General 10th April 1885.

A. S. Cameron, Colonel

APPENDIX VII

Nelidov to Giers, private letter, very secret,
Buyukdere, June 23/July 5, 1888.[7]

Ne soyez pas étonné de me voir revenir brusquement à la question de l'occupation du Bosphore. C'est que depuis quelque temps les événements semblent se précipiter en Orient. Les Autrichiens et les Anglais ne se gênent pas pour aller de l'avant; l'Allemagne elle-même semble encourager leurs convoitises, – et si le partage de la Turquie a réellement été ébauché en principe, – nous n'avons pas de temps à perdre pour tendre la main vers ce qui nous est nécessaire. Le bruit de voyage à Pétersbourg de l'Empereur Guillaume II m'a paru une occasion excellente pour exposer quelques idées à ce sujet, qui se résument en ceci: 1) pas d'accord possible avec l'Autriche qui est de mauvaise foi et de difficile composition; 2) pas d'arrangement sur les questions secondaires, surtout celle de Bulgarie, qui trouveront naturel-

7. From the collection of the private papers of N. K. Giers.

lement leur solution quand l'affaire principale sera réglée. Autrement nous donnerons un prix énorme pour quelque chose qui ne le vaut pas; nous nous étions garanti par nos arrangements de 80 et 84 la réunion de la Roumélie Orientale avec la Bulgarie, et lorsqu'elle s'est faite – c'était contre nous. Or aujourd'hui c'est de la solution de toute la question d'Orient contre nous que nous sommes menacés. Avec cela la situation intérieure ici devient très grave. Nous risquons une révolte militaire, des désordres à Constantinople même, et peut-être la chute du pouvoir au point que la sécurité politique, résultant pour nous de la fermeture des détroits deviendrait absolument illusoire. Et la Porte, impuissante, serait exposée à toutes les interventions étrangères. Nous avons bien [fait] de croire que les "alliés" y préparent, tous ensemble et chacun séparément. Nous devrions en faire autant, et l'occasion d'un courant plus sympathique entre nous et l'Allemagne m'a paru on ne peut plus favorable pour voir ce qu'on pourrait faire. Mais il va de soi qu'avant de risquer un mot, il faudra savoir si Bismarck *peut* et *veut* aller aussi loin que cela nous serait nécessaire. Je ne suis guère compétent pour en juger. Mon rôle doit se borner à indiquer ce qui se présente sur place, du coin d'observation qui m'est réservé. J'ai la conscience d'avoir, à ce point de vue, rempli strictement mon devoir. Il ne me reste qu'à Vous demander pardon pour le long exposé que j'ai fait officiellement et que je crois devoir corroborer par ces lignes.

Le Sultan est plus que jamais en proie à la peur. L'indiscipline et la pénurie du trésor deviennent réellement inquiétantes. Il y a eu des faits d'insubordination fort graves, – et il ne manque réellement qu'*un homme* pour que l'écroulement commence. Mais la race est si dégénérée que cet homme même ne se trouvera probablement pas. La pourriture durera, mais la situation politique sera de moins en moins rassurante. . .à moins d'un miracle ou d'un changement absolument inattendu.

BIBLIOGRAPHICAL NOTE

This account is based primarily on the following documentary collections: (1) five sets of documents from the Ottoman foreign ministry archives (*Hariciye Arshivi*) in Istanbul (*Russie* 9/86; *Russie* 9/87; *Egypte* E263/46A; *Bosnie-Hercegovine* 535/76; and in particular *Mer Noire* 20/6); (2) two volumes on the Straits question in the Public Record Office in London (F.O. 78/4271 and 4272); and (3) documents on the Danubian problems in 1870-71 in the *Haus-, Hof-, und Staatsarchiv* in Vienna (*Administrative Registratur* F34/S.R. 48). In addition, as will be seen in the footnotes, the regular correspondence to be found in the Public Record Office and the *Haus-, Hof- und Staatsarchiv* concerning the events discussed has been utilized.

Certain books were also of great value to this study. Because of the large amount of material available on the diplomatic history of the years discussed, no attempt will be made to cite all of the important works. The books mentioned below are limited to those which were used extensively in the text or which the author believes might be of interest to the reader. Other citations will be found in the footnotes.

Published Documents Two collections relating directly to the Ottoman Empire are J. C. Hurewitz, *Diplomacy in the Near and Middle East: A Documentary Record: 1535-1914* (New York, 1956) I, and Gabriel Noradounghian, *Recueil d'actes internationaux de l'Empire Ottoman* (Paris, 1902), III (1856-1878). Documents on the Russian denunciation of the Black Sea clauses and the Treaty of London can be found in J. Lepsius, A. M. Bartholdy, and F. Thimme (eds.), *Die Grosse Politik der Europäischen Kabinette, 1871-1914* (Berlin, 1922), II, pp. 3-25, and the British Blue Book *Accounts and Papers,* LXXII (1871), [C-245, C-265, C-267, C-314], pp. 1-178. This latter volume gives also the texts of the protocols and the treaty. The Penjdeh incident is covered in *Grosse Politik,* IV, pp. 109-128; Ministère des affaires étrangères, *Documents diplomatiques français, 1871-1914,* first series (Paris, 1929-), VI; and *Accounts and Papers,* LXXXVII (1884-85), [C-4363, C-4387, C-4388, C-4389, C-4418], pp. 21-380. For the Bosnian crisis G. P. Gooch and Harold Temperley (eds.), *British Documents on the Origins of the War, 1898-1914* (London, 1928-29), IV and V were used extensively.

In addition to this diplomatic documentation, particular mention must be made of the two sets of Granville correspondence edited by Agatha Ramm: *The Political Correspondence of Mr. Gladstone and Lord Granville, 1868-1876* (London, 1952) 2 vols., and *The Political Correspondence of Mr. Gladstone and Lord Granville, 1876-1886* (Oxford, 1962), 2 vols. This material has been supplemented with other letters from the Granville correspondence to be found in the Public Record Office.

Memoirs Of the numerous memoirs left by European diplomats covering the second half of the nineteenth century the most interesting for Ottoman politics is N. P. Ignatiev, "Zapiski Grafa N. P. Ignatieva (1864-1874)" (Memoirs of Count N. P. Ignatiev), published in 1914 and 1915 in *Izvestiia Ministerstva Inostrannikh Diel.* Of almost equal importance are the books of two German representatives at Constantinople: Hajo Holborn, ed. *Aufzeichnungen und Erinnerungen aus dem Leben des Botschafters Joseph Maria von Radowitz* (Berlin, 1925), 2 vols., and Ludwig Raschdau, *Ein sinkendes Reich* (Berlin, 1934). Other memoirs are cited in the footnotes. Although other diplomats such as Sir Henry Elliot, Friedrich Beust, and A. P. Izvolsky, who play a prominent role in these pages, have written accounts of their experiences, the emphasis is usually on other issues than the question of the Straits. This generalization is also unfortunately true for four Turkish memoirs covering these years: Ismail Kemal Bey, *The Memoirs of Ismail Kemal Bey,* edited by Sommerville Story (New York, n.d.); Izzet Pasha, *Denkwürdigkeiten des Marschalls Izzet Pascha,* edited and translated by Karl Klinghardt (Leipzig, 1927); General M. Moukhtar Pacha, *La Turquie, l'Allemagne et l'Europe* (Paris, 1924); and Mehmed Said Pasha, *Said Pashanin hâtirati* (Said Pasha's memoirs) (Istanbul, 1328), 3 vols.

General Background For a discussion of conditions in the Ottoman Empire the reader is referred to Roderic Davison, *Turkey* (New Jersey, 1968), and in particular to the same author's *Reform in the Ottoman Empire, 1856-1876* (Princeton, 1963). No similar book exists in English for the period of Abdülhamid II. The general diplomatic background is covered in the following surveys: M. S. Anderson, *The Eastern Question, 1774-1923* (London, 1966); William L. Langer, *European Alliances and Alignments, 1871-1890* (New York, 1956); and Barbara Jelavich, *A Century of Russian Foreign Policy, 1814-1914* (Philadelphia, 1964) and *The Habsburg Empire in European Affairs, 1814-1918* (Chicago, 1969).

The Straits Question Because of its importance in diplomatic history in both the nineteenth and the twentieth century the problem of the Straits has been the subject of numerous books and articles. Of major significance for this subject are two Russian studies. The first, Serge Goriainow, *Le Bosphore et les Dardanelles* (Paris, 1910), is based on Russian archival material. It covers primarily the question of the Straits at the London Conference, but it also discusses the Berlin Congress and the Salisbury declaration. Although Goriainow argues the Russian side on the major issues and does make some questionable statements, this book is indispensable for the subject, particularly in view of the lack of other Russian documentary sources. The second study, A. N. Mandelstam, "La Politique russe d'accès à la Méditerranée au XXème siècle," Académie de droit international, *Recueil des cours* (1934), XLVII, pp. 603-798, is of interest for the background of the Bosnian crisis.

Other books of value for this study are: Ettore Anchieri, *Costantinopoli i gli Stretti nella Politica Russa ed Europea* (Milan, 1948); Erik Brüel, *International Straits* (London, 1947), II; B. A. Dranov, *Chernomorskie Prolivy* (The Black Sea Straits) (Moscow, 1948); Harry N. Howard, *The Problem of the Turkish Straits* (Washington, 1947); Coleman Philipson and Noel Buxton, *The Question of the Bosphorus and the Dardanelles* (London, 1917); and Cemal Tukin, *Osmanli Imparatorluğu devrinde Boğazlar Meselesi* (The Problem of the Straits in the Ottoman Period) (Istanbul, 1947). Mention should also be made of P. N. Mishev, *La Mer Noire et les Dêtroits de Constantinople* (Paris, 1899), and the German dissertation Grigore Dendrino, *Bosphorus und Dardanellen* (Berlin, 1914). The following articles, although they cover a wider period than this discussion, are also recommended: Y. Hekmet Bayur, "Boğazlar Sorumunun Bir Evresi, 1906-1914" (A Phase of the Straits Question), *Belleten,* VII, 1943, pp. 89-215; Tevfik Biyiklioğlu, "Birinci Dünya Harbinde (1914-1918) ve Mondros Mütarekesi Siralarinda (30 Ekim 1918- 11 Ekim 1922), Boğazlar Problemi" (The First World War, 1914-1918 and the Period of the Treaty of Mondros, October 30, 1918-October 11, the Straits Problem), *Belleten,* XXV, pp. 81-93; Harry N. Howard, "The United States and the Problem of the Turkish Straits: the Foundations of American Policy (1830-1914)," *Balkan Studies,* III:1 (1962), pp. 1-28; J. C. Hurewitz, "Russia and the Turkish Straits: A Revaluation of the Origins of the Problem," *World Politics,* XIV (October, 1961-July, 1962), pp. 605-632; William L. Langer, "Russia, the Straits Question and the European Powers, 1904-08," *English Historical Review,* XLIV (1929), pp. 59-85; William A. Renzi, "Great Britain, Russia and the Straits, 1914-1915," *Journal of Modern History,* LXII:1 (March, 1970), pp. 1-20; and George B. Zotiades, "Russia and the Question of Constantinople and the Turkish Straits during the Balkan Wars," *Balkan Studies,* XI:2 (1970), pp. 281-298.

The London Conference With the exception of Gorianiow most of the books listed here concentrate on the negotiations leading to the conference and not on its proceedings. Kurt Rheindorf, *Die Schwarze Meer (Pontus) Frage, 1856-1871* (Berlin, 1925) discusses the issue in the years after the Crimean War. The immediate preliminaries of the conference are described in G. Troubetski, "Les Préliminaires de la Conférence de Londres," *Revue d'Histoire diplomatique,* XXIII (1909), pp. 108-138, 359-396, and in two books by W. E. Mosse, *The Rise and Fall of the Crimean System* (London, 1963), in particular pages 158-183, and *The European Powers and the German Question, 1848-1871* (Cambridge, 1958), pp. 333-358. The conference is also the subject of Heinrich Mertz, *Die Schwarze Meer-Konferenz von 1871* (Tübingen dissertation, n.d.).

On the question of the Danube at the three conferences, in Paris in 1856, in London in 1871, and in Berlin in 1878, three books were of use: J. P. Chamberlain, *The Regime of the International Rivers: Danube and Rhine* (New York, 1923); Henri Heynal, *Le Droit du Danube International* (The Hague, 1929); and G. Kaeckenbeech, *International Rivers* (New York, 1962). Also of value were R. R. Baxter, *The Law of International Waterways* (Cambridge, Mass., 1964), and Paul Gogeanu, *Dunărea în relatiile internationale* (Bucharest, 1970).

The Eastern Crisis, 1875-1878 This period has perhaps received more attention than any other pertaining to the "Eastern Question." For the diplomacy of these years the reader is referred in particular to three excellent books: B. H. Sumner, *Russia and the Balkans, 1870-1880* (Oxford, 1937); W. N. Medlicott, *The Congress of Berlin and After* (London, 1938); and Dwight E. Lee, *Great Britain and the Cyprus Convention Policy of 1878* (Cambridge, 1934). Sumner has an extensive annotated bibliography (pp. 675-698).

The 1880s and the Penjdeh Incident For British policy after the Congress of Berlin extensive use has been made of C. J. Lowe, *The Reluctant Imperialists* (London, 1967) 2 vols. Russian policy and the alliance with the German courts is analyzed in S. D. Skazkin, *Konets avstro-russko-germanskogo soiuza* (The End of the Austrian-Russian-German Alliance) (Moscow, 1928). The most valuable descriptions of the Afghan border crisis in 1884 and 1885 are to be found in Rose Louise Greaves, *Persia and the Defense of India* (London, 1959), pp. 53-58, and D. P. Singhal, *India and Afghanistan, 1876-1907* (Melbourne, 1963), pp. 107-132. The Bulgarian crisis is discussed in Charles Jelavich, *Tsarist Russia and Balkan Nationalism* (Berkeley, 1958). The sections on Batum are based on B. Jelavich, "Great Britain and the Russian Acquisition of Batum, 1878-1886," *Slavonic and East European Review,* XLVIII (January, 1970), pp. 44-66.

The Bosnian Crisis This account has been based primarily on *British Documents on the Origins of the War* and the Mandelstam article, both cited previously. Of interest for Russian policy is also I. V. Bestushev, *Borba v Rossii po voprosam vneshnei politiki* (The Struggle in Russia over Questions of Foreign Policy) (Moscow, 1961). The general European background and the crisis itself are described in Luigi Albertini, *The Origins of the War of 1914* (London, 1952), I, pp. 190-257, and Bernadotte E. Schmitt, *The Annexation of Bosnia, 1908-1909* (Cambridge, 1937).

INDEX